# Language Arts and Environmental Awareness

*To my husband and son,
James E. and James M. Roberts*

# Language Arts and Environmental Awareness

100+ Integrated Books and Activities for Children

Patricia L. Roberts, Ed. D.
California State University, Sacramento

LAMAR UNIVERSITY LIBRARY

Linnet Professional Publications ■ 1998

GE
70
R63
1998

© 1998 Patricia L. Roberts. All rights reserved.
First published 1998 as a Linnet Professional Publication,
an imprint of The Shoe String Press, Inc.,
North Haven, Connecticut 06473.

Library of Congress Cataloging-in-Publication Data

Roberts, Patricia, 1936–
    Language arts and environmental awareness:
  100+ integrated books and activities
  for children/by Patricia L. Roberts.
      p.  cm.
    Includes bibliographical references and index.
    ISBN 0-208-02427-1 (alk. paper).
    1. Environmental education—Bibliography.
  2. Environmental sciences—Study and teaching (Elementary)—Bibliography.
  3. Language arts (Elementary)—Bibliography.  I. Title.
Z5863.E55R63   1998
[GE70]
016.3723'57—dc21                                    97-32638
                                                               CIP

The paper in this publication meets the minimum requirements
of American National Standard for Information Sciences—
Permanence of Paper for Printed Library Materials,
ANSI Z39.48—1984.∞

Design by Abigail Johnston

Printed in the United States of America

# Contents

Introduction / vii

**I. Involving Children in Language**
Ages 5–8 / 3
Ages 9–14 / 25

**II. Involving Children in Listening**
Ages 5–8 / 49
Ages 9–14 / 65

**III. Involving Children in Folk Literature**
Ages 5–8 / 85
Ages 9–14 / 104

**IV. Involving Children in Reading**
Ages 5–8 / 119
Ages 9–14 / 137

**V. Involving Children in Speaking**
Ages 5–8 / 187
Ages 9–14 / 204

## VI. Involving Children in Writing
Ages 5–8  /  227
Ages 9–14  /  243

Appendix I: Environmental Agencies and Organizations  /  277

Appendix II: Periodicals That Publish Children's Work  /  279

Index of Book Titles, Authors, and Illustrators  /  283

Subject Index  /  291

# Introduction

This book is for teachers, librarians, and parents who want to develop children's awareness in environmental education as well as integrate the content with the building and refining of language arts skills. Though most states say that each school district must adopt environmental education and integrate it into the curriculum, there is a lack of content guidelines and books on this topic which makes some teachers turn to a serendipitous collection of materials that they gather together. In response to this lack of materials, this book presents environmental awareness topics in clear terms that will appeal to children's curiosity, interest, and sense of action.

## Need for Environmental Awareness Education

Environmental problems are increasing and children's interest in protecting the environment is growing. The tremendous need for recognition and understanding of our earth's radically changing environment has never been greater than it is today. The recent emphasis on widespread abuses of the oceans, global warming, endangered species, and cleaning up environmental waste may be only the tip of the iceberg of impending environmental needs. The persistence of those who pollute the oceans and lands, the pervasive smog and smoke where people live, and the proliferation of actions and accidents that pollute the environment are not occurrences of history, but are a contemporary part of the news related to everyday life in America.

## viii  Introduction

According to a recent national poll of youths, ages eleven to eighteen, by Washington-based polling firm, Peter D. Hart Research Associates, it is children, not parents, who worry more about the declining environment and who also do more about it (Koenenn, 1992). The Hart report also says that a "green revolution" is coming from the new generation of children and teenagers because no issue ranks as highly as the environment in shaping the world in which they are growing up. Other results from the Hart report indicate the following:

- A majority of youths identified *themselves* as the member of the family who is most concerned about environmental issues and a majority of their parents agreed.

- Sixty percent of the youths said that they have been left worse off environmentally than their parents and forty-five percent of their parents agreed.

- Sixty percent of youths identified recycling and buying environmentally compatible products as the issues where they try the most to influence their parents.

From this report and other contemporary comments, today's youths appear to be a generation burdened with water and air pollution, ozone thinning, species endangerment, toxic waste, abuse of resources, diminishing habitats such as rain-forest shrinkage, and other environmental problems. These environmental problems have generated recommendations by David W. Orr, founder and co-director of the Meadowbrook Project, an ecological education center in Fox, Arkansas. The recommendations are shown in the following figure centered around Orr's suggestion that "All education can be environmental education":

## All Education Can Be Environmental Education

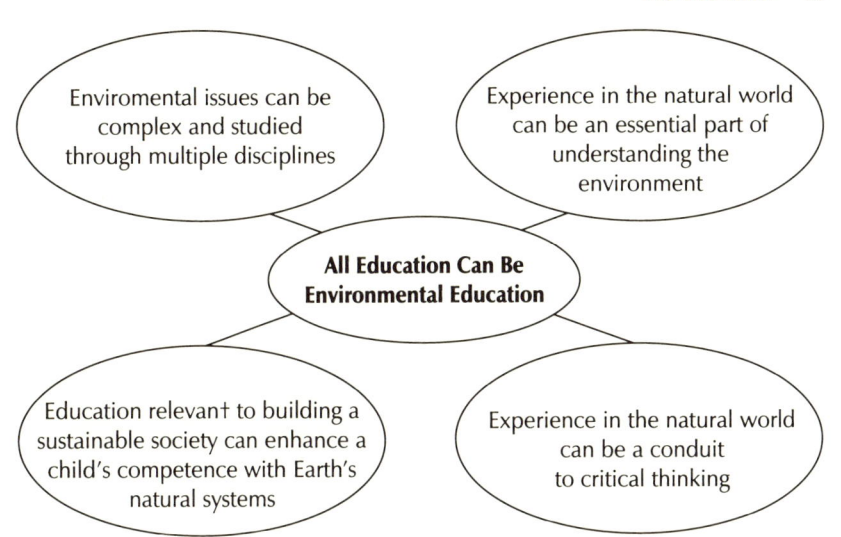

- Enviromental issues can be complex and studied through multiple disciplines
- Experience in the natural world can be an essential part of understanding the environment
- Education relevant to building a sustainable society can enhance a child's competence with Earth's natural systems
- Experience in the natural world can be a conduit to critical thinking

In addition to supporting Orr's call that all education can be environmental education, the emphasis in this book is on integration between environmental awareness and the skills of language arts. The standards for English Language Arts developed by the National Council of Teachers of English and the International Reading Association (1996) guide the activities that follow each children's book in this resource. For the purpose of this book, the standards are considered as an entity of language arts and English skills, all interrelated. The standards indicate that children should focus on the use of language, develop listening skills, and read different types of texts. They should be guided to participate in activities and projects where they get involved in public speaking to communicate effectively, use writing mechanics appropriately, and engage in different writing strategies. Briefly, the standards indicate that children need to be able to accomplish the following:

1. Use spoken and written language for the purposes of enjoyment, persuasion, exchanging information, and learning about a particular topic of interest; develop competence in English and understanding of content across the curriculum;

3. Adjust spoken and written language vocabulary and style to communicate effectively with audiences and for different purposes;

4. Respect diversity in language use, patterns and dialects across cultures, ethnic groups, geographic regions, and social roles;
5. Read a range of literature in many genres to build an understanding of human experience;
6. Read a range of texts—fiction, nonfiction, classic, and contemporary works—to acquire new information to respond to the needs and demands of society and the workplace; read for personal fulfillment and to build an understanding of themselves and of the cultures of the United States and the world;
7. Use different writing process elements, e.g., narrative writing, procedural writing, to communicate with different audiences for a variety of purposes;
8. Conduct research on issues and interests by generating ideas and questions and by posing problems; gather, evaluate, and synthesize data from a variety of sources such as print and nonprint texts, artifacts, or people, and communicate their discoveries in ways that suit their purpose and audience;
9. Use a variety of resources such as databases, computer networks, libraries, or videos to gather and synthesize information and to create and communicate knowledge;
10. Apply knowledge of language structure, language conventions of spelling, capitalization and punctuation, media techniques, figurative language, and genre to create and critique;
11. Apply strategies to comprehend, evaluate and appreciate texts; draw on prior experience, their interactions with others, their knowledge of word meaning and other text, their word identification strategies, and their understanding of sound–letter correspondence, sentence structure, context, and graphics;
12. Participate as knowledgeable, reflective, creative, and critical members of a variety of literacy communities.

The way children think about caring for a variety of habitats, life forms, and resources can be shaped by education—taught by others in the home, at school, and in society. Through education, children's awareness of Earth's natural resources can be broadened and librarians and teachers are in an ideal position to lead the way toward developing environmental awareness in a positive way that integrates the language arts skills. Indeed, an integrated approach to developing an earthwise consciousness can be woven into language arts skills for children that eventually may mold truly aware citizens who value Earth's environment, its creatures, and finite resources.

Integrating language arts with the content of environmental awareness is an informational path to help children toward the goal of developing their understanding and appreciation of the environment as they also build and refine their language arts skills. The interest and need for this integration across curriculum areas is expressed in current and contemporary teaching methods, textbooks, and professional writings. Reflecting this interest, this resource focuses on integration instruction related to language arts and environmental education and will give librarians, educators, and others a viable aid that furthers education's current interest about this type of instruction for all ages and that helps develop an interdisciplinary theme approach to the topic as suggested in educational materials currently on the market.

## How to Use This Book

This resource book looks at carefully selected children's literature in a distinct way—as a tool to help children develop an environmental awareness while they polish their language arts skills. Through the exposure of literature related to the environment and carefully designed activities related to language arts, children will be encouraged to develop an understanding of what is going on in our environment and show their appreciation and respect for the living things and resources we have on Earth. Features in this book include the following:

- **Introduction and related adult readings.** The introduction focuses on the rationale for an integrated language arts-environmental awareness approach and provides the basis for using children's literature to achieve the goal of integrating content about the environment with developing language arts skills. Adult readings and resources are included.

- **Bibliographies.** In the language arts sections, librarians, teachers, parents, adults who work with children's groups, and others will find helpful bibliographies—quality children's books that focus on environmental awareness and literature-based activities. The bibliographies not only will assist adults as they use children's literature as a vehicle for developing environmental awareness but also will be a resource for integrating language arts into a curriculum of appreciating, studying, and protecting the environment.

The bibliographies have language arts headings—language, listening, folk literature, reading, speaking, and writing. Each bibliography presents environmental awareness books and activities for children in the elementary and middle school (ages 5–14). Part I, Involving Children in Language, includes books of poetry that emphasize the authors' appreciation of reflections about the beauty and wonders of nature. In Involving Children in Listening, Part II, there are books that lend themselves to developing listening skills, i.e., books with information about endangered animals, ones that give directions, and those that provide details about ecosystems or creatures' dependence on their habitat. Part III, Involving Children in Folk Literature, includes legends, myths, and "how-and-why" tales that reflect some of the beliefs about nature held by Native Americans and others. Involving Children in Reading, Part IV, has entries representing different genres related to environmental awareness. As an example, several entries are books of activities for children who want to read to follow the directions to complete a project that interests them. Part V, Involving Children in Speaking, includes books and activities that lend themselves to communicating orally, such as summarizing a biographee's contributions to conservation after reading the person's life story. Involving Children in Writing, Part VI, has books and activities that reflect the use of capitalization, punctuation, and writing mechanics as children communicate with those around them. Several books can become a springboard for a child's private and public compositions.

The books in each part are entered by the author's last name and followed by complete bibliographic information. For ease of use, each part is divided in two. The first section suggests books and activities for children ages 5–8, and the second, books and activities for children ages 9–14.

- **Literature-based language arts activities.** The activities suggested for use with each book include procedures for using environmental awareness content in an integrated way with language arts skill development. Each book in the bibliographies is followed by not only a language arts activity suitable for classroom use but also by a home activity. In some entries, the classroom activities can be adapted for home use and the home activities for classroom use.

- **Reference use.** Librarians, teachers, administrators, school counselors, camp directors, Scout leaders, and parents will find this text valuable as a personal and professional reference. University and college instructors can use this resource as a supplement for a graduate or undergraduate course in children's literature, language arts teaching methods, literacy, and science/social science methods. School librarians, summer school workers, day care workers, and camp counselors will find the material in this resource valuable for seminars, workshops, and summer programs.

- **Appendixes and indexes.** Names and addresses of environmental agencies and organizations and of periodicals that publish children's work are appended at the end of the book. An author, illustrator, and title index is provided for the titles of children's books. A subject index concludes the book.

## Summary

This book is intended to be a starting point for caring teachers, librarians, and parents who find themselves challenged by a growing number of children who are, to a larger and larger degree, anxiously in search of understanding why they are environmentally worse off than their parents. While even the most skilled educator, parent, and citizen cannot change immediately the air and water pollution and other problems of the environment faced by the children they work with, they can, themselves, be positive role models as adults who realize that there are resolutions to the problems and that individual action can make a difference. Furthermore, they can enhance children's language arts skills by selecting quality children's literature and activities that guide children not only toward an awareness of the environment and what they can do to protect it, but also toward integrating language arts skills that reflect the standards for the English-Language Arts. This book is a call for creative instruction and action toward that goal.

## Readings and Resources

Alliance for Environmental Education, PO Box 368, The Plains, VA 22171. Provides teacher training workshops and develops curricula for environmental education.

Earth Generation, PO Box 2005, Midland, MI 48641. Offers "The Earth Generation" teacher's guide for middle school and junior high students. The activities emphasize the scientific method rather than just writing about a political point of view.

Education Development Specialists, 5505 E. Carson St., Suite 250, Lakewood, CA 90713. Offers one unit per grade, K-6, about air, energy, land, and water. Includes teacher's guide, black line masters, posters, activities, and tests.

ERIC: Educational Resource Information Clearinghouse, 1200 Chambers Road, Room 310, Columbus, OH 43212. Has database and library related to science and environmental education.

Environmental Defense Fund, 257 Park Avenue South, Suite 16, New York, NY 10016. Inquire about current projects and information.

Farstrup, Alan E., and Miles Myers, editors. *Standards for the English Language Arts*. Urbana, IL: National Council of Teachers of English/Newark, DE: International Reading Association, 1996. Results of a four-year project to ensure children become proficient users of language so they succeed in school, career, and independent learning and participate in our democracy. The project involved educators, parents, researchers, and others, nationwide.

Global Relief, PO Box 2000, Washington DC 20013. Write for information about current materials.

The Greenhouse Crisis Foundation, 1130 17th Street NW, Washington DC 20036. Write for information about available materials.

National Science Foundation, 1800 G Street NW, Washington, DC 20550. Inquire about foundation-supported projects and related information.

Sierra Club, 730 Polk Street, San Francisco, CA 94109. Inquire about available materials.

Toshiba/NSTA Exploravision Awards Program, 1940 Wilson Blvd., Arlington, VA 22201–3000. Phone: 703–243–7100. For information, encourage the students to write to inquire about an annual technology awards contest cosponsored by the National Science Teachers Association and Toshiba Corporation. First place winners receive $10,000 savings bonds.

The Union of Concerned Scientists, 26 Church Street, Cambridge, MA 02238.

US EPA, Information Access Branch, Public Information Center, 401 M Street SW, PM-211B, Washington, DC 20460. Offers the Environmental Protection Agency List: Environmental Education Materials for Teachers and Young People, Grades K-12. This is a list of private and public organizations that provide educational materials.

# 1 • Involving Children in Language

# Involving Children in Language: Ages 5–8

- **Armour, Richard (1974).** *Sea Full of Whales.* Illustrated by the author. New York: McGraw-Hill. Ages 7–8.

**Environmental context:** Appreciation of world's largest living mammals

In this book, Richard Armour offers poetic expressions that show his feelings for the largest creatures in the world. He also tells what a mammal is, why a whale is a mammal, and discusses the two basic types of whales. Other facts are given, e.g., most people erroneously think a whale's blow hole is a water spout and the author clarifies this: "It's air the whale's held/ In its lungs till it's hot." The verses highlight an environmental consciousness about these mammoth beings. Full-color paintings.

**Activity: "A Whale Mural"**

**Language arts focus:** To use language to communicate with others for different purposes; to develop vocabulary through a telephone call and to prepare a poetry mural.

Ask the children what they could do to help monitor the beautiful wild whale by talking to someone via a telephone call in your area's Department of Natural Resources. Ask, "What could we do to help preserve the integrity of this magnificent creature? What can we do to help protect the whale and its habitat? What other questions do you want to ask the resource person?" Write the children's questions and suggestions on a

**4   Language Arts and Environmental Awareness**

large sheet of paper to display in the room. Perhaps some of the children's queries will be about widespread abuses in the whale's environment, i.e., pollution (some dolphins now contain DDT levels higher than ever before); poaching (marine life is being illegally caught which reduces the ocean's food supply); and overfishing (a practice which causes whales and dolphins to drown in nets).

Before the phone call to a resource person, have the children prepare for the call by researching the whale's biology and habitat. Ask the children to select two group representatives to make the telephone call to a resource person and ask the group's questions. Discuss making the actual phone call, phone manners, how to conduct a brief phone interview, and other directions you think will be helpful to the children. Have the two report what was learned back to the group. After the phone call, have the children prepare a whale mural to record the information gained from the phone call and to display the findings from their research:

1. Guide the children in drawing a whale to scale on mural paper in the room, an activity that integrates math with the topic. To do this, cut a photocopy of a whale apart and give each child a piece of the whale shape. Have the children use rulers and enlarge the piece they have by drawing it on a large sheet of paper. For example, if the piece measures one inch, have them enlarge it to ten (or twelve) inches. Have the children cut out the pieces and assemble them on the mural to make an enlarged picture of a whale.

2. Record a whale's characteristics or ways to care for its habitat in a poetic form. Encourage the children to write about a whale's traits and behavior or about protecting the ocean in their own original poems, and if appropriate, use one or more of the following forms. Have the children write their poems on small whale-shaped pieces of paper to paste around the larger whale shape on the mural:

    - The *acrostic poem* is a poem where the first letter of each line is part of a word that can be read vertically. The lines do not have to rhyme. Example for the word *Whale*:

**W**et and wild in the ocean
**H**ere comes the huge mammal
**A**t great speed, then greater speed
**L**ingering deep, floating shallow
**E**very bit a giant in a watery world.

- The *different-portrait poem* asks the children to identify with the largest creature in the ocean: "I am a whale and I . . ."

- The *if or then poem* can begin with the words, "If I were a whale, then I . . ."

- The *one-word poem* shows ways to value one word as a poetic image in itself—the image itself has meaning. For example, the word *whale*, written on the back of a small origami whale, can turn the paper whale into a one-word poem that becomes the first poem to "swim" across the mural.

- The *sound poem* does not have to have any meaning beyond having sounds, i.e., "These are the sounds I think a whale makes."

- The *map poem* is a drawing or picture that shows an area and its important features. For instance, a map poem of a whale can have its features labeled in the form of free verse.

**Home Activity**

If your child is interested in corresponding with Maris Sidenstecker, a marine biologist and cofounder of the environmental group called "Save the Whales," invite your child to write to the biologist in care of Garnier-Weythman Productions, 19700 Fairchild, Irvine, CA 92715. Encourage your child to ask questions of the biologist about what is going on currently to save the whales and care for their environment. Ask your child, "In what ways can you help the whales?"

Suggest reading together *An Ocean World* by Peter Sis (Greenwillow, 1992, ages 5–7). This story has a *Free Willie* theme: a whale raised in captivity is returned to the ocean. Select together the words in the book that describe the whale and the care it gets from humans. Write the words in a list. Underline the words your child knows.

**6** Language Arts and Environmental Awareness

### ■ Behn, Harry (1966). "Trees." In *The Golden Hive.* New York: Harcourt, Brace Jovanovich. Ages 8 up.

**Environmental context:** Importance of trees

In this collection, the author remembers his childhood in over forty poems that reveal his memories about the world around him and he records his thoughts about people, creatures, and natural wonders. In "Trees," he says they are the kindest things he knows for they do no harm but "simply grow." He details other recollections about these leafy sentinels and what they offer to other living creatures: they provide shade for animals; serve as a gathering place for birds; supply fruit to eat; and provide wood to make people's houses. These nostalgic verses underscore the author's ecological awareness of nature and living things.

**Activity: "Ecological Poetry Break"**

**Language arts focus:** To participate in poetry recitation; to experiment with different oral interpretations

Tell the children that they will have an opportunity to take part in an ecological poetry break at different times during the day. To help the children become familiar with a poem for this activity, read aloud some favorite verses related to the environment. Use different voices for different lines to demonstrate ways of orally interpreting the words to the children. Show the poem on the board, an overhead transparency, or class chart so you can point to the words as you read them again and ask the children to read along with you. Have the children participate in the following verbal exercises:

1. Mention to the children that as they all read together, you will select different lines to mumble quickly. When the children hear your mumbling, it will be their signal to chime in and say all the words they know in the lines.

2. Elicit the children's suggestions for oral interpretation of the words (loud, soft, fast, slow).

3. Divide the children into groups and have each group practice reading aloud one of the verses to get ready to present the poem together

to another group or the whole group or to another class. They can incorporate any of the group's suggestions for an oral interpretation.

4. If appropriate, have the children choose actions to perform as they read the poem and let the children hold a copy of the poem so they do not have to recite the poem from memory.

5. Let the children read and perform their poems at different times during the school day, i.e., returning from recess, as an "ecological poetry break."

**Home Activity**

Invite your child to make an ecological self-portrait. Pencil-sketch the outline of your child's body shape on butcher paper and have your child draw his or her face and hair. Have your child cover the chest area of the outline with a collage of magazine or newspaper pictures of items related to caring for trees or other ecological actions that interest your child. Have your child dictate one sentence about each picture. Ask your child to design a pair of shorts, socks, and shoes on the figure outline with an ecology motif that he or she colors or paints. Display your child's body-outline in the home and encourage your child to add more pictures to the environmental collage as he or she finds them.

■ **Buchanan, Ken, and Debby Buchanan (1994).** *It Rained on the Desert Today.* Illustrated by Libba Tracy. New York: Northland.

**Environmental context:** Restorative power of water for living things

This book is a description of the coming of a long-awaited storm in a desert in the Southwest and tells the authors' appreciation of the natural beauty found in this habitat. Told in free-verse, the text focuses on the arid scene as well as its plants and animals as the environment changes from a sunny day to a stormy one interrupted by bright flashes of zigzag lightning. The text also provides a model for a reader to write about its theme—that water has the power to refresh and restore living things. Full-color illustrations.

## 8  Language Arts and Environmental Awareness

**Activity: "Telephone Talk"**

**Language arts focus:** To role-play phone calls to partners; to use spoken and written language vocabulary and style to communicate with an audience to exchange information

Invite the children to look again at the illustrations in *It Rained on the Desert Today* with you and ask them to respond to the approaching desert storm with their own thoughts and feelings about a rain storm. Have them tell about any experiences they have had on a rainy day or during a storm. After they have responded to the experience of what it was like for them in such weather, ask them to divide up with partners and take turns talking in the role of a child who visits the desert on a stormy day and sees the effect that water has on living things. Have children choose partners and make "imaginary phone calls" to one another to tell what they know about the importance of water in a desert habitat from their point of view. After the phone calls, ask the children to do "fast writes," i.e., writing as fast as they can to record what they heard during the phone call about the need for water in a desert habitat. Have the children take their writing home to show a relative what they learned about this type of environment.

**Home Activity**

Take a trip to the library together and look at a world atlas. Find a map of the world with some names of the countries and deserts indicated. Say the name of a desert and have your child point to the area. For follow-up, invite your child to listen to language in an activity called "Desert Animal Drama." Read aloud a brief paragraph about a desert animal twice. The first time, ask your child to listen to the paragraph and decide how the animal might move. Then during a second reading, ask your child to act out the motions he or she has selected.

- **Bunting, Eve (1996). *Sunflower House.*** Illustrated by Kathryn Hewitt. New York: Harcourt. Ages 5–6.

**Environmental context:** Humans' effect on environment

Related to a child's natural surroundings, Bunting's rhyming couplets are used to tell the story of a young boy who plants sunflower seeds in

## Involving Children in Language: Ages 5–8    9

a circle and watches them grow into tall golden-brown flowers. He waters them and when they are taller than he is, their nodding heads turn to the center of the circle. They make a roof for a space that the boy calls a sunflower house. The boy and his friends play in the house all summer and sometimes sleep out in it at night. When the leaves turn brown and the stalks fall down, the boy fills his pockets with seeds to eat. Some of the seeds are eaten by the birds and others fall on the ground waiting to grow again next year. The story focuses on action children can take, such as planting seeds, and on the important impact people make on their natural surroundings. Watercolor and colored pencil illustrations.

**Activity: "Sunflower Rhymes"**

**Language arts focus:** To recognize and create rhymes

Create original rhyming couplets with the children to complete the sequence of "One, two, three . . . ; four, five, six . . . ." Write the sequence on the board. For the first couplet, ask the children to think of words that rhyme with the word *three* and write the words on the board, e.g., *bee, fee, friendly, key, me, knee, pea, sea, see, tea, tee,* and *we*. Then, have the children think of rhymes for the word *six,* and write the words on the board. Encourage the children to suggest rhyming couplets related to the story by using the list of words on the board to complete the couplets aloud. Examples can include the following lines:

> One, two, three
> Friends play with me.
> Four, five, six
> We plant a sunflower mix.

Have the children record the finished couplets on paper and illustrate them for a display to show how children can affect the environment by planting flowers.

**Home Activity**

Together with your child, look for sunflowers growing in local gardens or fields as well as any that are available at a grocery store, nursery, or fruit stand. See how many other varieties of flowers your child can name and have him or her smell the flowers. Invite your child to purchase sunflower seeds and grow some of these tall flowers for the local birds. Talk with your child about what materials he or she will need to do this and help gather them. When the seeds in a sunflower head are ready, use a utensil to loosen them and lay them out to dry. Put the seeds in a commercial feeder for the birds or make an original feeder of your own—perhaps using stale rolls, bagels, pita bread, tortillas, or bread slices covered with peanut butter and seeds.

■ **Edwards, Richard (1993).** *Ten Tall Oak Trees.* Illustrated by Caroline Crossland. New York: Tambourine. Ages 5–7.

**Environmental context:** Humans' and environment's effect on trees

Edwards's ecological counting book shows the effects that industrial progress, nature, and time have on a grove of ten oak trees as they are eliminated one by one. This book has a rhyming text that counts down from ten as the centuries pass and the trees diminish. Seasons come and go and people's clothing changes to show many years passing through different historical periods. Over the years, humans find new uses for the wood that the trees supply. Examples of the various images in the environment are made with vigorous language for a reader to enjoy. For example, a brewery "booms" as barrels are made, the wind "screams," and nearby highways "snarl." The final pages are wordless and show a view of a new oak tree's life cycle as a young boy walks through a barren field in the rain. He picks up an acorn, plants it in a pot, and watches it sprout. Watercolor paintings.

**Activity: "Read All About It"**

**Language arts focus:** To use language creatively and imaginatively in response to news headlines; to read to acquire new information

Show the children some news headlines related to problems in the environment, i.e., water and air pollution, toxic waste, energy crisis, population increases, food shortages, and other topics. Write the headlines on the board and ask the children to talk about how trees, in a real or imaginary way, might help solve the problems mentioned in the headlines. Have each child select one of the headlines, team up with a partner to talk about the problem, and then cooperatively write a news release that would tell how there has been a "wonderful and amazing discovery" about trees that would help solve the problem. Encourage children to make their news releases believable. Have the children divide into small groups to read their news releases aloud to one another. Display the pages on the bulletin board and then bind them together to make a class book titled *Trees Can Help*.

**Home Activity**

Have your child list all the types of trees he or she can. Then together, underline the ones your child has seen. Invite your child to select a favorite tree and make a leaf sculpture as a way to memorialize it. First, have your child sketch a leaf on the inside of a box lid. Next, show your child how to make a sculpture from salt and flour dough. Encourage your child to tell you what he or she is doing while following these directions:

1. Mix 3 tablespoons of salt with 1 tablespoon of flour and add water to get a doughy consistency.
2. Continue mixing and making enough dough in small amounts to cover the sketch.
3. Add food coloring to the dough to represent different parts of the leaf—dark green, light green, yellow, red, brown, and so on.
4. Pat the dough over the sketch, so that it forms a model of a leaf.

Let the leaf dry overnight and display it as a sculpture. If appropriate, have your child write a key or legend on an index card to label the favorite tree and to identify the leaf's parts according to the colors used.

## ■ George, Lindsay Barrett (1996). *Around the Pond: Who's Been Here?* Illustrated by the author. New York: Greenwillow. Ages 5–6.

**Environmental context:** Appreciating habitat of pond creatures

George's book introduces a child to the heron, river otter, wood duck, and other creatures that live near or in a pond. In the story, two children walk in a nature area to pick blueberries for a pie but they are soon distracted by the sights they see and by the items they find along a well-worn deer path. With each discovery, they ask, "Who's been here?" and the book turns into a guessing game. The reader must turn the page to find each answer—an animal, bird, or fish in its natural habitat. Notes on the creatures are appended at the back of the book. Bright gouache paintings.

### Activity: "Draw-Trade-Write"

**Language arts focus:** To use language about nature in telling stories; to adjust spoken and written vocabulary and style to communicate effectively

Tell the children they will have an opportunity to draw a story about nature in six pictures. Give each child three blank pages stapled together. After they draw their picture stories in sequence on the front and back of each sheet, have partners trade stories. Continue:

1. Give the children each three sheets of *lined* paper stapled together, and have each write a story about the illustrations that they received.

2. When the written stories are finished, have the children return the pictures to the original writers. Then give them each another set of three sheets of *lined* paper stapled together, and have them write their own stories for the pictures they originally drew.

3. Have the children sit together in pairs and read aloud the two stories that were written about the one set of illustrations. Encourage them to tell what is alike and what is different in the two stories. Have the children make additions, deletions, and changes to their stories if they want to do so.

### Home Activity

Engage your child in an observation activity, "In Nature I See. . . ." Begin the activity by saying:

> Earth, Sky, Tree, Tree, Tree,
> I see something you don't see.

It's close to you and close to me.

It is something that _____ (*describe the natural phenomena or animal, plant, insect, etc.*).

Ask your child to guess what it is. When your child guesses correctly, he or she takes a turn and describes something in nature for you to guess.

- **Heller, Ruth (1981).** *Chickens Aren't the Only Ones.* Illustrated by the author. New York: Grosset & Dunlap. Ages 5–8.

**Environmental context:** Appreciating oviparous (egg-laying) creatures

In Heller's book, the main idea is that chickens aren't the only creatures who lay eggs, and the author introduces several egg-laying creatures: chickens, frogs, fish, snails, snakes, spiders, and various insects. There is a rhyming text and interesting facts are given for many of the creatures. Here are two examples: the largest egg is laid by the ostrich and the smallest by the hummingbird; and two mammals from Australia lay eggs—the spiny anteater and the duckbill platypus. Bright full-color paintings.

**Activity: "Eggs-amination"**

**Language arts focus:** To make observations; to exchange information

Invite the children to observe the outside of an egg with a magnifying glass. Discuss, "What do you notice?" If appropriate, have a child carefully crack the egg over a container and examine the crack and then the inside of the shell. Continue the discussion with, "What do you guess or hypothesize or predict that the membrane is for in the egg?" (Protection and insulation). "The yolk?" (Food source). "And the two spiral bands?" (To secure placement of the yolk on top of a growing chick). Encourage the children to sketch and label what they have observed on egg-shaped paper they have cut and then participate in a whole group discussion to tell what they have learned about this natural construction.

**Home Activity**

Have your child listen to similarities and differences in language through sounds, words, and rhymes from Heller's *Chickens Aren't the Only*

*Ones*. Introduce word play in an activity called "Green Thumb Up." First, give your child a green thumb by placing a small drop of green food dye on one thumb. Then, pronounce two similar or dissimilar words aloud (trees-bees, rain-ran) and have your child indicate if the words sound the same or different in their endings. If the words sound the same, ask your child to put his or her thumb up and if the words sound different, have your child put his or her thumb down. After this word play, encourage your child to tell you what he or she has learned about nature's egg-laying creatures from the information in Heller's book.

■ **Janovitz, Marily (1996).** *Can I Help?* Illustrated by the author. New York: North-South Books. Ages 5–6.

**Environmental context:** Planting a garden or caring for plants

In this story a father and son, Wolf and Cub, are gardeners who enjoy working together as they prepare the soil. Though Cub is ready and willing to help Wolf in the garden, some humorous things happen as they pull weeds, mow grass, hoe the soil, and plant the seeds. After their chores are done, the two workers reward themselves for their hard work with a mutual hug and a restful nap. The text is rhymed and makes the gardeners' actions easy to listen to, i.e., "Do the mowing" and "Help with hoeing." Bright watercolor illustrations.

**Activity: "Lawnmower Language"**

**Language arts focus:** To develop and expand gardening vocabulary; to apply knowledge of word identification and sentence structure skills; to use spoken and written language to review vocabulary

After reading aloud *Can I Help?*, distribute word cards to the children with words from the story (*hoe, weeds, lawnmower, seeds, soil*, and so on). Tell the children they will participate in a fast "lawnmower" language activity. One child designated as the first "lawnmower" reads his or her word card (*weeds*, for example), and quickly says, "I've got the weeds. Who's got the _____?" and names another word from the story. The child with the called word card quickly continues with, "I've got the _____. Who's got the _____?" and names another word from the story. Encourage the children to do this at a brisk pace (as fast as a lawnmower can go) and have them continue until all the word cards related to the story have been read aloud.

As another activity, discuss the idea of a garden fundraiser to help purchase seeds to plant in an area on the school grounds. Invite a gardener to class to talk about what plant types would grow best in a school garden and about planting a garden as a way for the children to make a positive impact on the school environment. Have the children prepare a proposal about planting a garden to present to the principal and a representative from the school's ground and maintenance crew. Consider the following complementary activities for the children:

1. With the required school permission, have the children plant the garden and encourage them to repeat some of the rhymes from the story as they do the chores and make up their own rhyming lines as they talk to one another. For instance, the children can repeat, "Help with hoeing," and offer their own words in rhyme—"Wind is blowing," "Sweat is showing," "Nose needs blowing," "Hard work, hoeing," "Water's flowing," "Weeds need mowing," or "Keep on going."

2. Related to weeding and caring for the garden, let some volunteers, wearing disposable gloves, collect weeds from the garden at the end of each week. Have the children place the weeds on a scale and weigh the amount that is collected that week. Keep a record of the weight on a chart in the classroom and keep a list of other unwanted items (paper, trash) found in the garden.

**Home Activity**

Give your child several gardening catalogs and let him or her use the information to plan a garden for an area or container outside. Have your child measure the space to see how many plants he or she will need. Ask your child to plan the garden on paper and sketch and label the plants he or she would like to grow. Help your child order the seeds or tools from the catalogs in preparation for a spring planting.

## 16   Language Arts and Environmental Awareness

■ **Jeffers, Susan, reteller (1983).** *Hiawatha.* Illustrated by the reteller. New York: Dial. Ages 6–9.

**Environmental context:** Native American and wildlife relationship

Near the shores of Gitchee Gumee, Hiawatha is raised by his loving grandmother, Nokomis, the daughter of the moon. Nokomis nutures him and teaches him many things about nature. He learns about every bird and beast: their language, their names, and their secrets. He talks with the beasts when he meets them and sees them as part of his family—he calls them his brothers. This *Hiawatha* version is based on the stories of an actual Onondaga chief and is woven together with other tales from Indian folklore that are found in Henry Wadsworth Longfellow's poem, "The Song of Hiawatha," written in 1855. Bright full-color paintings.

**Activity: "Bird Sanctuary"**

**Language arts focus:** To use language to accomplish a purpose; to conduct research on interests; to adjust spoken language and style to communicate with others through poems and songs

Discuss with the children the idea of developing a bird refuge—perhaps called Hiawatha's Bird Sanctuary—on the school grounds with a fundraising activity to purchase trees and shrubs to plant that will attract birds native to the area. Ask volunteers to research some trees and plant types that will attract birds in the area and also watch the ads in the paper for the best prices. Continue with the following actions:

1. Help the children prepare and present a proposal about the purchase to the school principal and a representative from the school's maintenance crew to obtain any required school or district permission.

2. Copies of the proposal also can be sent to adults in the children's homes to notify them about the project.

3. Solicit the help of any interested parents or relatives—perhaps a parent works for a local nursery and can tell the children something about tree and plant types that attract local birds; or perhaps a relative is a biologist and can visit the group to pass along information about the birds native to the area and their habitat.

4. Schedule a time to plant the trees and shrubs, and if needed, have the children design invitations and invite the parents and relatives to attend the planting. Have the children select tree poems to recite and songs about trees to sing to celebrate the conclusion of the planting activity.

**Home Activity**

Encourage your child to attract birds to the yard or neighborhood area and prepare a breakfast, lunch, or dinner for a bird by tying string around rinds of oranges or grapefruits filled with seeds. Tie the rinds to a tree branch. As alternatives, popcorn can be strung on thread and hung on the branches, or a pine cone can be covered with peanut butter and rolled in bird seed. Tie the items with string to a tree limb. Additionally, invite your child to make bird sketches and research in a bird guide or informational book the names of the birds that he or she sees at the feeders throughout the year. If appropriate, keep a bird guide in a waterproof bag near the feeder. Invite your child to write a description of one of the birds without using the bird's name. Read the description aloud and guess which bird it is. Write a bird description of your own and have your child guess.

■ **Lewis, J. Patrick (1991).** *Earth Verses and Water Rhymes.* Illustrated by the author. New York: Atheneum. All ages.

**Environmental context:** Cycle of changing seasons

In this collection, Lewis offers verses that show an appreciation for the seasons and an ecological consciousness about how they affect the habitat of living things. The words poetically describe cool winds in fall, light snowflakes in winter, and tall leafy trees in spring and summer. As an example, the author mentions that shade trees can be nature's parasols and calls them Earth's umbrellas that "bloom out of reach." This book complements a study about a changing environment. Full-color illustrations.

**Activity: "Twisted Twig Wish"**

**Language arts focus:** To recite and illustrate rhymes; to exchange information

## 18 Language Arts and Environmental Awareness

Invite the children to go on a short nature walk in the nearby neighborhood or park to collect some twisted twigs. Back in the classroom, select one of the twisted twigs to pass around and ask the children to make their wishes for positive changes in the environment as they hold it. Invite the children to say aloud

> Juniper, hickory, walnut, fig
> Make a wish on a twisted twig.

and make a wish about any positive changes in the environment they would like to see or about some action they could take individually or as a group. Record the children's remarks on the board. Have them select one of the remarks and illustrate it on art paper folded in half similar to a greeting-card format. On the left-hand side, have the children sketch a scene the way it is now in the environment and on the right-hand side, have them make a drawing to show the positive changes in the environment they have wished for with the twig. Let volunteers tell about the changes they drew and what they can do to help bring about some of the changes. The children could then give their greeting card illustrations to someone they know who cares about the environment. This is also an activity that could culminate with Earth Day.

### Home Activity

With your child, introduce an activity called "Going on a Trip This Season" and ask him or her to listen as you say, "I'm going on a trip this season and it is _____ (fall, winter, spring, summer). I will _____ (state something that you will *take* or *do* or *see* related to the season). Invite your child to repeat your words and add what he or she will take or do or see on the seasonal outing. This is an activity you and your child can do together on walks, bike rides, long trips, and car rides through the changing seasons.

### ■ London, Jonathan (1996). *Fireflies, Fireflies, Light My Way.*
Illustrated by Linda Messier. New York: Viking. Ages 5–7.

**Environmental context:** Harmony of life forms

In London's book, a reader is introduced to a community of living creatures who survive in a swamp together—crawdads, catfish, and wood ducks. The sharing of a mutual habitat is emphasized as a young boy repeatedly calls out to the fireflies and asks them to lead the way to where the creatures play. He visits different groups of animals in turn—beavers, muskrats, and even night-loving raccoons. He follows the fireflies to still more places until several amphibians (alligators, frogs, and turtles) are found. Finally, the boy reaches a pond where all of the creatures are playing harmoniously together. Bright acrylic illustrations.

**Activity: "Mutual Habitat Sketches"**

**Language arts focus:** To expand vocabulary; to use spoken language to communicate descriptively with others

Mention to the children that just as the boy saw living creatures surviving in harmony in the swamp, they can think of all the living creatures that live near their home, yard, neighborhood, or park area in a mutual habitat. Perhaps they have noticed birds, butterflies, bees, crickets, spiders, and other creatures and can mention them. Encourage them to repeat the boy's words, "Fireflies, fireflies, light my way," or "Lead me to the place . . . where turtles play," and to insert their own words to name the creatures they have seen . . . e.g., birds, butterflies, bees, and Granddaddy Longlegs. Further, have the children think of a gathering place (backyard, park, grassy area, nature reserve) near their homes where several living creatures can survive together and describe the scene to others in the group. Ask the children to sketch the scene on posters to show the creatures living in harmony. Have the children tell what could interrupt the harmony of the creatures' survival and what they could do to help the creatures continue to live together as they do now. Display the posters around the school to help other children recognize that many living creatures can survive together in a mutual habitat.

**Home Activity**

Introduce your child to songs about nature by singing the words and tapping your fingers and feet to keep the time to the music heard on *Grandpa Art's Nature Songs for Children* by Arthur Custer (Carle Place, NY: Cimino Publishing Group, 1992, ages 5–8). Custer (Grandpa) presents cassettes that entertain and inform your child about creatures in the environment. Your child will hear about bird migration in "Grover the Plover," the life cycle of a butterfly in "Meta-mor-pho-sis," and the ways bugs help the environment in "Send Me Bugs." For each song, suggest that your child imagine the creature's habitat. For the butterfly's habitat, for instance, ask your child to imagine that he or she is waiting in a large shrub with a roof of protecting leaves and the sun is shining with warmth. Ask, "How do you feel? What is going on around you?"

As another activity, have your child move a crayon across paper in time to the music for a few minutes. Stop the music and invite your child to use the resulting shape to make a picture of a creature or object in the environment.

■ **McCloskey, Robert (1957).** *Time of Wonder.* Illustrated by the author. New York: Viking. Ages 7 up.

**Environmental context:** Appreciation of the sea; recognition of a storm's power

In McCloskey's story set at the end of summer, a vacationing family in their Maine island home realize a fierce storm is approaching. They take a trip to the mainland for food and gasoline and notice people putting out extra hundred-pound anchors and chains to secure their boats. Back on the island, the family brings in wood, fills their generator with gas, and waits for the first wind and rain. The wind grows stronger, whips up the waves, and snaps off tree branches. As the storm increases, Mother reads a story to the children and everyone sings "Mine Eyes Have Seen the Glory" as loud as they can. When the family sees the moon through the window, they realize that the storm will soon be over and they go to bed. The next day they see reminders of the hurricane before they prepare to leave the island. There are broken trees, jagged holes, debris, and storm-flattened sunflowers. Watercolor illustrations.

**Activity: "Environmental Awareness"**

**Language arts focus:** To increase vocabulary; to use language for enjoyment and for communication; to read procedural writing

Just as Mother read a story to her children in McCloskey's book, have the children read stories to one another and sing songs just as the *Time of Wonder* children did. If appropriate, suggest that the children plan a presentation of their environmental awareness and invite others to hear their stories and songs. Have them use *recycled* paper to write or decorate invitations to students in another class or to someone in the home. Have the children also use the paper to write their own menus for refreshments such as a flower pot cake and record directions for indoor or outdoor non-competitive games or other environmentally related activities after listening to the stories and singing songs. Involve the children in planning and making decorations and favors and treats related to the theme. For example, the children can make the following recipe for "Flower Pot Cake" with your supervision. Let the children mix and match flavors and colors and be creative:

**Flower Pot Cake**

1 cake mix
32 oz. whipped cream or artificial whipped topping
2 large instant puddings and milk required in package directions
1 large package favorite chocolate cookies
2 or 3 packages of gummy worms
clean flower pot ($9\frac{1}{2}$" tall, $10\frac{5}{8}$" diameter)
artificial flowers
clean trowel

At home, bake cake according to directions on box. Bake on cookie sheet or slice thinly when baked. Bring to class. Prepare pudding as for pie. Crush cookies. Fold pudding, whipped cream, and cookies together, saving some cookies for "topsoil." Line flower pot with plastic bag. Alternate layers of cake and pudding mixture to top of flower pot, adding gummy worms as you go. Put cookies on top for soil, and arrange flowers. Drape gummy worms over edge. Keep chilled. Serve with a trowel. Serves 25–30.
(*Courtesy of Barbara L. Brovelli-Moon, California State University, Sacramento*)

In further preparation for the environmental celebration, have the children search through the yellow pages to locate a shop that sells paper

## 22 Language Arts and Environmental Awareness

plates and cups made from recycled materials and serve the refreshments with them. Show a video of Dr. Seuss's *The Lorax* as a finale.

**Home Activity**

After reading *Time of Wonder* with your child, locate some poems related to the story and read them together. Point out the words you like best in your favorite verses. As an example, you can read a poem related to McCloskey's final question on the last page of his book, "Where do hummingbirds go in a hurricane?" One choice is David McCord's poem "Birds in the Rain" in *One at a Time* (Boston: Little, Brown, 1974, all ages). This is a rhythmic response to the question for a child to ponder. For another related poem, read aloud David McCord's "The Wind" (also in *One at a Time*) and emphasize his descriptive phrases of "Wind I-am-blowing" and "Washed in the blue."

■ **Ray, Mary Lyn (1996).** *Mud.* Illustrated by Lauren Stringer. New York: Harcourt, Brace. Ages 5–8.

**Environmental context:** Cycle of seasons

One night, a thaw at the end of the winter season turns the old snow and the muddy roads into puddles of water and holes filled with mud—and this is just the environment that attracts a young girl one early spring day. She takes off her shoes and puts her feet and hands in the mud. The text about the girl's playfulness and joy is a free verse poem that describes what she sees (nearby hills, oak trees, daffodils); what she hears (the squish and squeak of mud holes); and what she does (digs and dances) in the spring mud. Bright acrylic paintings.

**Activity: "Mud Is . . ."**

**Language arts focus:** To increase awareness about seasonal phenomena through writing and reading; to write free verse

Show the children a way to write free verse about spring mud by using the definition of mud from the dictionary or an encyclopedia and writing it on the board: Here's an example: "Mud is . . . dirt that is soft, wet, and sticky." Show the children how to recopy the definition in a free-verse format. Have the children suggest additional descriptive words about mud and include their words in the verse. The writing might look something like the following:

> Spring mud is . . .
> Soft as _____ (*have the children give suggestions*)
> Wet as _____ (*have the children give suggestions*)
> And sticky as _____ (*have the children give suggestions*)

Encourage the children to celebrate the seasonal cycle of nature by writing their own free verse poems for a bulletin board about a phenomenon related to each of the other seasons. Here are some suggestions:

1. A summer hurricane is . . . as large as a _____ /as powerful as a _____ /and has strong, swirling wind and heavy rain;
2. A fall fog is . . . as misty as _____ /as cloudy as _____ /and stays close to the ground or a body of water;
3. A winter blizzard is . . . as strong as a _____ /as cold as a _____ / and has very heavy snowfalls and wind.

To help the children recognize the seasonal changes that occur in the habitat of their area's flora and fauna, ask them to prepare a class bulletin board to display their verses about the phenomena in each season. For instance, the children can research different questions and prepare displays for the board that reflect the answers, e.g., for a winter scene, the children can prepare a snow-covered bird house in a winter blizzard with information about birds that migrate, or draw fog-shrouded shrubs with facts about butterflies that migrate in the fall. They can make paper trees and branches that bend over from the force of a summer hurricane or make a cross-section of the spring ground with information about mud and the creatures that live below ground. Schedule a class meeting so the children can present their ideas for the seasonal display before they implement them on the board.

**Home Activity**

Help your child become aware of the sounds in spring, summer, winter, and fall, and encourage your child to turn on a portable audiotape cassette recorder and make a recording on different days during the different seasons. Perhaps your child would be interested in recording sounds on his or her birthday, Earth Day, Saint Patrick's Day, or other days special to him or her. Have your child ask family members and friends to guess what is making the sounds in the recordings. Ask your child, "What noise pollution, if any, is heard on the tape?" Together, make a list of all the different causes of noise pollution the two of you can name in one minute as well as suggestions for reducing any noise pollution around the home.

# Involving Children in Language: Ages 9–14

■ **Chandra, Deborah (1990).** *Balloons and Other Poems.* Illustrated by the author. New York: Farrar, Straus and Giroux. Ages 9–14.

**Environmental context:** Humanlike behavior attributed to nature by poets

In Chandra's collection of verses, several of the poems anthropomorphize nature's features. For example, a discontented sea acts like a child as it slides slowly back on "slippery hands and knees," and the fog is a creature who wants its wet back "rubbed." Additionally, the leaves of autumn act like people when they scuttle, tumble, and grieve for summer as they call out their "Goodbyes!" Black line drawings.

**Activity: "Personification in Nature Verses"**

**Language arts focus:** To increase use of written language vocabulary with personification in nature verse; to apply knowledge of figurative language

After reading aloud several examples of personification from *Balloons and Other Poems* or another selection of verses, show the children some of the ways the author composed comparisons about nature with metaphors and similes and tell the children they will have an opportunity to think of and write metaphors and similes of their own about nature scenes. To initiate this, encourage the children to search through magazines to find travel advertisements and help the children to see how the ad-writers use poetic words about the natural beauty to catch the eyes and ears of a prospective tourist. Have the children cut out and collect these advertisements, read the ad words aloud to one another, and try their hand at composing metaphors and similes about nature based on the messages in the advertisements. In the list that follows, there are some expressions similar to the ones they can find and rewrite:

1. In an advertisement about Alaska, a child reads "great rivers of shimmering ice, majestic snow-capped mountain peaks," and composes a comparison: "Alaska's rivers are flowing mirrors that shimmer and reflect."
2. In an advertisement about Canada, the words "through icy blue waters where whales and porpoises play, past mountains that rise from the sea, and islands, frosted green" might motivate a child to write words similar to these: "Canada is a living quilt with patches of blue water, white mountains, and green land."
3. In an advertisement about Puerto Rico, a child reads about San Juan, "silky sand, whispering trade winds, the clicking of castanets, the cobblestone streets," and writes: "Puerto Rico is like a child's playground with silky sand and windy whispers."

Have the children create "nature banners" with metaphors and similes to display in the room.

**Home Activity**

Encourage your child to read aloud to you the comparisons in Sylvia Cassady's *Roomrimes* (Crowell, 1987, all ages) or another poetry source. Help your child find some verses describing nature—perhaps Cassady's lines that compare a clam shell to a parlor and a greenhouse to a bottle of summer floating in the winter snow. Ask for a point of view from your child: "How is a clam shell like a parlor? How is a greenhouse like a bottle of summer?" Invite your child to copy his or her favorites or write original comparisons about nature on paper to make a poster to display in your home. Point out that the key to writing comparisons is to think of ways in which two things are alike.

■ **Esbensen, Barbara Juster (1974).** *Echoes for the Eye: Poems to Celebrate Patterns in Nature.* Illustrated by Helen K. Davie. New York: Harper and Row. Ages 9 up.

**Environmental context:** Patterns in nature

Esbensen's words poetically point out some of the various patterns and shapes that can be seen in the environment. Her main idea is that this will help a child see nature in a new and different way—as "eye-echoes." An eye-echo is a repeating pattern of geometric shapes in nature and includes branches, circles, meanders, polygons, and spirals. Watercolor illustrations.

**Activity: "Eye-echoes"**

**Language arts focus:** To use spoken and written descriptive words to express appreciation of patterns seen in nature; to use the writing process of a word web to communicate with others

Discuss Esbensen's concept of "eye-echoes" with the children and have them search for patterns, e.g., they can find circles by looking at the end of a smaller branch found on a nature walk or by looking at the larger rings of a tree trunk in an illustration or a teacher-drawn diagram. Point out that a person can tell the age of a tree by counting the rings of a tree or by counting its rings of branches. Have the children make "eye-echo" name tags to send a message to others that they have observed some patterns in nature. To do this, let the children sketch an eye-echo pattern they have seen on a small square (4" × 4") of adhesive-backed paper. Have them write some words that describe the pattern on the tags. Tell the children to write their names on the tags and wear them for the day.

Additionally, draw a web on the board with the title, "Echoes for the Eye," at the center, and draw lines that radiate from the center outward. At the ends of the lines, draw ovals labeled with the headings, "Branches," "Circles," "Meanders," "Hexagons," and "Spirals." Discuss the headings and have volunteers sketch chalk outlines to show examples of patterns they have seen that reflect branches, circles, hexagons, and other eye-echoes.

## 28  Language Arts and Environmental Awareness

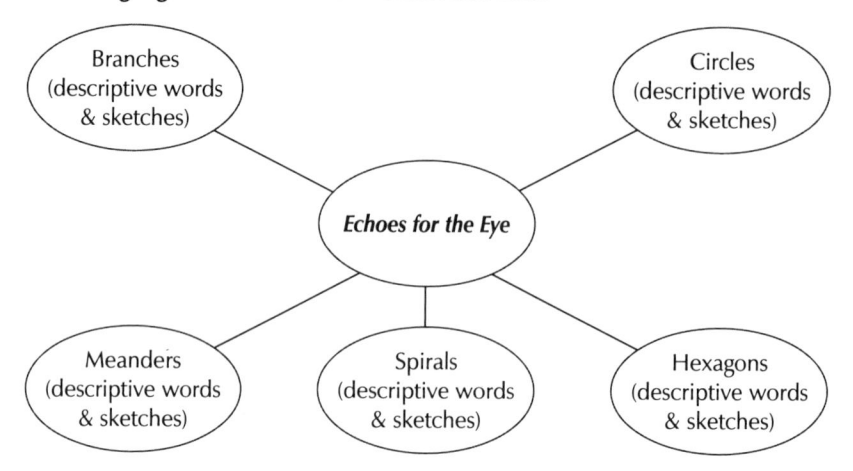

```
  Branches                                  Circles
(descriptive words)                    (descriptive words
   & sketches)                              & sketches)
            \                              /
             \                            /
              \                          /
               Echoes for the Eye
              /          |           \
             /           |            \
            /            |             \
  Meanders           Spirals          Hexagons
(descriptive words) (descriptive words) (descriptive words)
   & sketches)       & sketches)       & sketches)
```

For each heading, elicit the children's descriptive words about the eye-echoes they have seen and write them on the web. Have the children draw their own copies of the web, write in their choices of descriptive words, and draw the sketches they want for examples. Display the webs in the room and then collect them for a class book. Make it available for independent browsing and reading.

**Home Activity**

Encourage your child to sketch some of the patterns he or she sees in nature or finds in illustrations from books, magazines, and newspapers. Take time to have your child talk to you about what he or she draws. Encourage your child to organize the pattern collection in a paper-plate book. Have your child group the patterns into categories and add headings (Circles, Spirals, Branches) for each at the top of the plates. Punch one or two holes in one edge of the paper plates and tie them together with yarn or string. Have your child add plates to make a title page, table of contents, index, and if needed, a glossary. Encourage your child to illustrate the paper plate pages, number them, and show the book to a family member or a neighborhood friend. Invite your child to tell others what steps he or she took to complete the book of patterns.

■ **Froman, Robert (1974).** *Seeing Things.* Illustrated by the author. New York: Crowell. Ages 9 up.

**Environmental context:** Observations of the environment

Froman's book offers new ways of seeing things in nature through concrete poetry shapes—a way the writer shows his consciousness of, and an appreciation for, the environment. The author discusses what a "seeing" (concrete) poem is and says it is very *visual* because it has words that take a shape that helps turn on a light in someone's mind. The author then shows the words in the shape of a light bulb. There is another example in the poem, "Dead Tree." Froman considers the lifeless tree as a monument to its past and arranges his words about this message in the shape of a tree trunk and branches. Haiku examples reflecting thoughts about nature are also included. Full-color paintings.

**Activity: "Concrete Nature Poetry"**

**Language arts focus:** To express messages about nature through concrete poetry; to apply knowledge of poetry to create original lines

Mention to the children that they will have an opportunity to write their own messages about nature in a concrete poem. First take the children outside to observe the Earth's floor to find something to write a poem about for the activity. Assign each one a square-foot patch of dirt on the edge of the playground along with a ruler, a digging tool, and note paper. Have the children dig into the dirt and take handfuls of soil from the patch to observe. They can also measure what they find (size of pebbles, rocks, roots, leaves), sketch the shape of the items, and record some characteristics of the soil (wet, crumbly, dry, lumpy, fine, dark brown, light tan) on the note paper.

With the children back inside the classroom, have them refer to their notes and discuss the various shapes of items observed in the dirt patches. Have volunteers draw the outlines of some of these shapes on the board and talk about the idea that *any* of the shapes can be used to write one's own individual poems about the earth—there's almost no limit to the shapes the children can make for their poems. Further, invite the children to talk about any favorite concrete poems they have

**30   Language Arts and Environmental Awareness**

read and have them tell what they liked about the way the words are shown on the page and the way the shape interests them. Then ask the children to write their own concrete poems about something in nature—encourage them to write about something they observed in the dirt dig—and arrange the design of the words into a shape that is a part of the main idea in the poem.

For the children interested in additional shapes in which to write poetry, suggest they write their poetic words in one of the following forms:

- **Honeycomb shape poem.** This is a six-line poem with each line numbered and written around the outside edges of a hexagon.

- **Nautilus shape poem.** This is a form where the words of the poem spiral round and round similar to the spiraling shell of the nautilus.

- **Tower shape poem.** This is a form that has an equal number of words or syllables on each of its floors to tell about a view as seen from a great height—it could be an overhead perspective of a tall craggy rock, a slowly moving glacier, or a smoking volcano or the view as seen by a child looking down at a dirt dig, by an animal high on a mountainside, by a circling bird. The child selects the number of floors for the poem. Here is an overhead perspective of a bird who notices a city's development replacing nature:

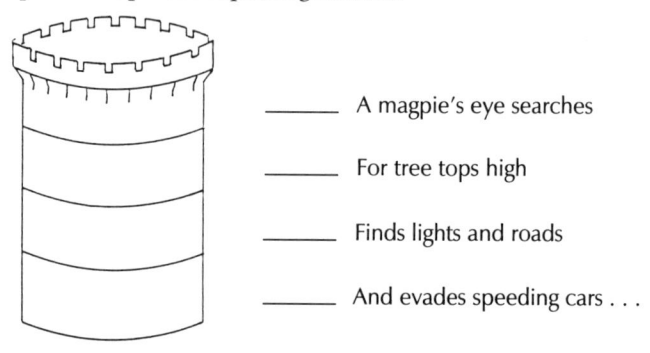

_____ A magpie's eye searches

_____ For tree tops high

_____ Finds lights and roads

_____ And evades speeding cars . . .

After the children write their concrete poems, ask volunteers to read some aloud, and collect all of the writing. Display the poems in a class book titled *Concrete Poems about Nature*. Place the book in a reading area so interested children can browse through the pages and read one another's nature poems independently.

**Home Activity**

Invite your child to extend his or her language further by thinking of "nature think-clinks," rhyming word pairs related to nature's creatures or their habitat. To compose a nature think-clink, ask your child to think of a noun and then an adjective for the noun that "clinks" into place in his or her mind. For instance, if your child thinks of *tree*, ask your child to think of adjectives related to tree (such as *leafy*) and choose one to make a nature think-clink such as *leafy tree*. Encourage your child to include some nature think-clinks when writing his or her own nature poems.

■ **Frost, Robert (1959).** *You Come Too, Favorite Poems of Young Readers.* New York: Holt, Rinehart & Winston. Ages 14 up.

**Environmental context:** Seeing nature as motivation for composing poetry

This collection of poems presents Frost's thoughts about the land and the people in the Massachusetts, Vermont, and New Hampshire areas. The poems are chosen from several works for which Frost received Pulitzer Prizes: *New Hampshire* (1923), *Collected Poems* (1930), *A Further Range* (1936), and *A Witness Tree* (1942). Included are such familiar poems as "A Hillside Thaw," "Mending Wall," and "Stopping by Woods on a Snowy Evening."

**Activity: "Croaking Voice Poetry"**

**Language arts focus:** To orally interpret nature poetry; to use spoken language vocabulary to communicate with others and to exchange information

Point out to the children that the American poet Robert Frost was born in San Francisco, moved to New England farm country at the age of ten, had difficulties in school, grew up to be a schoolteacher, and gained recognition as a poet in Britain during his stay there from 1912–1915.

Most importantly, Frost was affected by his life in farm country, where he supported himself by farming for several years, and tried to make things understood about the land through his poetry. He said that he wrote because he felt that he *had* to make these things understood. When he read his poetry aloud, listeners noted that he read in a "croaking" voice.

Invite the children to listen to one of Frost's poems as you read the verses aloud. Ask them to decide if he accomplished his purpose of making his thoughts and feelings understood about the environment from *their* point of view. Discuss, "In what ways do you agree or not agree that Frost made his thoughts about the land understood through his poems?" Additionally, engage the children in reading one of Frost's poems with each child reading one line. Have the children listen to a tape of Frost reading his poetry and encourage the children to read their lines in Frost's manner.

**Home Activity**

Together with your child, read aloud "The Gift Outright" from *The Poetry of Robert Frost,* edited by Edward Connery Lathem (Holt, Rinehart & Winston, 1969, ages 12 up) in recognition of Robert Frost. Mention that Frost was honored as the first poet presented in "Voices and Visions," a 1988 PBS series about America's best-known poets, and that he read this same poem at John F. Kennedy's presidential inauguration. Talk about the following with your child: "In what ways do the words of the poem tell you Frost's feeling for the land? Do you agree with Frost's point of view about the land being 'our' land? Why or why not?"

■ **Lavies, Barbara (1992).** *The Atlantic Salmon.* Illustrated by the author. New York: Dutton. Ages 9 up.

**Environmental context:** Appreciation and observation of nature in informative text and pictorial essay

In Lavies's book, a reader discovers the impact that humans have on the salmon as a species—humans have polluted, built dams, and overharvested. The text reveals the struggle of the salmon and its attempts to survive in its environment as it migrates from salt to fresh water and back again. A reader interested in photography also will appreciate the description of the author's homemade equipment that she used to take the photographs. The equipment enabled her to take underwater photos for her picture essay of the salmon's life cycle. Full-color photographs.

**Activity: "A Life Cycle"**

**Language arts focus:** To express thoughts through poetry; to adjust vocabulary and style to communicate with others

Elicit words from the children that reflect the life cycle of the salmon and write their suggestions on the board. Help the children transform the words into a septolet, with seven lines and fourteen words, such as the one that follows. This example is based on the text in Lavies's book. Point out to the children that the septolet poetry form has a break in the pattern.

| | |
|---|---|
| *(2 words)* | Salmon migrating |
| *(2 words)* | Salt water |
| *(2 words)* | Fresh water |
| *(2 words)* | Back again |
| *(break)* | |
| *(2 words)* | Water low |
| *(2 words)* | Pumps grind |
| *(2 words)* | Salmon gone |

Record the children's septolet on a chart, read it together as a group poem, and have the children draw their own small illustrations of the salmon to create a border for the chart. Display the poem in the classroom.

**Home Activity**

Explore with your child the "three R's" related to reading a nature poem: referring, reasoning, and reflecting. For referring, ask your child to tell you what he or she knows about the topic just from reading the title of a selected nature poem. For reasoning, ask your child what he or she thinks will be learned from the words of the poem. For reflecting,

## 34  Language Arts and Environmental Awareness

have your child reread or listen again to the poem and then tell you what he or she feels about the topic after hearing the poetic words a second or third time.

■ **Livingston, Myra Cohn (1992).** *I Never Told and Other Poems.* Illustrated by the author. New York: McElderry/Macmillan. Ages 9 up.

**Environmental context:** Observation of nature through a variety of verses

Livingston's collection has a variety of poetic forms that reflect upon nature. The forms include the following: cinquain (five lines with two, four, six, eight, and two syllables, respectively); couplet (two lines usually rhymed); haiku (three short lines with five, seven, five syllables, no rhyme); tercet (three lines usually rhymed); and quatrain (four lines, rhymed or not rhymed). The subjects selected for the verses include such topics as the sounds crows make, the beauty of Niagara Falls, and observing the moon. This selection is useful in introducing different poetic styles and word arrangements that portray nature scenes for the children. Line drawings.

**Activity:** *"Ah-h-h* Haiku"

**Language arts focus:** To express thoughts about nature through a Japanese poetry form; to respect poetic patterns from another culture

Read aloud some of the haiku examples from Livingston's book and mention to the children that writing haiku is special—it usually is saved to record a specific event in nature or an observation that brings an *ah-h-h* from deep within the writer. Ask the children to think of a time when they said *ah-h-h* to appreciate something that was going on in the natural world around them. Ask, "Was it the first time you saw a litter of chubby newborn puppies or mewing kittens?" "Was it when Willie the whale was finally freed?" "Was it something you saw on a nature show on television?" Invite the children to tell about any event in nature that brings an *ah-h-h* to them. Suggest that you will go on an *"Ah-h-h* Haiku Nature Walk"* with them on the next foggy day so they can ob-

## Involving Children in Language: Ages 9–14   35

serve nature in this type of weather. On the walk, involve children in one or more of the following observations:

1. Encourage them to look for events that bring an *ah-h-h* to them. Tell them that after the walk, they will have an opportunity to share their *ah-h-h* moment with others by creating haiku posters to display around the school to encourage others to appreciate the environment.

2. Direct the children to look closely at trees, shrubs, flowers, and living creatures through the fog so they can see nature and its creatures in a way that's different from what they see on a sunny day. For example, on a gray day, they might see shadows they haven't seen before or notice the dark forms of trees and birds' nests, or see plants against a light gray sky that seem to take on a different shape or thickness than when seen against a light blue sky on a sunny day.

3. Suggest that the children look for different forms in nature—maybe spider webs or bare tree branches—that can appear to change their dimensions in the fog. One of these forms can become an *ah-h-h* moment for them when the familiar shape becomes unfamiliar or looks different in the gray environment.

Back in the classroom, read more haiku poetry aloud and discuss the choice of words that are used to express the thoughts about nature. Have the children suggest their own words and phrases about the walk they took and write their words on the board. Ask the children to think of ways to use some of these words to write about what they saw in a haiku form. If appropriate, have them include the season of the year in some way in the poem so they can be more precise about the haiku moment they are recording in this activity.

### Home Activity

Read aloud examples of haiku to your child and suggest any of the following books for independent reading:

> *Cricket Songs* (Harcourt, 1964, ages 8 up) and *More Cricket Songs: Japanese Haiku* translated by Harry Behn (Harcourt, 1971, ages 8 up) have nature moments by Japanese poets;

## 36  Language Arts and Environmental Awareness

*Flower Moon Song* by Kazue Mizumura (Crowell, 1977, ages 8 up) has original haiku created by a Japanese-born American;

*Haiku: The Mood of the Earth, Haiku Vision,* and *Fly with the Wind, Flow with the Water* are original haiku reflections by Ann Atwood (Scribner's, 1971, 1977, 1979, respectively, ages 8 up);

*In the Eyes of the Cat: Japanese Poetry for All Seasons* by Demi (Holt, 1992, ages 7–10) has translations of Japanese haiku and tanka about living creatures, with the selections organized by seasons; tanka are short poems of five lines—the first and third lines are quite short and the second, fourth and fifth, a bit longer;

*In a Spring Garden* by Richard Lewis (Dial, 1964, ages 8 up) introduces the form of haiku as nature poetry.

- **Miller, Moira (1988). *The Search for Spring.*** Illustrated by the author. New York: Dial. Ages 10–14.

**Environmental context:** Spring as a metaphor for the meaning of life

In this story, poetic language is intertwined into a quest that takes place in the Middle Ages as a young inquisitive boy searches for the meaning of life through the metaphor of looking for spring. In the summer, a small boy's parents cannot explain to him where spring has gone and so he starts a journey to find spring for himself. During his travels, he studies for years with a wise man who tells him that spring has "gone with the wind." The boy leaves and searches for the wind. During his journey, he shares his food with a bird who helps him look for both the wind and the spring, and the boy in turn, protects the bird from the cold and snow during the winter until the warm weather comes. Finally, a woman, who is the boy's mother and lives in a nearby farmhouse, tells him that spring is all around him. She recognizes her boy and realizes he has grown into a young man sensitive to nature and life. Full-color illustrations.

**Activity: "Dawn and Dusk Conversations"**

**Language arts focus:** To engage in conversation and record observations about nature; to conduct outdoor research on interests and gather data; to communicate observational discoveries to others

During spring or summer when sunrise gives enough light to observe the environment, invite the children to see what is going on in nature at dawn in an area close to them, i.e., the backyard, front yard, the neighborhood, view from a window, edge of a nearby park, and so on. Have the children, accompanied by an older person or a friend, take notebooks and talk to their companion about what they observe. They can record their thoughts, feelings, and reflections about what they see—especially the creatures and what they do in the early morning environment. Suggest to the children that they repeat the activity in the same location at dusk and compare and contrast the behavior of creatures they also observed in the early morning. Remind the children to practice safety and always take someone with them; further, they should get permission from a guardian or parent if they plan to leave their family's yard or area. A compare-and-contrast set of notes in a child's notebook might look like this:

        Dawn _____ (date)     Dusk _____ (date)

1. Creature I saw:    _____   _____

   What was going on: _____   _____

2. Creature I saw:    _____   _____

   What was going on: _____   _____

Ask volunteers to report their observations back to the group and read their notes aloud. Conclude the discussion with, "Did you notice any polluting or littering that affected the environment at dawn? (Perhaps heavy early morning traffic of "big rigs" and double tanker trucks with polluting exhaust; early commuting coffee drinkers littering with paper cups.) Dusk? Is so, what are some of the actions you could take to help care for the environment you observed?"

**Home Activity**

Help your child create a visual display of poetic words that evoke images of nature after listening to or reading poetic expressions such as those found in *The Search for Spring*. To do this, have your child draw a large circle in the center of a sheet of paper with the heading, "Poetic Expressions about Nature I Like." From the circumference of the circle, ask your child to draw several lines radiating outward and then smaller circles at the end of each line. In each small circle, ask your child to write one of the titles of a nature story or a poem your child likes. On the line between the small circle and the central one, your child could write the poetic expression about nature he or she liked best in that narrative or verse. Display the poetic expressions in a place your child selects in the home.

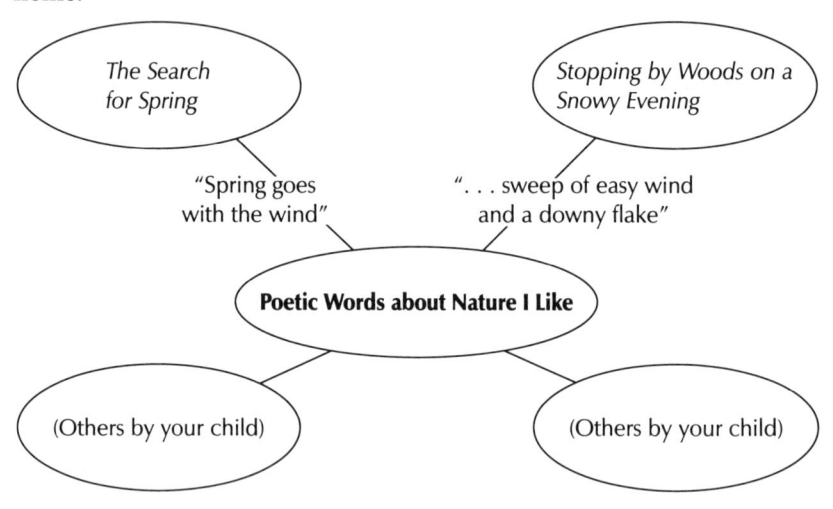

```
      ( The Search         )          ( Stopping by Woods on a )
      ( for Spring          )          ( Snowy Evening          )
              \                              /
         "Spring goes              "... sweep of easy wind
         with the wind"              and a downy flake"
                    \              /
              ( Poetic Words about Nature I Like )
                    /              \
      ( (Others by your child) )    ( (Others by your child) )
```

- ■ **Swann, Brian (1988).** *A Basket Full of White Eggs: Riddle-Poems.* Illustrated by Ponder Goembel. New York: Orchard. Ages 9 up.

**Environmental context:** Observations of nature

In Swann's book, a reader's environmental consciousness and observational skills, particularly of wildlife, can be tested with the riddle-question, "What am I?" Riddles about creatures and other aspects of nature are found in the book and a child can guess the answer from the clues in the accompanying illustrations. For example, a riddle about a forest animal from the Visayan people in the Philippines gives these clues: "No roots, no leaves— / So full of fine branches."

### Involving Children in Language: Ages 9–14    39

A reader asks the question, "What am I?" and looks at the illustration for a clue to the answer. The picture reveals the antlers of a brown deer hidden in the green leaves of a heavily wooded forest. The answer is found on the answer page at the end of the book. The riddles are multicultural, from Africa, Alaska, Arabia, Italy, Lithuania, Mexico, the Philippines, Turkey, and Yucatan. An author's note is included. Bright watercolor and colored pencil illustrations.

**Activity: "Nature Riddle: What Am I?"**

**Language arts focus:** To ask and answer riddles about nature; to apply knowledge of the riddle-writing process; to develop respect for nature riddle use in different cultures

Review the definition of a riddle with the children (it's a tricky or difficult question to be answered by guessing) and display an illustration showing a riddle about something related to nature from Swann's book. Explain to the children that each illustration they will see has a riddle about nature—especially its creatures—and the children can guess the answer to a riddle that goes along with a particular illustration. To do this, engage the children in the following activites:

1. Provide them with separate index cards bearing riddles that accompany the illustrations. Distribute the riddle cards to the children to read aloud and have them ask the riddle of one another as you show the appropriate illustration.

2. For example, show the illustration of the resilient red salmon leaping up over small waterfalls to return to their freshwater home to spawn. Invite the children to tell what they see in the picture. Hand out the index card with the accompanying riddle from the Ten'a people in Alaska printed on it. It states that unnamed creatures are riding upstream in their "red canoes." Have a child read the riddle aloud and ask, "What am I?"

3. Invite other children to guess the answer to the riddle. Have a child turn to the last page of the book to read the answer aloud and verify the children's guesses. Invite the children to discuss anything they know of that could endanger salmon as it is "riding upstream" (re-

## 40  Language Arts and Environmental Awareness

turning to spawn). Encourage the children to tell of ways they could help protect the salmon and its habitat.

4. Repeat the activity with the other topics of nature riddles such as the butterfly, the deer, and the fox's tail. Discuss any environmental concerns—effect of human pollution on salmon, toxic waste, deforestation of deer's habitat, and so on—related to each riddle answer.

5. Use the riddles about the living creatures to introduce different habitats in different countries or regions of the world. Begin with the riddle about the deer from the Philippines. Ask children what they know about the habitat in the Philippines. Explain that the riddle you are going to read is based on what a person could see in that habitat.

   Point to the Philippines on a world map. Read the riddle about the deer aloud and list on an index card what the children know about the habitat in the Philippines and any questions they have about it. Have children look for information about the Philippines. They could start by finding out more about the type of deer that live there. Encourage them to discover other animals that live there too. Display the riddle, along with some facts the children collect, near the Philippines on the map. Repeat the activity and encourage children to learn more about new habitats from other countries by reading other riddles. Attach the riddles to the map near the countries of origin. The children can add facts about each habitat.

**Home Activity**

With your child, read aloud several nature riddles from Swann's book and suggest that the two of you write your own riddles about the environment. Have your child print the riddles on sheets of paper and then draw pictures to illustrate the answers. Invite your child to show the pictures to someone at home or to a friend, and read the nature riddles aloud so others can guess the answers. Discuss any environmental concerns—water pollution, air pollution, diminishing habitats, toxic waste, and so on—related to the answer for each one.

- **Worth, Valerie (1972). *Small Poems.*** Illustrated by Natalie Babbitt. New York: Farrar, Straus, & Giroux. All ages.

**Environmental context:** Observations on life forms in nature

Worth shows her appreciation of living things in this collection of verses, and writes about a variety of subjects found in the environment. She describes daisies in golden banks, zinnias with petals in neat flat rings, and grass casting up seeds and hiding schools of mice. The poems either convey surprise, conclude a thought, or give information about nature's plants and animals. For example, in "Zinnias," the author surprises a reader when she announces that she wishes she were *like* the zinnias. In "Tractor," Worth refers to the vehicle as a large brown grasshopper—a comparison that might surprise a reader, and in "Grass," she gives an unusual insight when she refers to mice as attendees in rustling schools. Black line drawings.

**Activity: "Surprise! A Poem Ends"**

**Language arts focus:** To increase enjoyment of language about nature through a poem's ending; to exchange information found in poetry

Point out to the children that nature poetry can have an unexpected ending and surprise someone who reads it. For example, a good ending in a poem about plants and animals can do several things. It can: 1) sum up the meaning of the entire poem; 2) state the unexpected in some way; 3) give additional information; or 4) conclude a thought. Ask the children to reread some of their favorite poems about nature and look carefully at the endings to see if they can discern which endings are ones that summarize the poem, which ones say something unexpected, and which ones perform other functions such as giving facts or finishing a thought. Have the children report their findings to the group and write each ending (as well as what each ending does) on the board. Here are two examples of endings found in *Small Poems*:

| Endings | What the ending does |
| --- | --- |
| I wish I were like zinnias (in "Zinnias") | concludes the thought |
| hides whole rustling schools of mice (in "Grass") | informs |

### Home Activity

Read aloud to your child Eve Merriam's imaginative and poetic words about a creative way to solve a problem by pretending to crawl "inside it" and giving "a good substantial sneeze." These are poetic suggestions found in *Fresh Paint* (Macmillan, 1986, all ages). Ask your child to think about how someone could help resolve an environmental problem and imagine what the problem would be like if your child "crawled inside it" and "gave a sneeze" as Merriam suggests. Have your child select a problem related to the environment (perhaps one in the local newspaper) and write a news item (crawling inside) about it that could tell how someone did something (giving a sneeze) to help resolve the problem.

■ **Wright-Frierson, Virginia (1996).** *A Desert Scrapbook: Dawn to Dusk in the Sonoran Desert.* Illustrated by the author. New York: Simon & Schuster. Ages 9 up.

**Environmental context:** Desert ecosystem

Using a conversational tone in the text, Wright-Frierson gives her impressions, thoughts, and appreciative feelings about some desert creatures and the landscape of their habitat, an environment with very little rain and vegetation. She starts her dialogue at dawn and takes a reader along with her to explore the Sonoran Desert in the Southwest through the day and ends her narrative at dusk. She emphasizes ways the creatures have adapted to the extremes of the desert climate—blistering heat and freezing cold. For instance, a reader learns that some of the small desert animals burrow underground during the heat of the day and come out at night to eat, and that plant-eating animals get the water they need from plant juices. Watercolor sketches.

### Activity: "Changing a Grassy Plain to Desert"

**Language arts focus:** To engage in discussion about cause and effect; to use spoken language to communicate effectively with an audience

Tell the children that they will help turn a felt board scene of a grassy plain into a desert. Have the children make copies of outlined figures (backed with felt or flannel) of grass, plants, settlers, cattle, sheep, bison, prairie dogs, ravens, coyotes, insects, and rodents. Ask the children to place the figures on the felt board at the appropriate time as they contribute to a discussion about the following cause-and-effect happenings that can change a grassy area into a dry desert. Begin with a background of a green grassy plain with figures of grass and plants, then have the children make the following contributions:

1. Place figures of bison on the grassland scene. Place figures of settlers on the grassland scene along with figures of cattle and sheep and create the conversations the settlers might have had as they look at the richness of the grassy plains that will be food for their cattle and sheep.

2. Make up the dialogue the settlers would have about the bison when the bison competed with their livestock for the grass. Remove the bison from the board. Talk about how settlers hunted bison herds and killed the animals.

3. Place figures of prairie dogs in the scene and have the children suggest what the settlers said about them when the openings to their tunnels become dangerous to the settlers' livestock. Settlers poisoned or shot prairie dogs because their cattle tripped in the ground holes and injured themselves. Remove the prairie dogs.

4. Place figures of coyotes in the scene and have the children suggest conversation between two settlers about what to do to the coyotes because they are killing the sheep and cattle. (Settlers poisoned them.) Remove the coyotes.

5. Place figures of ravens in the scene and have the children create a conversation between two naturalists about the effect that feeding off a poisoned coyote has on the birds. (Birds are poisoned in turn.) Remove ravens.

6. Place figures of insects and rodents in the scene and have the children suggest a dialogue between two naturalists. They can talk about the fact there are few birds to feed on the insects and rodents, which are increasing in number. The land is beginning to suffer from related plagues. Add additional figures of insects and rodents.

7. Add more figures of cattle. Have two children create a conversation between two settlers about letting their sheep and cattle roam freely

**44  Language Arts and Environmental Awareness**

to overgraze the land and nibble the grass down to the roots. Have two other children create the dialogue between two naturalists as they talk about what happens when there are fewer and fewer grass plants and erosion of the grassy plain occurs. (To show that the once-green area is starting to erode and change into a brown desert environment, add more figures of cattle and remove some of the figures of grass and plants.)

8. Have the children fold a sheet of art paper in half. On the left-hand side, ask them to draw their interpretations of a once-grassy plain that is in natural balance, and on the right, their view of a grassy environment after it changes into a desert. Collect the artwork and put the drawings in a binder in a nearby reading area. Encourage the children to look at one another's interpretations of the changes in this environment.

**Home Activity**

Ask your child to listen to or read an informational book about the desert and identify sentences that he or she can write in a free-verse format (no rhymes). Demonstrate this for your child by reading aloud a definition of the desert from the dictionary or an excerpt from an informational book and then writing the words in free verse on paper. For example, a definition of the word *desert* from *The Lincoln Writing Dictionary for Children* (Harcourt Brace Jovanovich, 1988) looks like this in free verse:

> A desert
>   is a very
>     dry . . .
>       area of land,
>         sandy,
>           with little plant life.

Select a plain white inexpensive T-shirt and let your child choose textile paints to write his or her free verse (or an environmental message) on the shirt for others to see. Your child can decorate the shirt with scenes of the environment to draw attention to the words. Here are some sample messages: "Celebrate the desert"; "A delicate desert balance"; "I'm one with the desert"; and "Protect desert habitat."

- **Zerner, Amy, and Jessie Spicer Zerner (1993).** *Zen ABC.* Illustrated by the authors. Boston: Tuttle. Ages 9 up.

**Environmental context:** Experience in nature of "no thing"

The Zerners are mother and daughter authors and with this alphabet book, they introduce the concept of Zen, the idea of understanding one's own being in nature through meditation. In their words, Zen is the natural experience of "no thing." To explain the concept of Zen and no thing further, they tell a brief story about a fish who asks a queen fish about the characteristics and location of its habitat, the sea. The queen replies that the fish lives, moves, and has its being in the sea; that the sea is within the fish and without it; that the fish is made of the sea and will end in the sea; and that the sea is the fish's own being.

To illustrate that Zen is part of a living creature's own being, the authors select a Zen-related word for each letter of the alphabet and expand the meaning of each key word through a haiku (nature poem) or a zoan (an unanswerable question such as "what is the sound of one hand clapping?") or a phrase from classical Zen literature. Colored collages and pen-and-ink drawings.

**Activity: "Sijo Twists"**

**Language arts focus:** To use vocabulary about the environment in poetry; to express thoughts about nature through a Korean poetry form; to respect diversity in language use and poetic patterns from another culture

For those special children who enjoy writing haiku after hearing the examples in *Zen ABC* and who also are interested in another way to record their thoughts about the environment, introduce Sijo poetry. Sijo poetry is a form of nature verse from Korea, and it can be introduced, read, shown, and discussed with selections from *Sunset in a Spider Web* by Virginia Olsen Baron (Holt, Rinehart & Winston, 1974, ages 10 up). After hearing or reading examples of this type of poetry, a reader may

### 46  Language Arts and Environmental Awareness

notice that Sijo poems have three lines, e.g., the first line states the main idea or theme, the second line elaborates on it, and the third has a twist that is a contrast to the main idea. Encourage the children to experiment with the following as they write:

> To include an example of a twist, a child can leave a sentence unfinished to make the poem open-ended and to allow individual reflection by a reader or listener. Example:

> The smell of leafy trees in fall
> fog and wet grass
> and car exhaust . . .

Have the children work with partners to record their thoughts about nature in the three-line Sijo form. Ask several volunteers to read their verses aloud to the whole group. Encourage the children to listen for the language twists, and elicit their reactions.

**Home Activity**

Encourage your child to write his or her poetry on original bookmarks (paper cut about 2" × 6") to show his or her appreciation of nature—perhaps demonstrating the Zen idea that each creature's habitat is within and without each living thing. Invite your child to give the bookmarks to family members and friends. Also, encourage your child to display more verses on other items such as room banners, wall posters, and hanging mobiles to decorate the home.

# II · Involving Children in Listening

# Involving Children in Listening: Ages 5–8

- **Arnosky, Jim (1996).** *Crinkleroot's Guide to Knowing Butterflies and Moths.* Illustrated by the author. New York: Simon & Schuster. Ages 5–7.

**Environmental context:** Life cycle of butterflies and moths

Old Crinkleroot, a nature guide, carries his snake friend, Sassafras, coiled around his hat, and walks through grassy areas and woods to identify various species of butterflies and moths for a reader. He describes the caterpillars that change into butterflies or moths, what flowers appeal to them, how they sip nectar, pollinate plants, and what the insects' life cycle is like. Drawings show the insects in actual size. Watercolor illustrations.

**Activity: "Can Hear, Can't Hear"**

**Language arts focus:** To listen attentively for details; to exchange information

Mention to the children that you are going to read aloud from *Crinkleroot's Guide to Knowing Butterflies and Moths*. They are going to hear facts about the flowers and plants, such as milkweed, that appeal to butterflies and what behavior the insects perform in their habitat. Divide the children into three groups. Choose one or two in group three to wear soft ear plugs. Ask the children to listen attentively for different purposes.

## 50 Language Arts and Environmental Awareness

1. Ask group 1 to dictate the words they heard that were most interesting to them. Write the words on a chart.
2. Ask group 2 to dictate the words they heard that made a picture in their minds. Write some of their dictations as examples on a chart.
3. Ask group 3 to describe an insect or flower from the book to the children who are wearing ear plugs. Invite a child who heard the information to tell the facts aloud to one of the children who did not hear the information. Then, ask this child to summarize with, "You told me that. . . ." Other children can volunteer any information that is left out.

As a further activity, invite the children to use the information they received from the book to select and grow flower seeds that attract butterflies. Ask, "Which flower seeds should be purchased and planted for these colorful winged insects?" Write the names of the suggested flowers on the board. Purchase the seeds and have the children plant different seeds in paper cups in the room and care for the seedlings as they grow. Let the children take the plants home to give to someone they know who is interested in caring for butterflies and other living things in the environment. Ask the children to make suggestions to others in the home about ways to encourage butterflies to live in their yard and how to care for the plants butterflies like.

### Home Activity

To acquaint your child with noises in his or her home environment that get in the way of attentive listening, have your child make a list of things that interfered with his or her listening that day. Your child can develop a list similar to the following and then draw the items on a noise pollution map that indicates your child's surroundings:

1. Windows were open and could hear other kids or traffic outside
2. Planes overhead
3. People talking
4. Lawn mower and other machinery outside was noisy
5. Radio, disc player, or television in room made noise

Elicit your child's comments about suggestions for reducing the noises and implement those you can. Help your child draw a map of the home.

Ask your child to suggest the locations of noise pollution on the map and write the causes of the noise pollution there. Display the map on the refrigerator or other place where it can be readily seen.

■ **Bunting, Eve (1993).** *Night Tree.* Illustrated by Ted Rand. San Diego: Harcourt Brace Jovanovich. Ages 6–8.

**Environmental context:** Sharing food with wildlife

Bunting's story depicts a family's Christmas tradition of sharing their food with the creatures in a nearby forest. Every year, the family journeys out to decorate a living Christmas tree in the woods with apples, popcorn balls, and sunflower seeds. Instead of putting paper-wrapped presents beneath the tree, they leave pieces of apple, bread crumbs, and nuts. Bright watercolor illustrations.

**Activity: "Tree with Edibles"**

**Language arts focus:** To use language for the purpose of creating a tree of holiday treats for wildlife; to conduct research on interests and gather data; to use vocabulary to communicate reports to an audience

Ask the children to listen to *Night Tree* as you read it aloud to find out what one family did to make a tree of food treats for local wildlife in the winter. Tell the children that just as the family in Bunting's story decorated a tree in the woods with edibles for local wildlife, they will have the opportunity to create their own tree. To do this, take a nature walk with the children to locate a suitable tree or tall shrub on the school grounds. Urban children may use a tree in a container. Ask the children during the walk to look for signs of wildlife that might be interested in eating treats from the tree.

Back in the classroom, you can engage the children in talking about the kinds of birds and animals they saw in the area and list the names on the board. Ask the children to volunteer to research the creatures to find out what they eat. Write the children's names beside the bird and animal names to record which child will be responsible for the information:

## 52 Language Arts and Environmental Awareness

| Birds and Animals and What They Eat | Volunteers |
|---|---|
| A bluejay eats _____. | Carlos |

After the research, have the children report their findings and make a list on the board of the food items to put on the tree. On the appointed day, ask volunteers to bring the food from home and set aside a time to visit the tree and decorate it. Plan to visit the tree again so the children can determine what has been eaten. Have them guess (predict, hypothesize) which creature would nibble at what food.

### Home Activity

Invite your child to an environmental scavenger hunt in your home and prepare items for your child to find before the hunt. Make a list of birds or animals in your area and ask your child to find as many food types for the creatures on the list as possible. Your child can record the food types beside each creature's name. If some foods are not available in your home, hide pictures of them for your child to find. As a follow-up activity, the child can collect food items to put out to feed the birds and animals in your area.

■ **Fleming, Denise (1996).** *Where Once There Was a Wood.* Illustrated by the author. New York: Henry Holt & Co. Ages 6–7.

**Environmental context:** Importance of wooded habitat for living creatures

Fleming's story is set in a lush, green wooded area where wild creatures and plants thrive until they are replaced by a development project. This natural habitat flourishes with trees, flowers, shrubs, and grass, and is beautiful with butterflies and hummingbirds and other creatures until it is eventually destroyed. Many houses are built and the steep roofs and aluminum-framed windows replace the site where the tall trees and their encircling branches once stood.

Readers are given directions for making backyard habitats to rebuild part of any creature's natural habitat when it is destroyed. For example, a reader can use the information to prepare a garden area for butterflies and hummingbirds. A bibliography for further reading and notes on the work of the National Wildlife Federation are included. Full-color collage illustrations.

**Activity: "Bulletin Board Butterfly Habitat"**

**Language arts focus:** To listen to suggestions; to use spoken language vocabulary to create a bulletin board display; to apply knowledge of information

Invite the children to create a bulletin board to show a habitat that protects each stage of a butterfly's life cycle:

1. **Egg.** Ask, "How can we hide a butterfly's eggs?" The children can place colored tissue paper over insect eggs cut from paper to make the eggs less visible.
2. **Cocoon.** Ask, "How can we provide protection for a butterfly's cocoon?" The children can place leaves made from art paper over the cocoon to hide it in the display.
3. **Caterpillar.** Ask, "How can we make a caterpillar less visible to predators?" They can color caterpillars in counter shading, with the upper part of the body, which is normally light, colored dark, and the sides and bottom, normally in shadow, light.
4. **Adult.** Ask, "How can we protect an adult butterfly?" To protect the adult butterfly, the children can make butterfly wings with eyespots that resemble the eyes of animals to startle predators. Or they can cut flowers and leaves of flowers from art paper to place over the adult butterfly to give it protective cover. They also can sketch butterflies with wings that resemble dead leaves or patterns that look like bark, or make the wings transparent so foliage will show through them.

**Home Activity**

Invite your child to plant milkweed, cockle flowers, or other plants to attract some butterflies and observe the insects' behavior around the flowers. Talk about what you see: "What other creatures live on or around the plants that attract the butterflies?" (coexistence).

## 54 Language Arts and Environmental Awareness

■ **Guiberson, Brenda (1991).** *Spoonbill Swamp.* Illustrated by the author. New York: Henry Holt & Co. Ages 5–7.

**Environmental context:** Living creatures and their dependence on nature

Guiberson's book gives details about how wild creatures depend on the resources of the extensive swamps in Florida, Louisiana, and Texas for survival. Through the print and the accompanying pictures, a reader follows one day in the lives of the spoonbill and alligator families. The text points out that though the two species are different and natural enemies, there are similarities in the way they rely on the swamp for a habitat as they search for food, use the swamp for protective cover, and contribute to its ecosystem. Full-color photographs for illustrations.

**Activity: "Listen-Describe-Analyze"**

**Language arts focus:** To listen critically to analyze information for details; to listen carefully to comprehend and evaluate written and spoken descriptions

Read aloud excerpts from the book *Spoonbill Swamp* and then ask the children to divide into small groups. Give each group a photocopy of an illustration from the book and ask them to write a detailed description of the illustration. Collect the illustrations and display them on the chalk rail. Ask the first group to read aloud their description and have the other groups listen carefully to analyze it. Ask the children to identify the appropriate illustration from the chalk rail collection and then justify the decision for their choice. Let the children discuss why they could or could not identify the illustration. Repeat the activity with the other groups. Then have the children suggest guidelines for writing descriptions that will help them give accurate and detailed information to other. Write their suggestions on a chart for future reference when you repeat this activity with other nature books.

**Home Activity**

Introduce the activity "Swamp Exchange" to your child and some of his or her griends. Ask them to sit down on the floor. Tell them that they can take the role of swamp creatures and where they are sitting will represent the swamp habitat. Have the children suggest names of creatures in a swamp habitat and write the names on index cards. Collect the cards and give one to each child. One by one, encourage the children to tell what they know about the creature whose name is on the card, and its habitat. Ask them to listen for the names of two swamp creatures that you call out. The two children who have those cards exchange places. When you say, "Swamp exchange!" it is the signal for all of the children to change places in their "habitat" to represent the movement of the creatures in their environment as they search for food, look for protective cover, and contribute to its ecosystem.

■ **Luenn, Nancy (1994).** *Squish: A Wetland Walk.* Illustrated by Ronald Himler. New York: Atheneum. Ages 5–7.

**Environmental context:** Ecosystem of wetlands

Wearing a raincoat and boots, a young boy sloshes through a wetland area and observes what is going on. He is surprised at some of the unusual things that the busy inhabitants are doing: hungry herons hunt for food; quick-moving mice search for seeds; and leisurely snakes and water striders swim by. The boy hears some sounds he hasn't heard before: the croaking of frogs and singing of blackbirds. He also becomes aware of some unusual smells—especially a peculiar odor coming from decomposing plants and an earthy scent from the nearby mud. The boy realizes that living things contribute to the wetland ecosystem and have their own niche in this type of environment. Bright watercolor illustrations.

**Activity: "A Shrinking Environment"**

**Language arts focus:** To listen to procedures; to use spoken language to exchange information with others and to communicate effectively with an audience

Tell the children that they are going to play the role of a creature—blackbird, heron, garter snake, frog, mouse, water strider, and so on—in a shrinking wetland environment. Each child will need to sketch and color ten objects (one each on ten small squares of art paper) to represent the things they think they need—food, water, protective covering from plants, and so on. For example, the children role-playing mice may want a lot of food and can sketch lots of seeds on several squares. Continue the activity with the following steps:

1. Give the children lengths of yarn (60") to place around them as they sit on the floor. Tell them that these circles represent their wetland habitat and they should put their nature sketches on the floor beside them inside the circle. Ask volunteers to show their pictures and tell what they have on the papers in their environment.

2. Tell the children that their wetland environments are going to shrink because of land development and housing projects and other causes. Ask volunteers to be "shrinkers" who will shorten each length of yarn. Have shrinkers take a tape measure, measure 12" on each child's circle of yarn, and with scissors, cut it off.

3. Have the children encircle themselves with the shorter yarn and consider the smaller area they now have. There may not be room for all of the paper squares that represent their needs. Tell them to move their paper squares if they have to, to keep them inside the circle, but to keep the squares flat on the floor. If there is no room for all the squares, ask the children to give some up to the "shrinkers." Have the children listen to one another as they announce, in the role of a wetland creature, what they just lost in their shrinking environment.

4. Repeat the activity, if appropriate, and let the children sketch other items they need in the environment when they are in the role of another wetland creature.

5. Elicit from the whole group ideas about the value of a wetland environment and write their ideas on a class chart titled, "A Wetlands Habitat":

    - It catches rain for well water;
    - It is a nursery for young fish and a hunting ground for water fowl;
    - It gives protection for birds and ground animals;
    - It provides watery homes for such creatures as snakes, water striders, and frogs.

Elicit the children's suggestions for ways people can stop the shrinking of a wetland environment so that the creatures can have the things they need to survive. Record the suggestions on the chart.

**Home Activity**

Ask your child to help you make a small pond and place a small wooden tub in the ground to make a miniature wetland area. If desired, add to the pond plants that give off oxygen, such as waterweed, arrowhead, rushes, waterlilies, or cattails. Invite your child to observe the pond daily to see the extent to which snails and other creatures are attracted to your yard's small wetland area.

- **Martin, Jr., Bill, and John Archambault (1988).** *Listen to the Rain.* Illustrated by James Endicott. New York: Henry Holt. Ages 5–8.

    **Environmental context:** Refreshing power of rain and value of water to living things

    In this book-length poem, the authors use the rhythm of sounds and lyrical words to help a reader experience a rain storm through language. The words reflect the changing sounds that can be heard during a rainy day, beginning with the slow, soft, sprinkle of raindrops and an insistent dripping. The verse continues with the sound of pounding rain and then ends by describing a fresh wet aftertime when the storm stops. Full-color watercolor illustrations.

    **Activity: "Choral Speaking: Rain"**

    **Language arts focus:** To increase enjoyment of language about rain through a cumulative choral speaking verse; to adjust spoken language vocabulary and style to communicate effectively with an audience

    Divide the children into four groups. Read the image-building language in *Listen to the Rain* aloud as an accumulating choral reading activity that uses pages 3–20 in this unpaged book. In this activity, the first lines can be read by group 1, the second set of lines can be read by groups 1 and 2, and the third set of lines can be read by groups 1, 2, and 3, until the

## 58 Language Arts and Environmental Awareness

reading is finished. Have the children in group 4 use art paper to draw and color pictures of creatures during the rain storm to hold up and display during the choral reading. Since the words describe a rain storm that increases in its intensity, add the children's voices from the different groups to increase the volume of the verse as the rain changes from a light tinkle to a heavy pounding, and simulate the changes in the storm. Display the pictures to show what creatures are doing in the rainy environment. There are two lines of text on each page of the book and the lines can be assigned in the following way:

**Group 1**

*(pages 3–7)*

Listen to the . . .
the whisper of . . .
the slow soft . . .
th drip-drop . . .
the first wet . . .

**Groups 1 and 2**

*(pages 8–12)*

Listen to the . . .
the singing of . . .
the tiptoe . . .
the splish and . . .
the steady . . .
the singing of . . .

**Groups 1, 2, and 3**

*(pages 13–20)*

Listen to the . . .
the roaring . . .
the hurly-burly . . .
topsy-turvy . . .
lashing gnashing . . .
the lightning-flashing . . .
thunder . . .
sounding pounding . . .
leaving all . . .
a mishy mushy . . .

Have the children invite the members of another class into the room and perform this accumulating choral-speaking verse for them. Before the performance, have the children briefly tell ways that clean or un-

### Involving Children in Listening: Ages 5–8 59

clean water—particularly in the form of rain—can affect living creatures in their habitat.

**Home Activity**

Help your child get further acquainted with the sounds of nature and the atmosphere's acoustics with *Thunder, Singing Sounds, and Other Wonders: Sound in the Atmosphere* by Kenneth Heuer (Dodd, 1981, ages 8 up). This book introduces ways of recognizing natural music with thunder rumbles, wind whispers, and things that make singing sounds. Encourage your child to use objects in the home and replicate some of the sounds that living creatures in nature might hear in their habitats.

■ **Parnall, Peter (1989).** ***Quiet.*** Illustrated by the author. New York: Morrow. Ages 5–8.

**Environmental context:** Appreciating living creatures

In Parnall's story, a young inquisitive boy stays motionless with apple cores and seeds sprinkled on his chest to attract some living creatures in a nearby wood. He is successful: an observant raven watches him from a nearby tree and an interested chipmunk comes close and investigates the apple pieces and seeds. As the boy stays still, several curious chickadees assemble and call out to others. He notices a mouse approaching through the leaves on the ground and watches a bumblebee land on a sweet apple core on his chest. The boy shows his respect for nature's creatures by not disturbing them or their habitat. Line drawings and watercolor illustrations.

**Activity: "Motionless in the Woods"**

**Language arts focus:** To listen or describe an experience through drama; to exchange information with others

Have the children pair up with partners and ask one child to take the role of the motionless boy, and the other, the roles of the various inquisitive creatures. The motionless child can respond to what is going on while the second child listens and acts out or pantomimes the motions of the observing bird, the curious chipmunk, the chirping birds, the approaching mouse, and the flying bumblebee. After this role play, have the partners trade roles so each child can play the role of the boy. Have the children gather as a whole group and lead a discussion about different ways to show respect for living creatures in the woods and fields. Record their comments on a class chart and display it in the room.

**Home Activity**

With your child, take a nature walk and list every creature the two of you see on the trip. Select one of the creatures and have your child listen to the following language chant as you insert the name of the creature aloud. Have your child say these lines with you:

> We were walking to the *(woods, pond, corner)* the other day,
> When we saw a _____ *(name of creature)* going our way.
> We said, "Dear, dear _____ *(name of creature)*, where have you been?"
> It said, "I've been to the *(woods, pond, corner)* and I'm going again."
> We said, "Dear, dear _____ *(name of creature)*, what did you see?"
> And this is what it said, you see.
> "I saw the _____ *(name something seen in nature)* and the _____ *(name something seen in nature)*."
> "The _____ *(name something seen in nature)* and the _____ *(name something seen in nature)*."

Repeat the chant aloud as you and your child identify other living creatures on your nature activity.

■ **Steiner, Barbara A. (1996).** *A Desert Trip.* Illustrated by Ronald Himler. San Francisco: Sierra Club. Ages 6–8.

**Environmental context:** Appreciating a desert ecosystem

With her mother on an overnight hiking trip in a desert canyon, a young observant girl experiences the outdoors. The girl enjoys her mother's company and shows that she pays attention to the wonders of nature around her. She describes what she sees and talks about the plants, the rock formations, and the climate. She pays attention to her surroundings when the two stop to rest and even comments on what they eat for their meals. The young girl shows a respect for everything that is around her in the natural environment. Watercolor illustrations.

**Activity: "You Told Me That . . ."**

**Language arts focus:** To listen or describe an experience; to listen attentively to summarize what is heard; to communicate effectively with others

Have the children team up in partnerships and tell one another about a time when they experienced nature with someone—it could be any experience—visiting the desert or beach, going on a walking trip to a nearby park, observing birds from a window, facing a flood time, or taking a rafting trip down a fast-moving river. Have each child think about what he or she wants to say to describe the experience—what the weather was like, who they were with, what they saw, where they stopped to rest and eat their meals—and describe it to the listening partner. In turn, the listening partner summarizes what is described with the words, "You told me that. . . ." Have the children trade roles. Encourage the children to mention any littering or pollution that they saw and tell what *they* can do to keep a nature area free of litter and other things that pollute or cause damage to the surroundings.

**Home Activity**

Invite your child to make a desert garden in a dish with layers of gravel, potting soil, and sand. Plant different varieties of cactus—perhaps someone at a local nursery can introduce the child to some of the interesting names of various types, i.e., chicken and hens, fish-hook, rat's tail, and rabbit's ears. Place the dish on a layer of rocks and once in a while, ask your child to pour water on the rocks to put moisture in the air around the desert garden.

■ **Tressault, Alvin (1992).** *The Gift of the Tree.* Illustrated by the author. New York: Lothrop, Lee & Shepard. Ages 6-8.

**Environmental context:** Trees are important habitats

Tressault's book shows nature's cycle through a story about an old dominant oak tree that grows and stands tall for over a hundred years. The tree manufactures energy from the sun, provides shade, prevents the soil from drying out, and is a buffer for the movement of air. As the tree matures, some living creatures gnaw at it—termites tunnel inside and woodpeckers puncture it with tiny holes. One by one, its great branches crash to the ground and the tree returns to the earth where new life takes over. As part of this new life, the fallen tree becomes a home to chipmunks, raccoons, and other creatures, and as it decomposes, it nourishes the next generation of the forest—several new young trees. Watercolor illustrations.

**Activity: "From Tree to Log"**

**Language arts focus:** To listen critically; to apply knowledge to make predictions; to listen attentively to synthesize data

Read aloud Tressault's book up to the part where the tree crashes to the ground. Stop at this point and ask the children to use any information they have heard in the story and predict (guess) what they think is going to happen to the tree. Some of the children may infer that the tree becomes the hub of a society of smaller creatures such as ants, termites, beetles, millipedes, centipedes, and snails. Write their predictions on the board. After they have made their predictions, ask them to listen carefully as you read the rest of the book aloud so they can compare their predictions with the text. Help the children verify and compare the predictions they made on the board with the book's text.

**Home Activity**

Invite your child to play a hide-and-seek habitat game with you by using the illustrations in Douglas Florian's book *Nature Walk* (Greenwillow, 1989, ages 5–7). In the story, two children walk with their mother in the woods and the illustrations show several animals camouflaged on the pages. Additionally, a cottontail rabbit can be found in every scene. You and your child can search for the animals that hide in the illustrations. Turn to the back of the book to find a key in the index and see small pictures of the animals that can be found.

■ **Weeks, Sarah (1994).** *Crocodile Smile: 10 Songs of the Earth as the Animals See It.* Illustrated by Lois Ehlert. New York: HarperCollins. Ages 5–8.

**Environmental context:** Protecting endangered species

If a reader has ever wondered how endangered animals might react to what is going on in their habitats, then this book is the one to select. The songs about the cheetah, egret, giant panda, Komodo dragon, and other animals comprise the text and are heard on an accompanying tape. Two examples are the giant panda's song and the cheetah's song: The panda wonders aloud about what is making the chopping sound it hears beneath its tree and the cheetah points out its habitat is shrinking and sings about the monkey and the machete that "swing" beneath the same sky. Full-color collage illustrations.

**Activity: "Round-the-Group Story"**

**Language arts focus:** To listen attentively for information; to conduct research; to use spoken language vocabulary to create a story and to communicate what is learned

Divide the children into small groups of three or four and ask them to research information about an endangered animal. From the facts they gather, have them develop a round-the-group story about the animal. To start a round-the-group story, one child begins and states the first sentence that he or she composes, a second child repeats the first sentence and adds a second sentence, and so on. The story stops when the last child in the group ends it. Repeat the activity with another endangered animal. Have the small groups reconvene as a large group and ask volunteers to tell what they learned about threats to endangered species from Weeks's book and the accompanying tape and activity. Ask, "What suggestions did you find to protect an endangered species?"

**Home Activity**

Together, sing some of the songs from *Crocodile Smile: 10 Songs of the Earth as the Animals See It* and clap along to keep time with your child. Suggest that your child imagine being in a dark green wooded habitat with a

### 64 Language Arts and Environmental Awareness

roof of tree branches and rain falling. Have your child continue imagining that every tree branch, leaf, raindrop, and animal is sending out an environmental message and replay several songs so your child can listen to them. Elaborate on the meaning of some of the phrases that are heard. For instance, ask your child, "What does it mean to you when you hear an endangered animal wonder aloud about the unfamiliar sounds in its habitat? (sounds of chopping and cutting of trees)". Replay the giant panda's song or the cheetah's song and encourage your child to chant along at various intervals with "Sad, chop, chop, chop, chop. . . ." For a related activity, ask your child to listen to part of a selected song. Before your child hears the entire song, have him or her review quickly the information about an endangered animal heard so far in the song.

# Involving Children in Listening: Ages 9–14

■ **Dunlap, Julie (1996).** ***Birds in the Bushes: A Story about Margaret Morse Nice.*** Illustrated by Ralph L. Ramstad. Minneapolis: Carolrhoda. Ages 9–10.

**Environmental context:** Studying backyard birds

Dunlap's book is the life story of Margaret Morse Nice (1883–1974) who studied birds in her backyard and built her reputation as an ornithologist. Nice's interest began in childhood and continued through graduate school where she studied biology. When she married, she continued to do her research on birds but also planned time with her family. Her firsthand observations were made throughout the seasons. A bibliography for further reading is included. Black-and-white drawings and photographs.

**Activity: "Nice's Success"**

**Language arts focus:** To listen to details and take notes for later reference; to participate in discussion

Tell the children that they are going to hear excerpts from the life story of Margaret Morse Nice, one of the first women to become a leader of a major ornithological group. Ask them to listen to find out what group she led, what she did as a young girl that her parents considered "unladylike," and what actions she took that show the children her determination to study birds. Read several excerpts aloud and have the children take notes so they can refer to details about Nice's life as they participate in a whole group discussion about her.

**Home Activity**

To help your child attract birds and become familiar with the ones in his or her own backyard as Margaret Nice did, invite your child to write and order a resource kit called "Learning About Our Backyard Birds" from the National Bird-Feeding Society (PO Box 23, Northbrook, IL, 60065–0023), a group that promotes the feeding and housing of wild birds. The kit (cost about eight dollars) contains bird quizzes to complete, charts to help your child identify birds, line drawings your child can color, recipes to follow for a bird feeder, and suggestions for making favorite bird snacks.

- **Facklam, Margery (1990).** *And Then There Was One: The Mysteries of Extinction.* Illustrated by Pamela Johnson. San Francisco: Sierra Club. Ages 9 up.

**Environmental context:** Extinction of Earth's creatures

In this informative text, Facklam examines reasons why animals disappear from the earth. She discusses such natural causes as earthquakes and floods, as well as human activities that cause near-extinction: hunting, destroying habitats, and polluting. The accident of the tanker *Exxon Valdez* in Prince William Sound is cited as one example of how humans can ruin a habitat in a particular area. Near-extinction, however, has been reversed by people who care about the environment and by those who have worked in environmental centers and passed legislation to save selected species. One such center is the Darwin Research Station on the Galapagos Islands where scientists have established conservation, protection, and breeding programs for creatures native to the islands. Citing these examples, Facklam states that people *can* do something about the negative environmental changes: people can keep the earth clean, stop polluting, and stop destroying the habitats of other living things. Black-and-white sketches.

**Activity: "What I Can Do"**

**Language arts focus:** To listen to points of view; to use spoken language to exchange information and for persuasion

Mention to the children that in Facklam's book they are going to hear several reasons why some animals become extinct—why they disappear from the earth. After listening to what is read aloud, have each child turn to another child and tell the information they heard. Then, have the children get into small groups by counting off 1, 2, 3, 4, to make groups of four and retell one another in the group what they heard in the book and what they can do to effect changes in the environment to prevent extinction of living things. Ask one of the groups (or all groups if there is time) to volunteer and record their information on audiotape. Afterwards, place the tape and recorder in an area of the room with headphones so the children can listen to the reasons for animal extinction mentioned by the other class members.

**Home Activity**

Talk with your child about the effects of funds and finances in your city and county on local nature areas. Discuss the following: "What do you think happens when these funds are available? Unavailable?"

Tell your child you are going to read aloud about some situations that could happen when funds are unavailable for nature areas and invite your child to make suggestions that would help the members of youth groups or adult groups who want to assist in each of the following situations:

1. What could be done if habitat and fire protection crews and "eyes and ears" patrols by unarmed park rangers are reduced due to lack of funds?

2. What help could be provided if swimming areas are closed and mowing and irrigation halted in some park areas?

3. What assistance could be given if repairs to buildings, barbecue grills, tables, fencing, and gates in nature areas are neglected or delayed?

4. What could volunteers do if staff for adaptive leisure services—recreational programs, social events and independent living training for developmentally disabled citizens—are reduced?

■ **Gordon, Esther S., and Bernard L. Gordon (1977).** *If an Auk Could Talk.* Illustrated by Pamela Baldwin. New York: Walck. Ages 9 up.

**Environmental context:** Extinction of Earth's creatures

The Gordons discuss the extinction of the great auk, a fast-swimming bird once hunted for food and feathers. In its time, the auk's feathers were a substitute for eider duck feathers and used in pillows and other bedding materials. Auk-hunting was organized and the birds, caught nesting and resting on land, were driven into stone pens and clubbed. Some of these pens are still seen today on Funk Island, Newfoundland. The auk became scarce and died out in the 1800s and all that a child can see today are several tall great auk specimens and dried eggs in museums such as the one in Dublin, Ireland. Bordered black-and-white drawings.

**Activity: "If an Animal Could Talk . . ."**

**Language arts focus:** To listen carefully for information; to conduct research about interests

Have the children research an extinct or endangered animal of their choice and use the information to prepare a monologue in the role of the animal. Ask the children to include what happened to cause the animal's extinction. If appropriate, have the children make masks of their animals' faces from paper plates and hold them up during their monologues. They can write their monologue lines on the back of the plate to facilitate the delivery of the lines. Have the children pair up, sit facing one another, and deliver their monologues to each other. Increase the size of the group and have two pairs meet together to make a group of four and have the children listen to one another's monologues again.

They can also choose partners and use their two animal masks as puppets. They can engage in the following situations for puppet play:

1. One endangered animal has a problem with its shrinking environment and can't think of a solution on its own. It meets another endangered animal and tells it about the problem. The second animal also has a problem within its habitat. The two see if they can help one another toward solutions.

2. One animal is an interviewer on an endangered animal television show. The other animal is one who has just returned from visiting a different habitat and can tell what is happening there.

3. One animal has heard some environmental news on the local television station. It finds the positive side of the news. Another animal speaks out about the negative side. The two see if they can help one another resolve the conflict in the two views.

Then, have all the children get together and ask a child from each group to tell about the monologue that generated the most discussion in this activity. Ask, "What does the activity motivate you to do to protect endangered animals you know about?"

**Home Activity**

Encourage your child to research information on the computer about an endangered bird, perhaps the bald eagle, California condor, Hawaiian stilt, prairie chicken, or the whooping crane. To do this, introduce your child to the Internet by going to a nearby library and trying out the computers. The librarians will help your child get started for free. With a computer, your child can get news about endangered species, information about birds, or send and receive mail from others interested in this subject.

The Internet connects the computer your child is using with other computers around the world through phone lines. A subscriber service, such as America Online, and software, such as Microsoft's Internet Explorer, help your child find what he or she wants on the Internet. Invite your child to tell other family members about the computer experience and what he or she learned.

## ■ Gordon, Esther S., and Bernard L. Gordon (1976). *Once There Was a Passenger Pigeon.* Illustrated by Lawrence Di Fiori. New York: Walck. Ages 9 up.

**Environmental context:** Extinction of earth's creatures

In the seventeenth century, great numbers of passenger pigeons blacked out the sun in New Amsterdam (now New York City) but today there are no more—the last one died in 1914 and is preserved in the Smithsonian Institute. The large birds (eighteen inches tall) were called "pigeons of passage" because of their wide-ranging migratory travels and were admired, sketched, and recorded by the ornithologist John James Audubon. In the 1600s, the seemingly endless supply of young squabs were hunted for food and used as targets in shooting contests. This thoughtless killing doomed the birds—a fate facing several birds today such as the osprey (fish hawk), snowy egret, Kirtland's warbler, and the sandhill crane. These birds are all in danger. To combat this, the authors ask for bird sanctuaries, conservation, more protection laws, educational programs about wildlife protection, and a ban on insecticides to save endangered animals from the fate of the passenger pigeon. Bordered black-and-white sketches.

**Activity: "A Mock Trial"**

**Language arts focus:** To prepare for and listen to a mock trial situation; to conduct research about interests; to use spoken and written language vocabulary to communicate effectively

Have the children conduct a mock trial to explore fully the situation concerning the hunting of the passenger pigeon. Bring the unidentified pigeon hunters (represented by body outlines on large sheets of paper as Hunter A, Hunter B, etc.) to trial. Prepare for the trial by involving the children in the following procedures:

1. Assign roles by a random drawing for judge, jury, alternates, attorneys, bailiff, court clerk, audience, court artists, and media representatives.

2. Give the children time to research their roles and prepare for the trial. For instance, audience members can research information

about the auk, the dodo, or other extinct birds and determine the extent to which they are or are not supporters of hunting a bird to extinction.

3. Ask the court artists to research information as a basis for making any sketches needed by the attorneys.

4. Ask the media representatives to research information about what happened to the pigeon. Some of the representatives can write brief news articles about the bird, while others prepare daily TV news reports about the trial.

5. At the end of each proceeding, have the media representatives read their news reports aloud to the whole group. If appropriate for their reports, they can quote some of the verses about the passenger pigeon, auk, and today's endangered animals from around the world found in *Advice for a Frog* by Alice Shertle with illustrations by Norman Green (New York: Morrow, 1995, ages 9 up).

**Home Activity**

Invite your child to research a situation concerning an endangered bird species in your area. Discuss the following: "What is going on currently? In what ways is the endangered bird being cared for and protected? How can you help protect the bird?" Ask your child to suggest ways that he or she can take action and show support for any of the following:

1. Bird sanctuaries
2. Conservation actions
3. Protection laws
4. Educational programs
5. Laws to ban insecticides

■ **Hare, Tony (1990). *The Greenhouse Effect.*** Illustrated by Aziz Khan. New York: Gloucester Press. Ages 9 up.

**Environmental context:** Need for increased use of energy alternatives

The author, chair of the British Association of Nature Conservationists and Plant Life, discusses the greenhouse effect—a phenomenon that

## 72  Language Arts and Environmental Awareness

explains how the earth stays warm and how global warming appears to be increasing from carbon dioxide, flurocarbons, and combustion. Temperature is a factor in the earth's ecosystem and it seems that it is getting warmer. Evidence of this is cited, e.g., there is an increase of carbon dioxide and other gases in the air as a result of combustion of coal, oil, wood, etc. Carbon dioxide and other gases trap heat (sun's radiation) near the earth's surface and contribute to a greenhouse effect on the earth's surface. In turn, the objects in the greenhouse radiate heat that can be reradiated back, thus adding to the warming effect. Some specialists warn of an increase in warmth in the climate and cite rising sea levels, rising air temperatures, rising gas levels in the atmosphere, and increasing natural disasters as evidence of this. The ways humans use energy and the ever-increasing pollution by gases may continue to affect the earth's balanced ecosystem and the health of the ozone layer. To cut back on greenhouse gases and the possibility of the overheating of the earth, the author calls for an increased use of energy alternatives and conservation. Full-color drawings.

**Activity: "Energy Use Affects Ozone"**

**Language arts focus:** To listen for information and to identify items; to conduct research through a survey; to exchange information

Since the use of energy alternatives will help cut back on carbon dioxide and other greenhouse gases that affect the ozone, the children can look for energy-efficient appliances and helpful actions by school personnel and others. Encourage the children to check for drafty windows, leaky faucets, running toilets, and other environmental waste. On the conservation side, have the children notice people who switch off lights and heating when not needed, people who use recycled materials, and those who take public transportation. Have the children make a list of what they find. Write the children's information about their items on the board in two lists, "Ozone Enemies" and "Ozone Friends." To further identify the items that are ozone friends, have the children design their own symbol from adhesive-backed paper. Ask the children to survey the classroom and school to label any items that are ozone-friendly (such as spray paint containers without polyfluorocarbons that help cut back on gases and do not poison the atmosphere).

Further, help the children get a sense of the changes (and energy requirements) that have happened since their great-great grandparents' time, and discuss the ways people's needs over the years have demanded certain items. To clarify this, ask the children to name any items in their school that would *not* have been in people's schools one hundred years ago.

Ask the children to suggest things they can do to save energy in their school environment and write their ideas on a class chart entitled "Ways to Save Energy in My School." For any of the following suggestions, have the children identify what they could do to act on the energy-saver idea or identify the adult who could respond to the suggestion.

**Ways to Save Energy in My School**

1. Turn off water faucets, repair leaky ones;
2. Turn off lights when not in use;
3. Turn off computers when not in use;
4. Replace inefficient bulbs with energy-efficient ones;
5. Lower the temperature of hot water heater(s);
6. Seal drafty windows;
7. Use reflectors in lighting fixtures;
8. Maintain furnace and air-conditioning units.

**Home Activity**

Help your child survey your home for ozone-friendly items. Have your child design and make as many ozone-friendly symbols as he or she needs for the items in the home. Let your child cut the symbols out of adhesive-backed paper, and with your permission, affix the ozone-friendly symbols to identified items at home.

As a follow-up activity, encourage your child to prepare a display of greenhouse-effect-related news items from daily newspapers and ask your child to read or listen to the first paragraph of each news article before placing it in a scrapbook or notebook in your home. Talk with your child about the importance of cutting back on the gases that are poisoning the atmosphere and the various ways this can be done. People can: burn less fossil fuel; conserve energy to cut down carbon dioxide in the atmosphere; use fewer aerosol products; and plant trees that absorb carbon dioxide. Encourage your child to keep adding articles to the book throughout the year.

■ **Knapp, Brian (1992).** *What Do We Know about Rainforests?*
Illustrated by Mark Franklin. New York: Peter Bedrick. Ages 9 up.

**Environmental context:** Appreciation and importance of rainforest

Knapp's book is a survey of the earth's lush rainforests, their climates and importance. Factual information is given: the tall trees in the warm, humid rainforests are the dominant living things in the environment and give the people there fuel, food, furniture, heat, and homes. The author points out that the trees also form the habitat for a variety of animal and plant species that are specifically adapted to the conditions of the rainforest habitat. Additionally, scientists are currently finding that the rainforests are a valuable source of medicines and food for people. Full-color photographs.

**Activity: "Rainforest Water"**

**Language arts focus:** To listen to observations of fellow students; to apply knowledge of procedures; to listen attentively to others; to respect diversity in language use when meeting in pairs for discussion

Point out to the children that some people need help in seeing the danger in destroying any forest; in Thailand, for example, the forests have been logged and reduced to only 20 percent of their former size in the last twenty years. The people there now realize the damage that logging causes. When the trees are cut, their roots no longer hold water in the soil, and each subsequent rainstorm does *not* absorb into the soil as it did in the past but runs off. This runoff causes floods that damage property and harm people. To demonstrate this, have the children select two

**Involving Children in Listening: Ages 9–14**    75

clear glass or plastic containers that hold water and complete the following:

1. Inside container 1, place clumps of weeds that have the ground still attached to them, and miniature figures of people, houses, animals, and so on.
2. In container 2, place only dirt along the bottom with the figures.
3. Place plastic wrap on the stage of an overhead projector (to protect it from water drops) and set container 1 on the wrap. Turn on the projector light so the action is projected on a screen or wall. Choose children to pour a measured amount of water down over container 1 to simulate a rainstorm and observe the action of the water and what happens to the figures.
4. Place wrap and container 2 on the overhead projector stage. Have other children pour the same amount of water down over container 2 and observe what happens.

Ask the children to meet in pairs and listen to one another as they tell what they observed and what meaning this activity has for them. Ask them to respond to these questions, "What information did you gain about the danger in destroying a forest? About the value of protecting and caring for a forest? What can you do to help protect a forest? Are the issues related to protecting a forest different or similar to protecting a rainforest? What are some of the different issues from your point of view?"

**Home Activity**

Invite your child to think of ways that trees in the rainforest and other areas are important (prevent erosion, provide homes for animals, furnish food for wildlife, etc.) and ways people use trees outside of their natural environment (for houses, furniture, toys, tool construction, food, tree sap for resin, and so on). Write the child's suggestions on a sheet of paper under two headings, "Ways Trees Help Nature" and "Ways Trees Help People." Ask your child to suggest ideas for a third

**76  Language Arts and Environmental Awareness**

heading, "Ways People Help Trees." Display the paper on the home refrigerator or other appropriate place.

■ **McCord, David (1980).** *One at a Time.* Illustrated by Henry B. Kane. Boston: Little, Brown. All ages.

**Environmental context:** Observing living things in nature

McCord, an award-winning poet, shows his appreciation of living things in the environment and writes verses about a variety of subjects seen in nature. His poems include: "Three Signs of Spring," "Every Time I Climb a Tree," and "Earth Song." Black line drawings.

**Activity: "Mystery Life Forms"**

**Language arts focus:** To listen carefully to a poem; to make interpretations of descriptions and hear suggestions of others; to listen attentively to others and respect diversity of language use by fellow students

Read aloud one of McCord's poems about a creature in nature and ask the children to listen for words that tell them something about the creature. Point out that the creature is named in the poem's title. Select a second poem such as "The Newt," "The Grasshopper," "All about Fireflies," "Snail," "The Starfish," or "Cocoon," and write the lines on an overhead transparency, a chart, the writing board, or tagboard strips for a pocket chart. Mask the title and any reference to the name of the life form in the poem so that the life form is a "mystery" to the children.

Cover up all the lines except the first and read it aloud. Have the children listen to the poem as it is read—one line at a time—and reveal each written line as it is read aloud. After each line, ask the children for their interpretations about what the poem is describing. Ask, "What is the 'mystery' life form from nature that the lines are telling you about?" Ask the children to listen carefully to each other as they make their guesses. When the answer is guessed, reveal the title and have the children tell their ideas about the importance of the life form to the environment. Then, show the entire poem and ask the children to read it aloud with you as a choral reading. Repeat the activity with another poem about another one of nature's life forms.

**Home Activity**

Introduce your child to some of the observations of living things and the environment written by different poets, such as David McCord's *One at a Time*, Robert Froman's *Seeing Things*, or Sylvia Cassady's *Roomrimes*, and ask your child to listen to the poems that you read aloud. As your child listens, give your child a post card and encourage him or her to sketch or draw a scene or picture prompted by the words. Invite your child to copy some lines of the verses on the card and mail it to a relative or friend.

■ **Peet, Bill (1970).** *The Wump World.* Illustrated by the author. Boston: Houghton Mifflin. Ages 9 up.

**Environmental context:** Effect of pollution

Peet's story sends the message that becoming aware of others' negative impact on the environment can lead to action. Blue-green fanciful creatures, the Wumps, respond with various cooperative actions when their Wump world is invaded by polluters. The Wumps figure out what to do and band together to respond to the unwanted intrusion that is ruining their environment. Watercolor illustrations.

**Activity: "Caring Actions"**

**Language arts focus:** To listen to directions and to dramatic portrayals by others; to use spoken language vocabulary to exchange information and/or persuade; to listen to background music and dramatize it with movements

Initiate dramatic activities with the children related to the environmental pollution happening to the Wumps and their habitat.

1. First, Have the children sit in a circle and act out several natural phenomena that could be seen in *The Wump World*, i.e., windy breezes moving in and out of the circle, clouds floating by, and tree limbs blowing in the wind.

2. Read aloud an excerpt from the story and ask the children for ideas for dramatizing the words with movements. Play a brief selection of

background music during the children's actions. Ask them to *show* others what is happening in the excerpt without saying anythinng, and without stopping any actions until the music stops.

3. Present the children with situations in which they can make decisions. Ask the children to consider what would happen if they were a character in a specific place (e.g., a Wump who faces intruders who are ruining the environment) and give their own original responses. Ask, "In what way can you act out your decisions?"

4. Introduce other books (poems, songs) about protecting the environment and follow up the stories with additional role-playing about what happens. For instance, read aloud *Who Cares?* by Munro Leaf (Lippincott, 1971, ages 9 up) to introduce the subject of caring about the effects of pollution, and have the children suggest what actions they can perform to music about this topic.

**Home Activity**

Play for your child some of the songs about environmental issues facing the world today heard in *Evergreen, Everblue* by Raffi (MCA Records, 1990). Sing the lyrics and keep time together. Talk about the words that tell of human dependence on the earth for survival, as well as ways the songs celebrate the life-sustaining capabilities of the earth. Encourage your child to tell you about any human negligence that pollutes the air, water, and soil, and harms the earth. Elicit comments from your child with, "What can you do to help care for the earth? To show that you care about changing the negative effects people have on the environment?"

■ **Scott, Jack Denton (1974).** *Loggerhead Turtle: Survivor from the Sea.* Illustrated by Ozzie Sweet. New York: Putnam. Ages 9 up.

**Environmental context:** Protecting endangered species

Scott's informational book discusses the habitat of a female loggerhead turtle, a now-endangered species that has remained unchanged for over 150 million years. The turtle always returns to Jupiter Island off the Florida coast to lay her eggs. Helped by the Turtle Boys, a group in the area that works specifically to save the loggerhead, most of the female's hatchlings survive the danger from predators and find their way back to the sea. The Turtle Boys work on twenty-four-hour patrols under a special permit from the Florida Department of Natural Resources and increase the chances of a turtle's survival when they drive away such predators as raccoons, crows, gulls, and other seabirds who attack the nests and the turtle hatchlings. The Turtle Boys keep records on weather, the type of predator, the condition of a raided turtle nest, and the number of eggs destroyed. Sometimes, the boys use an artificial hatchery and transport the hatchlings to the beach in safety. They also attach metal tags to some female turtles to trace the migratory movements of the loggerhead, for scientists still don't know the extent of its underwater journeys or what compels the female to lay her eggs on the very beach where she herself was born. The Boys measure the turtle and record the date and her weight so they can study her rate of growth if she is ever recaptured and identified by her tag. Black-and-white photographs.

**Activity: "Endangered Animal Sketches"**

**Language arts focus:** To listen attentively to information as a basis for making a sketch; to use spoken language vocabulary to communicate effectively; to use written language to describe something

Have the children fold art paper into four squares and listen to a child read aloud a sequence of sentences that describes the loggerhead turtle. Each subsequent sentence should give the children more information so they can make increasingly detailed sketches of this endangered species. For example, sketch 1 should be a minimal sketch of the species since a small amount of information is offered (see the example that follows). In contrast, the last sketch should be the most detailed since a large amount of information is offered. Encourage the children to listen and to use the information they hear in each sentence to draw a picture of a loggerhead turtle in a square on their paper. Sentences to read aloud can be similar to the ones that follow:

1. **Sketch 1.** "The loggerhead turtle is a living fossil with four legs and no ears. Draw a loggerhead turtle like this in square one."
2. **Sketch 2.** "Dark green on top and light green underneath, a loggerhead turtle blends into the dark water when seen from the top while

## 80  Language Arts and Environmental Awareness

hunting for its food. Its tail is a balance. Using this information and all the information you heard before, draw another loggerhead turtle in square two."

3. **Sketch 3.** "The loggerhead turtle has a shell that measures about four feet across and has eyes as large as coffee cups. It has a bony beak that is about the size of a man's head and it weighs about 300 pounds. It travels with others in herds. Using this information and all the information you heard before, draw another loggerhead turtle in square three."

4. **Sketch 4.** "A loggerhead turtle has a bony shell of plates on its back. The shell is made of flat, smooth plates that look like a knight's armor. Sometimes it has barnacles living on its shell and marine grass sprouting from its back. Sometimes the shell is cracked in places and the turtle's neck is very wrinkled. Using this information and all the information you heard before, draw a fourth and final loggerhead turtle in square four."

5. Elicit comments from the children about which sentences gave them the information they needed to sketch this endangered species. Have the children get in groups of two, and encourage them to write their own descriptive sentences to read to their partners as their partners make sketches based on the information they hear. To do this, have each child write four sentences, with each one having more information about an endangered animal. Let the partner fold a sheet of paper into four squares and sketch while the other reads the four sentences. Ask the children to change roles and repeat the activity.

6. In the whole group, have the children suggest guidelines that will help them write better descriptive sentences to read to others. Write the children's suggestions on an overhead transparency or class chart. Use the suggestions as a future reference when the group repeats the activity and considers the characteristics of another endangered animal.

**Home Activity**

Encourage your child to choose books about an endangered species in your geographical area from a nearby library. Read excerpts from the books to one another with both using a caring voice when reading aloud about negative effects that have happened to endanger a living creature.

Further, show your child how to skim through the books and put bookmarks in places where there is an informative message, an interesting ecological incident, a beautiful description of nature, or an eye-catching illustration about the endangered creature. With your child, take turns and read aloud from these selections to gather information about what current practices are affecting endangered species and the environment in your area.

# III ▪ Involving Children in Folk Literature

# Involving Children in Folk Literature: Ages 5-8

■ **Bouchard, Dave (1990). *The Elders Are Watching.*** Illustrated by Roy Henry Vickers. Tofino, BC, Canada: Eagle Dancer Enterprises. Ages 8 up.

**Environmental context:** Beliefs about interdependence of living things

In keeping with the Native American belief of *mitakuye oyasin* (every living thing is related), Bouchard's book offers a reader the voices of the Elders who remind everyone that life on Earth is interdependent. Since the beginning of time, the Elders have watched over the environment. They have seen some of it destroyed and point out that human promises to care for it have been broken to acquire a majority of money for a minority of people. The Elders support the belief that humans must understand the relationship of all living things on Earth and they call for an environmental ethic about caring for the planet. Full-color paintings.

**Activity: "All Can Live Together"**

**Language arts focus:** To recognize nature beliefs in prose; to exchange information about experiences

Ask the children to listen for examples that point out the message that "all can live together" as you read aloud a related story, Natalia Romanova's *Once There Was a Tree* (New York: Puffin, 1985, ages 8 up) with illustrations by Gennady Spirin. In this tale set in Russia, an old growth (mature) tree is split to the core by a lightning bolt and a woodsman

**86**  Language Arts and Environmental Awareness

trims it down to the stump which then becomes a small habitat for living creatures—ants, bark beetles, earwigs, and a frog. When a man rests on the stump, he thinks that he owns it since he believes he already owns the forest and the rest of the earth. The author asks, "Who owns the stump?" and invites a reader to consider that the ants own it, that the beetles own it, and so on. The question, however, is answered in the final part of the text when the author states that the stump or tree belongs to everyone because it "grows from the earth that is the home for all." After hearing the story, ask the children to share their personal examples of how all can live together in a common home, Earth.

**Home Activity**

Start a letter to your child about what you did at your child's age that made you realize that every living thing is related. For example, you could write that you observed nature's creatures during the summer, visited different habitats, read magazines about nature, or supported the charity groups that protect endangered animals. Ask your child to read this letter with you and talk with you about it. Invite your child to think of things to write in his or her own letter that show an ongoing awareness of the changing environment. Encourage your child to mail the letter to a relative, friend, or neighbor.

■ **Bowden, Joan Chase, reteller (1979).** *Why the Tides Ebb and Flow.* Illustrated by Marc Brown. Boston: Houghton Mifflin. Ages 7–8.

**Environmental context:** Beliefs about origins of tides

This "how-and-why" tale explains why the ocean has tides and emphasizes a relationship between humans and the environment. An old woman living alone has no hut and asks Sky Spirit for one but he is too busy for her request. She asks for a rock and he says, "Take one." She climbs into her stew pot, sails out on the ocean, and threatens to pull a rock from the hole in the ocean if the Sky Spirit does not keep his promise to give her some shelter. When she pulls up the rock, the ocean begins to pour down into the bottomless hole in the sea. So Sky Spirit sends a dog, a young maiden, and a young man to stop the flow but they join the old woman and love and protect her, keep her company, and promise to build a hut for her. The Sky Spirit also makes a bargain that if the old woman puts back the rock, she can borrow it twice each day to beautify her flower patch. To this day, when she takes the rock, the water goes down. When she puts it back, the water goes up, and hence the tides ebb low and then leap high to cover the shore twice a day. Heavy line drawings.

**Activity: "How-and-Why Tales about Nature"**

**Language arts focus:** To appreciate nature beliefs found in folk literature; to use spoken and written language to relate information about literary elements and stories that reflect phenomena in nature

Mention to the children that this is a type of tale that early people told to help explain what was happening in nature around them. Have the children pretend that this tale was told long ago because an early storyteller noticed the tides and wanted to explain why this happened to others. Read aloud the "how-and-why" story about the tides and ask the children to work in small groups to gather information about the elements of who, what, when, where, why; what the action was; and how the tale ended. Have the children record their information in a graphic web such as the one that follows:

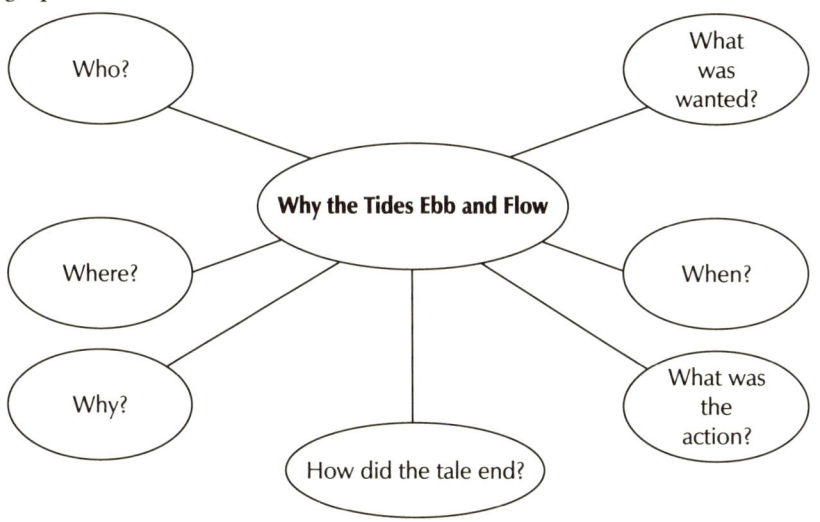

- Who?
- What was wanted?
- **Why the Tides Ebb and Flow**
- Where?
- When?
- Why?
- What was the action?
- How did the tale end?

## 88  Language Arts and Environmental Awareness

Ask the children to locate and read other "how-and-why" tales about natural phenomena. Have them write the bibliographic information about the tales on a chart labeled "How-and-Why Tales about Nature's Phenomena." An example could include the following titles:

**Natural Events**

- Daly, Niki, reteller (1995). *Why the Sun and Moon Live in the Sky.* Illustrated by the reteller. New York: Lothrop, Lee & Shepard. Ages 7–9. This is a why tale from the Inibio people about what happens when the Sea and her children visit the abode of the Sun and Moon.

**Seasons**

- Hodges, Margaret, reteller (1973). *Persephone and the Springtime, A Greek Myth.* Illustrated by the reteller. Boston: Little, Brown. Ages 8 up. This is a myth about Persephone who is released from Hades to bring spring.

**Others by the children**

Pointing to various book titles on the chart, discuss with the children, "Why do you think native people told these stories about nature? What do you think they wanted to say with these stories?"

**Home Activity**

Read aloud an informational article about the tides with your child. Mention that in the marine world, certain animals have a relationship with the ocean and respond to the tides with their own internal clocks. One example is the fiddler crab, which changes its colors according to the changing tides. It pays attention to its own internal tidal timepiece to do this and is dark when tides are low, pale when tides are high, and dark again at low tide. The crab is darkest when tides are lowest in the place where the crab lives and lightest when the tides are highest. Kept in laboratories by scientists, the crab also retains its ability to make its color changes in rhythm with the tides even when it is far *away* from its home near the tides. If your child is further interested in this topic of tidal rhythms in animals, suggest that he or she research the fiddler crab, herring, grunion, or the flat worm of the Brittany coast.

- **Bruchac, Joseph, reteller (1994).** *The Great Ball Game: A Muskogee Story.* Illustrated by Michael Caduto. New York: Dial. Ages 5–8.

**Environmental context:** "How-and-why" story about birds' characteristics

Some Native American storytellers' thoughts about why birds are banished to the south—their migration journeys—are explained in this tale. In Bruchac's story, the animals and birds argue over which group is better and decide to settle the argument with a ball game. Bat, small and weak, is not chosen for either team, but it is eventually Bat who wins the match for the animals, who then banish the birds. Full-color acrylic illustrations.

### Activity: "A Tale of the Birds' Banishment"

**Language arts focus:** To transform information from a story; to participate in discussion; to use spoken language vocabulary to exchange information

Have the children imagine that this tale was told long ago because early people noticed the migration journeys of birds and wanted to explain why the birds did this. Ask the children to reflect on what the land must have looked like long ago for the migrating birds as they traveled. Lead a discussion about the way the land looked for the following:

1. Water birds (cranes, ducks, geese, herons);
2. Grass and woods birds (eagles, grouse, owls, partridges, pigeons, quail, vultures, woodpeckers);
3. Songbirds (meadowlarks, mocking birds, thrushes, finches, wrens, blackbirds, bluebirds, orioles).

Elicit comments from the children about any birds they have seen migrating. Add your own input and that of a local biologist you've contacted. Identify the route (sometimes along waterways) that ducks and other migrating birds follow today to fly across your state. Have each child cut out a small silhouette of a flying bird and affix the shape to a state map in a migratory line to mark the pathway the birds take when they migrate.

**Home Activity**

Ask your child to imagine what your state looked like long ago for the animals (bears, coyotes, deer, foxes, wolves, mountain lions, rabbits, squirrels, wildcats, porcupines, badgers, raccoons). Give your child an outline map of the state and ask him or her to make decisions about which illustrations of mountains, valleys, waterways, fish, and animals to sketch or draw to show the environment long ago. Contrast your child's sketch with a contemporary map that shows the current local roads and highways and point out developments that have affected the environment—highways through mountains and valleys, dams on waterways, and business and housing developments in the habitats of various animals. Make a list with your child about the impact of this construction on contemporary wildlife.

■ **Clement, Claude, reteller (1986).** *The Painter and the Wild Swans.* Illustrated by the author. New York: Dial. Ages 5–8.

**Environmental context:** Explanation of natural phenomena in a legend
In this story, a Japanese painter is captivated by the sight of beautiful wild swans from Siberia and leaves his work to follow them. When he finds them on an island in an icy lake, he faces death from exposure to the cold but realizes that seeing their beauty is its own reward for his journey. With this reflection and acceptance, he is transformed into a wild swan and flies away with the others. Full-color watercolor illustrations.

**Activity: "Influenced by Nature's Beauty"**

**Language arts focus:** To develop and expand spoken language vocabulary through storytelling; to develop dialogue

Read or tell Clement's tale aloud. Have the children decide on what the Japanese painter in the story could tell as an anecdote to another character—perhaps a fellow worker or another painter or a family member. Have the children insert this character in the tale and suggest dialogue between the two. Elicit a variety of statements by asking, "What do you think the Japanese painter would say about the beauty of the wild swans? What do you think the new character would say about the birds or the environment? What short story (or stories) about these living creatures and their habitats could the Japanese painter tell the new character?"

**Home Activity**

Invite your child to write a story from the point of view of the wild swans in Clement's book. He or she could describe what the journey is like as the swans travel from Siberia, how it feels to be a swan during this migration, the ways humans alter the birds' environment, and ways that swans can affect a sensitive person who appreciates their beauty. Ask your child to read the story aloud to you.

■ **de Paola, Tomie, reteller (1983).** *The Legend of the Bluebonnet.* Illustrated by the author. New York: Scholastic. Ages 5–8.

**Environmental context:** Explanation of natural phenomena in legend

In this legend, a shaman tells the suffering Comanche people that a drought and famine has come upon them because the people are selfish. To show they are not selfish, they must sacrifice a treasured possession to the Great Spirits. The shaman says this action will restore life as it was before the famine. A small girl, She-Who-Is-Alone, is without parents or grandparents, but she is the only one to sacrifice a valued possession. She burns a warrior doll her mother made for her. When She-Who-Is-Alone places the doll's ashes on the hillside, many bluebonnet flowers appear and the people see the flowers as a sign of forgiveness from the Great Spirits. They recognize her contribution to the Comanche people and rename the small girl "One-Who-Dearly-Loved-Her-People." Full-color watercolor illustrations.

### Activity: "Telling Stories about Phenomena"

**Language arts focus:** To develop or expand vocabulary through storytelling; to exchange information about selecting and telling stories; to communicate effectively to an audience

After reading aloud the legend of the appearance of the first bluebonnet flowers, ask the children to select and tell a Native American legend or "how-and-why" tale about another phenomenon in nature and prepare the story by working in teams of two. Take time to discuss ways to select and tell stories with the children and elicit their remarks to write on charts in the room. Their remarks might include some of the following suggestions:

1. **How Can I Select a Story?** Choose a story you like (see the chart of "How and Why Tales" about nature in the activity for Joan Chase Bowden's book *Why the Tides Ebb and Flow*). Decide on a story your friends in class will also like.

2. **How Can I Get Ready to Tell a Story?** Read the story slowly. Reread it several times so you will know the words, rhythm, and flow of the language. Then tell the story out loud to yourself until the telling is fun for you.

3. **How Should I Tell the Story to Others?** Tell the story to a friend. Use enthusiasm. Use different voices for the characters.

Schedule time for the children to tell their stories in small groups or to the whole group as an audience.

### Home Activity

Invite your child to see the effects of drought as mentioned in *The Legend of the Bluebonnet* by deliberately *not* watering a house plant for several days. Ask your child to make sketches of the leaves as they wither. Have your child water the plant and then tell what happens when it receives water. Discuss how quickly the plant revives.

- **de Paola, Tomie, reteller (1988).** *The Legend of the Indian Paintbrush.* Illustrated by the author. New York: Putnam Group. Ages 5–7.

**Environmental context:** Appreciating beauty of plants

In this legend, a small boy, Little Gopher, uses his artistic skills to give a special gift back to his people. He paints the deeds of his tribe. As a reward, he is given magical paint brushes of bright colors—red, orange, and yellow. These colors enable him to paint his version of his environment, especially the colorful evening sky. When the brushes are discarded, they take root and bloom as Indian paintbrush flowers across the hillside. Full-color watercolor illustrations.

**Activity: "Beautiful vs. Ugly Environment"**

**Language arts focus:** To engage in conversation; to exchange information

Talk about the beauty of plants that the children have seen in their environment, such as the Indian paintbrush flower in this legend and in contrast, the ugliness that trash and pollution bring into an environment. Ask the children to walk around the school grounds with you to observe the plants growing in the area and to pick up trash. Have the children divide into four groups and give each group a paper trash bag and each child a pair of disposable gloves. Have one member of each group carry a separate bag for recyclable items that are found. Suggest that they take note of the pollution they can't pick up—smoke from stacks, car exhaust. Make sure they avoid touching dangerous items; leave them for a school maintenance person to dispose of at another time, especially pollutants such as cans of motor oil and old batteries.

Back in the classroom, involve the children in one or more of the following activities:

1. Have the children wash their hands with soap and water after touching trash.
2. Encourage the children to talk about the types of trash they found and the areas where the most trash was located.

## 94  Language Arts and Environmental Awareness

3. Ask one member of each group to show the bag of recyclable items that were found. Discuss the difference between recyclable items (aluminum cans, glass bottles, and newspapers) and biodegradable ones (fruit peelings, grass clippings).

**Home Activity**

Point out to your child the usefulness of biodegradable leaves from plants and trees. Invite your child to compost some leaves in the fall to recycle them and turn them into soil. Use a 20-, 30-, or 50-gallon drum with holes punched in the bottom and sides. Add leaves and other plant materials (fruit and vegetable peelings, coffee grounds, tomato vines, etc.). Throw in some twigs to help the air circulate in the pile. Wet the pile with water and cover it with a discarded rug or tarp. Stir the pile with a pitchfork or a sturdy stick several times throughout the season. In the spring, the pile will be a rich substance for you and your child to add to the soil.

- **Gershator, Phillis (1995).** *Honi's Circle of Trees.* Illustrated by Mimi Green. New York: Jewish Publication Society. Ages 5–7.

**Environmental context:** Planting seeds for generations to come

Gershator's story introduces Honi, an elderly legendary character, who selflessly wanders across the land of ancient Israel planting carob seeds that will grow for future generations to enjoy. Honi comes to a village where a friendly man remembers a rain miracle that Honi performed years before and encourages the old man to take a rest. Honi, reminiscent of Rip Van Winkle, awakens from what he thought was a nap and learns that seventy years have passed. He is confused and upset. He soon discovers, however, that he has been granted this extension of years so he can see his trees bear fruit for the people. Full-color watercolor illustrations.

**Activity: "A Story Character's View"**

**Language arts focus:** To recognize names; to create a bulletin board display; to conduct research about interests

Engage the children in creating a bulletin board about the importance of the carob tree (or other trees). On a display board, have the children show the different parts common to all trees, any patterns that they see in trees, and the names and functions of the parts of trees. Ask the children to design drawings to emphasize the importance and value of trees to other living creatures. To do this, the children can select one of the following projects:

1. Research the role that the carob tree plays in the lives of living creatures.
2. Research the name of the state tree and its importance. If there is no state tree, have the children plan a class contest to select a state tree. Who could they write to and propose their candidate for a state tree?
3. Other ideas suggested by the children.

**Home Activity**

Encourage your child to examine a variety of leaves and identify the leaf parts. After discovering that all leaves have the same essential parts, your child can sketch and label leaf parts on a line drawing. If appropriate, help your child compare the parts of a tree and its functions with similar parts and functions of the human body to relate the messages that "Every living thing is part of Earth's family" and "Living things are all related." Ask your child to copy the messages as captions for the drawing. Display the drawing in a place selected by your child.

■ **Glass, Andrew (1995).** *Folks Call Me Appleseed John.* New York: Doubleday. Ages 7–8.

**Environmental context:** Planting trees for generations to come

Glass's fictional story is about John Chapman and is a narrative that focuses on the friendship and caring feelings between John and Nathaniel, his younger half-brother. The text also expresses the brothers' friendly relationship with Native Americans they meet in their adventurous journeys. John also tells about some of the exciting experiences the brothers have while traveling in western Pennsylvania. A map and biographical notes are included. Full-color watercolor illustrations.

### Activity: "Adopt a Tree"

**Language arts focus:** To use spoken and written language vocabulary; to conduct inquiries into types of trees; to report and communicate effectively to an audience

Mention to the children that you want to adopt a tree and you want to know what would be the best tree to adopt in your area. Ask them to help you make a decision (would it be an apple tree?) and have them inquire of local nurseries or research in books about the types of trees that grow well in the region and their importance for people, birds, insects, and animals. Have the children report their findings back to the group. Record their findings on the board. For example, the name of a particular apple tree, MacIntosh, that grows well in an area can be recorded under the heading, "Tree Name."

| Tree Name | Area Found | Importance |
| --- | --- | --- |
| MacIntosh | Washington state | Provides fruit |

Have the children read aloud the information on the chart before making a decision about a type of tree to adopt. With the children, identify a tree of that type on the schoolground, or in a nearby park, to care for. Alternatively, purchase a sapling and care for the adopted tree in the room or in a large container just outside the classroom door. With the permission of the school administrator, plant the tree outside when it outgrows the container.

### Home Activity

With your child's assistance, plant a seedling of a fast-growing tree in a clear plastic container and watch the roots as they grow. Ask your child to make weekly sketches of the root growth that is seen. Every two weeks, ask the child to collect additional data, such as recording the amount of water given the tree, the number of leaves on the seedling, the height and width of the plant, and number of leaf sprouts or buds, if any. Ask the child to predict what value the tree will have for living creatures when it reaches maturity. Select a location outside for the tree and plant it there when it gets too large for the container.

- **Lacapa, Michael, reteller (1990).** *The Flute Player: An Apache Folktale.* Illustrated by the author. Flagstaff: Northland Publishing Co. Ages 8 up.

**Environmental context:** Explanation of natural phenomena in folktale

In this retold Apache tale, Lacapa relates the People's respect for every aspect of nature, even a small dying leaf that falls to the ground. This story is about a young girl and boy, a flute player, who are attracted to one another during an Apache hoop dance. The girl says that when she hears his flute, she will place a leaf in the river that runs through the canyon. The floating leaf will tell him that she likes his music. When the flute player leaves and join his companions for a long hunt, the girl becomes ill and dies before his return. To this day, when the people hear nature's echoes through the canyon and see leaves falling into the river, they say that the girl still likes the music of the flute player. Full-color watercolor illustrations.

**Activity: "Trash's Point of View"**

**Language arts focus:** To transform a Native American tale into a new creative story; to apply knowledge of story elements; to write a first person story

Ask the children to imagine what it would be like for the beautiful river and canyon in the previous story to be littered with forms of pollution. Ask them to imagine that the school grounds have been turned into a beautiful river and canyon area similar to the setting in the tale and tell them they will have an opportunity to look for forms of pollution. Give each child a small plastic bag and disposable gloves and take them outside on a tour of the school grounds—now an imagined river and canyon area. Have each child collect small, non-dangerous pollutants that are found. Be sure that each child wears gloves while picking up any trash and emphasize that large or dangerous objects should be left alone for the school grounds crew to dispose of at another time. Have the children wash their hands when they return inside.

Back in the room, have each child use one of the pollutants in his or her baggie as a basis for writing a creative story from the point of view of the pollutant that has found itself in the children's imaginary river and canyon area. For example, the children can write about how the pollutant or trash got into the water and wilderness, how it feels to be a pollutant, and ways in which the object could be recycled and disposed of before it pollutes the environment further. Ask volunteers to read their stories aloud. Collect the stories and place them in a notebook in a class reading area. Encourage the children to read the stories for independent reading.

**Home Activity**

Invite your child to go on a walk with you or another adult to observe the types of trash your child can find in the neighborhood. Locate the areas with the most trash, and note which items can be recycled as well as which items can be used for compost. Ask your child, "What can you do to help recycle the items you found?"

■ **Luenn, Nancy (1993).** *Song of the Ancient Forest.* Illustrated by Jill Kastner. New York: Atheneum. Ages 6–10.

**Environmental context:** Caring for a forest

Centered around the character of Raven, the trickster, from the stories of Native Americans of the Northwest, this tale is set in the earth's beginning. This is a time when Raven has the ability to see the future and the upcoming destruction of the forest in the name of progress. To give a warning, Raven sings a song about this to all around him but no one believes him. As time goes by, native people and their cultures vanish, pioneers who settle on the land change its original balance, and the forests begin to vanish. Still no one believes Raven's musical words about the destruction. When only a few trees in an old growth forest remain, Raven meets young Marni, a logger's daughter. Marni listens to Raven, hears the message, and understands his plea to save the forest.

She takes the warning home to her father, who tells his logger companions, but they only scoff at Raven's words. They stone Raven and as the bird's blood flows into the soil, the trees begin to sing and cause the men to run away in fright. Raven, true to his trickster nature, revives himself and again sings his song about the symbiotic relationship of living things in the forest. Raven's warning is emphasized in the song's finale:

> "Without the fungus, there is no forest,
> Without the forest, no circle of time, no circle of time...."

**Activity: "Brainstorming"**

**Language arts focus:** To think of alternate words to a song; to participate in group discussions; to synthesize information

Divide the children into small groups and ask them to think of similarities and differences between the ways pioneers used the land on which they settled and the ways the children and their families use the land today. Have them record their ideas on paper under two headings:

**Ways Pioneers Used the Land**  **Ways People Today Use the Land**

Back together as a whole group, the children can refer to their lists to suggest different words to Raven's song of warning and to emphasize caring for the land and its creatures with their own words. The following is a form to write on the board to elicit the children's words for the song:

| **Raven's Song** | **Our Song** |
|---|---|
| Without the squirrel, | Without the _____, |
| there is no owl. | there is no _____. |
| Without the salmon, | Without the _____, |
| eagle dies. | _____ dies. |
|  | (*other lines by the children*) |

**Home Activity**

Show your child several ecology-related laser video discs on a television monitor or program them into a computer disc to enhance your child's learning about what is going on in the forests and other habitats and to give your child quick access to thousands of visuals. If these visuals are unavailable at home, visit a nearby library with access to this technology. With a still-frame control, your child can observe phenomena and details that he or she may have only read about previously. A resource for this is *CD-Rom for Librarians and Educators: A Resource Guide for Over 300 Instructional Programs* by Barbara Head Sorrow and Betty S. Lumpkin (Jefferson, NC: McFarland, 1993). Other examples of video disc titles and sources include the following selections:

*Acid Rain* from National Geographic, Education Services Division, 1145 17th St. NW, Washington, DC 20036–4688.

*Animal Homes* from Churchill Media, 12210 Nebraska Ave., Los Angeles, CA 90025–3600.

*Our Environment* from Optilearn, Inc., PO Box 997, Stevens Point, WI, 54481.

■ **Rodanas, Kristina, reteller (1992).** ***The Dragonfly's Tale.*** Illustrated by the author. New York: Clarion. Ages 6–10.

**Environmental context:** Native American beliefs about effects of weather

In this Zuni legend, the Ashivi people waste their corn harvest and they are punished by the Corn Maidens with a drought-caused famine. When the people leave the famine area, a brother and sister are left behind and the boy makes a toy dragonfly for the girl from the corn tassels. The dragonfly comes to life and asks the Corn Maidens for help. In return, the Corn Maidens bless the land and make it fruitful again. Full-color watercolor illustrations.

**Activity: "Environment"**

**Language arts focus:** To brainstorm about different elements of the environment; to participate in discussion; to diagram a word web

Lead a discussion with the whole group related to the story and ask the children to brainstorm various subjects that could be studied around the topic of "Native Americans and the Environment." Write the children's ideas on the board in a list. Read the list aloud and then sketch a web on the board to write the subjects that could be investigated by interested children. The topics could be grouped under the headings of various subjects in a web such as the examples that follow:

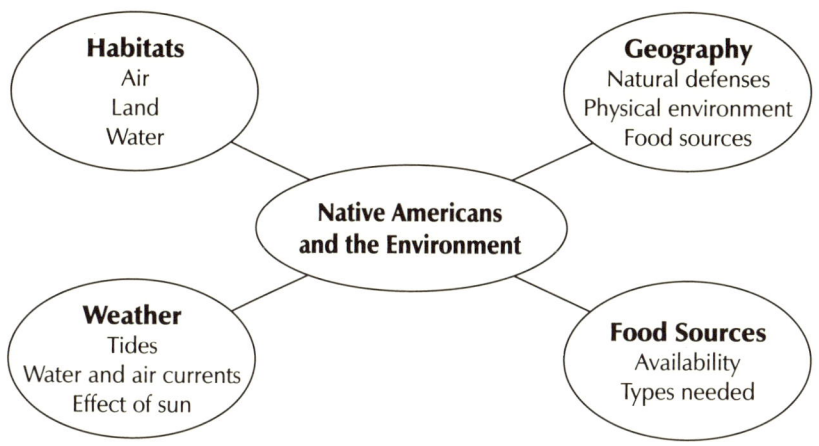

**Habitats**
Air
Land
Water

**Geography**
Natural defenses
Physical environment
Food sources

**Native Americans and the Environment**

**Weather**
Tides
Water and air currents
Effect of sun

**Food Sources**
Availability
Types needed

Have the children make their own individual copies of the web. Encourage the children to use the web as a reference in future conversations and other class activities related to the environment and beliefs of Native Americans. Encourage interested children to make further inquiries into the topics of their choice and report their findings back to the whole group.

**Home Activity**

Discuss with your child the meaning of the words "Earth's fruitfulness" as well as beliefs of some Native American tribes after reading aloud excerpts from the *Keepers of the Animals: Native American Stories and Wildlife Activities for Children* by Michael Caduto and the Abenaki author, Joseph Bruchac (Fulcrum, 1991, ages 8 up). In the book, Caduto and Bruchac retell several animal tales that focus on native people's relationship with the animal world and also include directions for environmental projects.

- **Steiner, Barbara (1988).** *Whale Brother.* Illustrated by the author. New York: Walker. Ages 7–8.

**Environmental context:** Recognizing Native American beliefs about caring for nature and its creatures

In Steiner's story, Omu wants to become a great carver of ivory like Padloq, a craftsman of his tribe. Padloq tells Omu that he can only make the bone come alive by learning to wait until he "sees" a carving in the bone, and by finding the stillness—waiting for something to burst forth—in the ivory. Later, when Omu is out in his kayak, he plays his harmonica and sees killer whales in a circle around him. Each day from then on, he plays his songs for the whales and they sing their songs back to him. One day, he notices a large male whale on the shore and sees that the whale cannot move and its skin is dry and dull. For five days, Omu sits with his whale brother, sings to it, and plays his harmonica. When one of the whales in the water tosses Omu a tusk of ivory, he begins to carve it and asks the whale's spirit to come into the ivory. When the whale gives up its life, the boy plays a song to accompany the whale as it goes to the Spirit World. When Omu finally returns home to his worried parents, he tells them what happened and how he finally found the stillness to carve the ivory tusk. Full-color acrylic illustrations.

**Activity: "Questions and Answers"**

**Language arts focus:** To participate in discussion; to audiotape information about whales; to use spoken vocabulary for questions and answers about interests

Read aloud excerpts from *Whales: Giants of the Deep* by Dorothy Hinshaw Patent (Holiday House, 1984, ages 10–11) and then discuss some of the facts about whales, the pronunciation of their scientific names, and any terms unfamiliar to the children. For this discussion, select a child to be a tape technician for the group. He or she will push the button to record information during the group's discussion and turn the tape over when needed. Ask the child to label the tape and place it with the book in a listening area or reading shelf. After a week, let another child erase the tape and use it again to record more questions and answers about another environmental topic in which the children are interested.

## Home Activity

Invite your child to make a whale body shape or shapes for a hanging mobile. He or she can cut shapes from colored felt and punch the edges with a one-hole paper punch to make holes for lacing. The shapes can be filled with newspaper or soft material, decorated, and laced together. Have your child tie yarn or string to the shapes and hang them from a coat hanger to make a mobile.

# Involving Children in Folk Literature: Ages 9–14

- **Bierhorst, John, reteller (1970).** *The Ring in the Prairie: A Shawnee Legend.* Illustrated by Leo and Diane Dillon. New York: Dial. Ages 9–13.

**Environmental context:** Explanation of natural phenomena in legend

In Bierhorst's retold tale, the Shawnee belief about how animals and birds came to be is the message. It begins when a magical ring wears through the sod in the prairie and becomes the landing site of a basket carrying twelve beautiful princesses, daughters of a star chief in the sky. Waupee, a tall and manly hunter, wins the youngest as his bride and she is happy until life on earth loses its appeal for her. She makes a basket and flies away in it with her son to go back to her father. When her son grows older, the star chief says that Waupee can come and live with them and to do this, he should bring along earthly gifts—one of each kind of bird and animal. Waupee takes only a tail, a foot, or a wing of each animal and he is carried along with the gifts up to the sky to live with the star chief. At a feast, the chief says that the guests might take any of the earthly gifts they like best. Those who select tails or claws are changed into animals and run off. Waupee, his wife, and son choose a white hawk's feather and each becomes a white hawk. They descend with the other birds to earth where they still live to this day. Full-color watercolor illustrations.

**Activity: "Bird and animal collages"**

**Language arts focus:** To use spoken and written language vocabulary to describe fauna

In the story, the star chief tells Waupee that he can live with his family in the sky and to do this, he should bring along earthly gifts—one of each kind of bird and animal. Invite interested children to make bird and animal collages from pictures showing a creature that Waupee might have chosen in its habitat. The pictures can be drawn or cut out from discarded magazines, newspapers, advertising flyers, and brochures. Display the collages and elicit adjectives from the children to describe what is shown in their artwork. Encourage the children to write lists of additional words about what the birds and animals might hear, see, smell, taste, and touch on index cards to place near the collage habitats.

**Home Activity**

Encourage your child to read several animal origin stories from Native American tribes and tell you about the way the stories express some native people's beliefs about the origin of birds and animals and their characteristics.

- **Cohlene, Terri, reteller (1990).** *Ka-ha-si and the Loon: An Eskimo Legend.* Illustrated by Charles Reasoner. Vero Beach, FL: Rourke. Ages 9–13.

**Environmental context:** Recognizing the animal-human relationship

Cohlene's story retells the legend of an Eskimo hero, Ka-ha-si, with an animal-human relationship as well as information about the way humans depend on the environment for their food. In the tale, Ka-ha-si acquires great strength and boldness and uses his abilities to rescue his people in times of peril. As a boy in the cold North, Ka-ha-si does not learn how to hunt or fish or play like the other children; instead, every day and night he stays asleep by his mother's lamp. One early morning, a beautiful loon awakens him with a message from his grandfather to tell him that each day he must eat four leaves from a magical bush and bathe in the icy waters of a stream. Ka-ha-si does this. When a season of hunger arrives for the villagers, Ka-ha-si suggests that the men hold a big walrus skin and throw him high into the air so he can see where the animals are hiding. When the men do so, Ka-ha-si sees walruses on a nearby ice floe and they paddle their umiaks into the water. Ka-ha-si is the first one ashore on the floe to hunt the animals to get food so his people can live. Later, the loon tells Ka-ha-si that his grandfather needs him and he paddles out to a giant whirlpool and allows the sea to swallow him up so he can be with his elderly relative. In the days that follow, people sing of Ka-ha-si's deeds as a hero of the people. Includes information on the customs and lifestyle of the Eskimos. Full-color acrylic illustrations.

### Activity: "Ka-ha-si's Actions"

**Language arts focus:** To respond to issues related to the story; to participate in essay writing to inform, explain, and persuade a reader toward a point of view

Encourage the children to write their own short paragraphs about walruses, telling their points of view. Everyone can read these at a later time in a class book. Ask them to express their thoughts about Ka-ha-si's actions of providing food for his hungry people. Before the children write, you may model the process by writing a short paragraph on the board or the overhead projector. Elicit the children's responses about some of the following issues:

1. To what extent do the children agree or disagree that humans have a right to hunt animals?
2. Do they believe (or not believe) that the hunting of a walrus is justified?
3. In what way do they realize the importance of walruses to Ka-ha-si's people and accept the value of a walrus and its importance to the native people as Ka-ha-si did?

### Home Activity

Take your child to the library to find some facts about arctic animals and ways they are or are not being protected. Have your child take paper and pencil to record his or her findings and make sketches of the animals that live in this cold environment. At home, let your child make an informational folder about the animals and use the library findings as reference material to write captions for the sketches.

- **Goble, Paul, reteller (1984).** *Buffalo Woman.* Illustrated by the author. New York: Bradbury. Ages 9–13.

**Environmental context:** Native American beliefs that living things are related

In this tale, the Native American belief about ways we are all related, a theme expressed by the Sioux from the Plains tribes as *mitakuye oyasin*, is portrayed through an animal-to-human transformation. A buffalo from the Buffalo Nation turns herself into a woman and marries a young man and says, "You have always had good feelings for our people. . . . My people wish that the love we have for each other will be an example for both our peoples to follow." In the author's notes, Goble states that the story teaches that buffalo and people were related and their lives closely interwoven. Early storytellers believed that retelling the story was *not* entertainment but strengthened the People's bond with the herds, encouraged the herds to return so that the People could live, and had a power to bring about a change within each person. It was felt that in listening to the story, the People might all be a little more worthy of their buffalo relatives. Full-color acrylic illustrations.

**Activity: "Relationship of Living Things"**

**Language arts focus:** To use spoken language to express views; to participate in a discussion

Ask the children to reflect upon what changes, if any, have happened to their thoughts because of the message of *mitakuye oyasin* in the story of *Buffalo Woman*. Discuss: "In what way do you realize that some people believe that every living thing is related? In what way could people try to be a little more worthy of our relatives in Earth's family?" Ask some volunteers to share their thoughts with the group. Invite interested children to read additional stories from the Native American culture and other cultures that they know about that send the message "living things are all related."

**Home Activity**

Read Paul Goble's *The Friendly Wolf* (Bradbury, 1974, ages 7–9) with your child. In the story, two children wander about during a berry-picking expedition and become lost in the hills. They are protected by a wolf who leads them back to the tribe. Talk about the wolf's help, and by comparison, ways dogs in contemporary life have helped people in different situations. Ask, "In what way does the story of *The Friendly Wolf* send the message that living things are all related? How do stories you know about ways dogs have helped people in times of need send the message that living things are all related?"

- **Lawlor, Laurie (1995).** ***The Real Johnny Appleseed.*** Illustrated by Mary Thompson. Chicago: Albert Whitman. Ages 9–13.

**Environmental context:** Planting trees for others

With the theme that one can help others in need, this biography has brief chapters about Appleseed's desire to provide apple trees for others, details about the times in which he lived, and facts about the people he befriended as well as the geography of the country where he traveled. Of note is the emphasis on Appleseed's character, including his interest in helping others, his friendship with Native Americans, his fondness for children, love of books, and his business sense about the value of trees. Full-color watercolor illustrations.

**Activity: "Appleseed's Story and Apples"**

**Language arts focus:** To relate literature to content study; to use spoken and written language vocabulary to show understanding of content across the curriculum

Mention to the children that studying the life of Johnny Appleseed can help them also learn about the history of apples and their place in people's lives. Invite the children to suggest ways they can learn more about the value of apples, and write their ideas in a list on the board. Examples can include visiting a nearby orchard, helping to harvest apples, talking to a grower about the grower's job and how apple trees are cared for during the seasons. Classroom activities might include learning how to dry apple slices, make apple juice, or construct doll-figures from dried apples. If appropriate for the class, relate the study of apples to different areas of the curriculum. Some examples include the following suggestions:

1. **Math.** Engage the children in counting apples; in cutting an apple in half to see the pattern of the seeds; in grouping apples according to attributes of color, size, type, and weight; in weighing (how many make a bushel?); in measuring the circumference of different types; and in counting the number of different types of apples in a grocery sack. Record the information on a class chart and display in the room.

2. **Reading.** Encourage the children to scan a variety of cookbooks to discover recipes that use apples. Have the children copy unusual recipes that use apples to make apple cookies, apple muffins, apple sauce, and apple butter. Have them copy their favorites to give to someone they know.

3. **Writing.** Encourage the children to write brief informational books about apples and what they have learned.

4. **Science.** Plan a field trip to a nearby store to buy different types of apples to taste and compare. Vote for a favorite apple and record the results on a class chart. Ask the children to poll their class or family members to find out each one's favorite type of apple and then, if appropriate for the climate, plant apple seeds from that favorite apple to start an apple tree for their family.

5. **Language arts.** Ask the children in small groups to read the poem "Johnny Appleseed" from *A Book of Americans* by Rosemary and Stephen Vincent Benet (Holt, 1986, ages 9 up). Have them copy the verses and cut the lines apart. Let them give the lines to another group and have the children in the receiving group decide *how* they will say what is in each four-line verse (loud voice, soft voice, apologetic voice, and so on). Encourage all of the children to chime in on a refrain after each verse:

### 110 Language Arts and Environmental Awareness

"Consider, consider
think well upon
the marvelous story
of Appleseed John."

Also related to language arts, suggest that the children perform a choral reading of Reeve Lindbergh's *Johnny Appleseed* (Boston: Joy Street /Little, Brown, 1995, ages 9 up). This is a biographical text about John Chapman and highlights his work as a naturalist and missionary. It has poetic lines in rhyme and brief selected sections will be suitable for reading aloud as a group chorus.

Further, suggest that the children "reserve" their individual inquiries about apples by listing them on the board. Beside each entry on the list, write the name of the child who announces that he or she wants to inquire into the topic. If appropriate, write the titles of books that could initiate a child's inquiry. The following examples include inquiries and book titles:

- **Inquiry 1: Jobs apples can provide for people.** _____ (*child's name*)
  Bourgeois, Paulette (1990). *The Amazing Apple Book*. New York: Addison Wesley. Ages 9–11. This book offers interesting facts about apples including natural history and historical background. It includes some recipes, games, and crafts for apples.

- **Inquiry 2: Where and how apples grow, climate needed for growth.**
  _____ (*child's name*)
  (*Book title supplied by the children*)

- **Inquiry 3: Ways apples are used by families** _____ (*child's name*)
  (*Book title supplied by the children*)

■ **Rose, Deborah, adaptor (1990). *The People Who Hugged Trees.*** Illustrated by Birgitta Safflund. Niwot, CO: Roberts Rinehart. Ages 9–11.

**Environmental context:** Human interdependence with other life forms on Earth

In this centuries-old folktale from India, Amrita, a girl who appreciates trees, understands the connection between the people and these tall leafy sentinels. She realizes that without the trees, there would be no survival for her people, for the trees guard the village from the sandstorms that blow through the desert and are markers for the water source. When the Maharajah's woodsmen arrive to cut the forest, Amrita and other villagers protect the trees by forming the first tree-hugging movement (a *chipko*) in Rajasthan, India. Watercolor illustrations.

**Activity: "Environmental Class Museum"**

**Language arts focus:** To present information; to participate in a brainstorming session to generate ideas; to use spoken and written language vocabulary for the purpose of developing a class museum; to read selections from literature to build an understanding of people's relationship to the environment

Tell the children that they will have an opportunity to show others what they know about the connection between people and the environment by preparing dramatized scenes for an environmental museum in their classroom. They can select scenes from favorite books and "freeze" the scene for others to see in the class's museum. To make selections, brainstorm themes with the children that make an impact on the environment in a positive (or negative) way, such as protecting trees from being cut, pollution of air and water by factories, and so on. Involve the children in the following steps to prepare an environmental museum:

1. Give them picture books related to this subject so they can get ideas for the scenes they want and have them decide on which ones should be in the group's environmental museum.

2. Have the children get into small groups with their books, select a scene that they can present as a group, and practice holding the scene in a frozen position. They can make simple props or backgrounds on butcher paper if needed. Tell the children that each scene will be an exhibit in the classroom museum and they can decorate strips of butcher paper to hang from ceiling to floor to separate their exhibit from the others.

## 112   Language Arts and Environmental Awareness

3. If needed, ask for volunteers to bring strands of clear mini-lights (from their home's holiday assortment) to illuminate each scene.

4. As a whole group, have the children design an invitational flyer announcing when their environmental museum will be open and inviting another class of children to visit.

5. On the day the museum is open, set up the groups in their scenes in the classroom and invite the guests to come in and tour the exhibits with two or three children in your class designated as official guides. Draw the window shades and turn the class lights off so the mini-lights draw attention to each exhibit. At each exhibit, have one child step forward out of the scene to narrate what is going on. Here is an example of what could be said in a scene depicting Amrita's *chipko*:

    > I am Amrita from India and I love the beautiful trees in my desert village because I know there is a connection between my people and the trees. Without the trees, my people could not live through the harsh desert storms, for the trees act like wind walls to keep the sand away. Without the trees, my people would not know where the water is in the desert, for the trees are a sign there is water below. One day, the royal woodsmen arrive to cut the trees and I take action and start the first tree-hugging movement in my village in Rajasthan. You see all of my friends in the village here behind me and they are protecting the trees from the woodsmen by hugging the tree trunks and standing in the way of the axes. If you want to know more about what happened, read *The People Who Hugged Trees* by Deborah Rose.

6. Have the visitors stop at each exhibit and listen to the narration.

**Home Activity**

With your child, tape-record a brief radio or TV news report that states *facts* about the effects of tree harvesting and other forest destruction. Then record a newscast by a commentator who states his or her *opinion* of the news about the cutting of trees (flooding, possible erosion, spotted owl report, human interest story, or animal interest story). Ask your child to listen to the two different presentations of the news and to note any differences in the information he or she receives. Ask your child to describe these differences. Discuss: "In what ways could you tell that information was a fact or an opinion?" As a follow-up activity, ask your child to transform his or her oral descriptions of the differences into a brief written paragraph to read to another family member.

- **Shaw-Mackinnon, Margaret (1996).** *Tiktala.* Illustrated by Laszlo Gal. New York: Holiday. Ages 9–11.

**Environmental context:** Protecting wildlife

In this human-to-animal transformation story, Tiktala is a modern Inuit girl who wants to carve soapstone. At a town meeting about the secrets of the traditional carvers, she discovers that she has to find her spirit helper and in her search, she is transformed into a seal. She swims with another seal, Tulimak, who does not trust humans, and she defends Tulimak's seal pup from a man determined to club it. Being with Tulimak, Tiktala finally understands the seal and how to carve its image. Full-color watercolor illustrations.

**Activity: "Transformation Story: Animal Helpers"**

**Language arts focus:** To transform information into an art form; to conduct research about interests; to exchange information

Ask the children to imagine that they need to find their animal helpers, just as Tiktala did, before they can truly understand an animal and how to sculpt, draw, sketch, or paint its image. Have them research an animal of their choice—its habitat, food, life cycle, protective coloring, predators—and take notes on what they find from their search. Tell them that their goal is to get enough information to satisfy them that they are beginning to understand the animal well enough to recreate its image in an art form. Have them report their findings about their selected animals to others in small groups. Ask the children to use the information they have gathered to make sculpted figures, drawings, sketches, or paintings of the animal. Display the artwork in the room and ask the

### 114   Language Arts and Environmental Awareness

children to write a paragraph of information about their animals on index cards to display next to their artwork.

**Home Activity**

Invite your child to select a favorite animal as the basis for a creative art project. Encourage your child to create a replica of the animal in some way—sketching, drawing, painting, sculpting—and include items from the animal's habitat in the project.

- **Young, Ed, reteller (1995).** *Night Visitors.* Illustrated by the reteller. New York: Philomel. Ages 9–11.

**Environmental context:** Respecting all forms of life

Young's Chinese folktale advocates respect for living things, no matter their size. Ants invade a family's storeroom and eat the grain, and the father prepares to get rid of the invading pests. A solution comes to Ho Kuan, a young boy, in a dream. He seals the storeroom so his father will not drown the ants, shows his respect for the creatures' lives, and succeeds in saving the insects from a watery fate. Black-and-white illustrations.

**Activity: "Research and Panel Discussion: Ants"**

**Language arts focus:** To conduct research about interests; to use written language vocabulary to prepare a report; to participate in a panel discussion; to communicate with an audience

Help the children collect photocopies of pictures of different types of ants. Make available printed materials on ants, what they do, and what they contribute to the environment. Have the children divide into groups and assign two or more different types of ants to each group. For a few days, let the groups do research about their types of ants. When the groups are prepared, write the name of one of the types of ants on the board. The group members assigned that type of ant walk to the front of the room and report as a panel on the group's findings. After all of the reports, have each child select his or her favorite type of ant, point out the work it does in the environment, and give his or her reasons for making that choice.

**Home Activity**

Ask your child to write or tell a description of a type of realistic ant that he or she knows about and draw or sketch a picture of it. Then, ask your child to write or tell a description of a fanciful super-ant (emphasize one that does outstanding things for the environment) that he or she imagines and illustrate it. Let your child compare the sketch of the imaginary ant with an illustration in an informational book and point out any differences that are seen. Then, ask your child to tell you why he or she gave the fanciful ant the characteristics it has, what it does to help the environment, and why it looks the way it does in the drawing. Contrast the information with what a realistic ant does to work in its habitat. Tape the sketches side by side and display in the home.

# IV ▪ Involving Children in Reading

# Involving Children in Reading: Ages 5–8

- **Castaldo, Nancy Fusco (1996).** *Sunny Days & Starry Nights: A Little Hands Nature Book.* Illustrated by Loretta Trezzo Braren. New York: Williamson Publishers. Ages 4–8.

**Environmental context:** Interacting with the natural world

Castaldo's informational book is a collection of activities on subjects such as sun, weather, trees, seeds, and birds. There are materials listed for each activity along with instructions and related additional things to do. Examples of some of the activities include making bird feeders from stale pastry, constructing plaster animal prints, drawing sand pictures, and making a hanging garden from a large sponge. Black line drawings.

**Activity: "What I Learned . . ."**

**Language arts context:** To read to select an activity and to read for directions; to use language to summarize

Ask the children to write or dictate brief four-page reports on the activity they selected to do. On each of the first two pages, have them summarize and illustrate the steps in the activity. On the third page, have them state how this activity helped them get acquainted with the natural world. And on the fourth page, have them write and respond to "What I learned about nature. . . ." Ask volunteers to read their final pages aloud to the group. Have the children mount the reports on art paper. If appropriate, punch holes in the upper corners of each page and thread yarn through the holes as a hanger to display the reports.

**Home Activity**

Help your child get acquainted further with what is happening to an endangered bird and learn more about that species. Encourage your child to make a bird stick figure puppet. Sketch the bird's head on a circle of poster board, cut out eye openings, and paste it on a tongue depressor handle. Encourage your child to tell what has been learned to a younger sibling or friend by talking behind the bird puppet. Your child may write some facts about the bird on the back of the puppet and read them aloud.

■ **Gilmmerveen, Ulco (1989).** *A Tale of Antarctica.* Illustrated by the author. New York: Scholastic. Ages 7–8.

**Environmental context:** Humans' effect on Antarctic habitat

Gilmmerveen's story is about some humans' inadvertent destructive approach to the habitat of the Antarctic penguins during a one-year period. The author personifies the penguins with the names Papa Penguin, Mama, and Junior. When Papa Penguin is coated with oil, Mama and Junior find a human who is their friend and lead him to Papa. Over a twelve-month period, the life cycle of the penguin and several factors that affect its survival are portrayed. The factors include oil spills, littering, and developers' bulldozers. Full-color illustrations.

**Activity: "A Business Letter"**

**Language arts context:** To read and listen for information; to compose a business letter

Tell children that they are going to become aware of the need to monitor and protect the Antarctic as a habitat for penguins and other creatures. Ask them to listen to the reading aloud of *A Tale of Antarctica* to find out the possible dangers that can affect the living things there. After the children listen to this information, elicit suggestions from them about what they could do to help protect the penguins and other Antarctic wildlife. One suggestion might be speaking out and writing to officials in business and government to protest ocean spills, pollution through littering, and the takeover of habitat by developers. Ask them to dictate what they would say and write their words on a chart in a business letter form.

**Home Activity**

With your child, read aloud Gilmmerveen's *A Tale of Antarctica,* and write an environmental recipe together for protecting the penguins' habitat against destructive approaches. Read the ingredients aloud together. Here is an example of a recipe:

> Take one penguin family (Papa, Mama, and Junior)
> Mix in a cold Antarctic land
> Add a way to speak out against oil spills
> Add a way to stop overdevelopment of the environment
> Add a way to stop littering
> Put it all together to make a quality habitat for penguins.

■ **Glaser, Linda (1996).** *Compost! Growing Gardens from Your Garbage.* Illustrated by Anca Hariton. Brookfield, CT: Millbrook. Ages 5–8.

**Environmental context:** Refuse in a home garden

Glaser's book is an introduction to the sound environmental practice of using compost (rich nutritious earth) in the garden and explains how this can be made from home refuse. Kitchen scraps, food waste, yard clippings, organic wastes, and other plant material form the base of compost. Nature turns these materials into earth filled with nutrients. When compost is added to gardens, lawns, and potted house plants, it creates healthy plants, and builds and renews the soil. Questions and answers about composting are included. Bordered watercolor illustrations.

**Activity: "Preparing and Using Compost"**

**Language arts context:** To read for information; to read hand-written notes for literal meaning; to conduct survey research

**122  Language Arts and Environmental Awareness**

Ask the children to interview people they know in their neighborhood about the different ways they prepare compost for their gardens and lawns. Have the children take notes on the interviews. Encourage the children to read their notes to one another in small groups. With the children's help, make a list of different ways to create compost collections for yard and garden use. Write the list on the board. Have the children read the list aloud and select one way that they would like to try at home.

**Home Activity**

Introduce your child to the contributions of earthworms in creating compost by reading aloud excerpts from the book *Worms Eat My Garbage* by Mary Appelhof (Seventh Generation, 1996, One Mill Street, Suite A 26, Burlington, VT 05401-1545). If interested, purchase worms and a plastic bin to compost the family's food waste.

■ **Grindley, Sally (1996).** *Peter's Place.* Illustrated by Michael Foreman. New York: Harcourt Brace. Ages 5–7.

**Environmental context:** Ocean pollution

Grindley's story is set at sea. When a ship comes too close to shore and breaks apart on the rocks, the oil slick pollutes the water and the oceanside location that a young boy, Peter, often visits to feed the seals and the eider ducks. The animals have difficulty surviving after their fur and feathers become coated with oil. To help care for them, Peter joins with others to scrub away oily deposits from the rocky shore. Peter's favorite animals survive their ordeal, but although the ocean begins to return to a balanced state, reminders of the accident still remain. Soft watercolor illustrations.

**Activity: "Effects of Oil Spills"**

**Language arts context:** To select and critically read passages related to oil spills; to discuss oil spill effects; to express a point of view

Show the picture in the book of the oil-covered bird to the children, and in an audience-reading situation, have the children read aloud as a group the words in the story that describe the oil-spill accident. Then, tell the children they are going to have the opportunity to simulate the effects of an oil spill similar to the one they read about in the story. To do this, have a child put a small amount of cooking oil in a clear glass container on the stage of an overhead projector. Ask a few children to dip feathers in the oil to see the ways the feathers are affected. The projector will magnify the effect. Remember to turn off the projector lamp occasionally so the oil does not get overly hot and become a safety hazard.

Distribute paper towels, oil-covered feathers, and paper cups filled with water and a detergent to the children. Have them use the materials to clean the oil. Ask the children to wash the feathers and observe what goes on. Have them record their thoughts on paper about what they did and put the pages in a class book for others to read. Based on this activity, elicit ideas from the children about the best way they could think of to clean up an oil spill.

**Home Activity**

Encourage your child to write a letter about environmental awareness to someone, real or imaginary, about what is going on in his or her environmental life. For example, your child can explain what he or she knows about the effects of oil spills on living things and their habitat, or mention several actions he or she is taking to care for animals affected by oil spills and other disasters. Encourage your child to give details about a part of the environment that he or she really cares about—that's "in the blood." Mention that your child can write the letter in a chatty or sad way and praise someone who helps or complain about someone who hinders the protection of the environment.

■ **James, Betsy (1995).** ***Blow Away Soon.*** Illustrated by Anna Vojtech. New York: The Putnam Group. Ages 5–7.

**Environmental context:** Value of wind to living things

The warm friendship between young Sophie and her grandmother, who live in the desert, is the focus of James's story. When Sophie says she doesn't like the wind blowing at night, her grandmother promises to help her understand this. The next day, the two walk together along the cliffs and in the desert canyons so Sophie can collect treasures from the land (some sand and grass, a feather, and an ancient shell). Sophie helps her grandmother build a small stone altar (a place to offer treasures to the wind) that her grandmother calls the Blow-Away-Soon. The two talk about how the wind helps the life cycle of living things and Sophie's relationship with her grandmother deepens as she begins to appreciate how wind affects the changes in the rest of the natural world. Full-color illustrations.

**Activity: "Environmental Notebooks"**

**Language arts context:** To read notebooks with written facts and opinions

Tell the children that they will have the opportunity to make notebooks about how wind helps living things when they observe some land on your school grounds that you have asked to remain unmowed and unweeded for a period of time. Leaving the area unmowed and unweeded is helpful in studying the effect of wind on seeds of growing grass and weeds. Tell the children that they can become temporary owners of "Ecology Circles" of the unmowed land. Give each child a clear, plastic container top (you can purchase clear container tops from a local grocery's delicatessen), and ask the children to cut a large circle out of the tops to make a ring. As often as possible, take a walk with the children to the outdoor area and have them lay the rings on the ground to frame the areas that the children are studying. The ring forms a boundary around the area a child is observing and helps a child stay focused on a specific location and not the entire area. Encourage them to study the changes there—particularly any due to wind—over the days, weeks, and months. Each day that the children walk, ask them to look for several examples of evidence that wind has effected the area or that plants and animals use the wind in some way. Observations during a nature walk can include the following:

1. Observe milkweed, a dandelion seed, or other seeds on the ground in the "Ecology Circle" or blowing through the air. Notice if you sneeze because you might be sensitive to plant pollen in the air.

2. Look for the wind blowing a spider's web within the ring's area or for differences in insect life on a windy day, a calm day, etc.
3. Observe leaves of trees blowing to the ground (to eventually decompose and enrich soil) or for evidence of drying soil, wet soil, and so on within an "Ecology Circle."
4. Look for evidence of pollutants (paper and other items) blown into the ring's area.

During each walk, have the children record their facts, the changes over time, their opinions about what is going on, and sketch what they see in notebooks. In class, ask them to trade notebooks. Have them select three sketches in the notes they receive and write a sentence or two about each sketch. Have the children return the notes and their sentences to the notebook owners. Engage them in reading one another's observations of the changes and ask them to look for the differences between *facts* and *opinion*. As they notice what facts are given and what opinions are offered, have them give feedback about facts and opinion to one another. Each writer can make additions, changes, or deletions to his or her notebook.

As a follow-up activity, invite the children to use their bodies to represent concepts related to the effects of wind, i.e., evaporation of water, precipitation that blows. Have the children create the movements and introduce language that describes their actions. For instance, they can demonstrate movements that show a spider's web blowing a distance on a windy day.

**Home Activity**

Each day for a selected month, have your child record an entry about an environmental event happening in the news in an ecology diary (three-hole binder) entitled "Earthmonth: A Diary of My Planet." Your child can record something from the newspapers, the radio, or the television news—perhaps reports about clean air, global warming, tropical storms, hurricanes, earthquakes, floods, monsoons, and so on. At the end of each week, have your child reread the entries together with you to determine any patterns or trends that he or she can identify from the entries, i.e., maybe your child sees an increase in reports about the migration of living creatures to northern areas to escape global warming, or reads about an increase in reports about misuses and abuses of the ocean waters. If appropriate, ask your child to illustrate some of the pages and give the writing to someone in the family to read.

- **Jaspersohn, William (1996).** *Timber! From Trees to Wood Products.* Illustrated by the author. Boston: Little, Brown. Ages 5–7.

    **Environmental context:** Importance of planting new trees in place of harvested trees

    Jaspersohn's informational book is a view of what happens to harvested trees as the wood becomes products for people. The logging process is described, from cutting trees and delivering the timber to wood mills to making boards and paper that are turned into various products. The process is shown in photographs and the text discusses the ways paper, plywood, and veneer are made. There is further information about timber products, recycling, and how lumber is dried. Full-color photographs.

    **Activity: "Read and React: Replanting Trees"**

    **Language arts context:** To make predictions; to read and research a topic of inquiry

    Elicit the children's reactions to trees being used for wood products and ask individuals to explain some of their reactions (agreement or disagreement) to the harvesting of trees. Let the children's comments begin their inquiries into why (and how) various companies replant seedlings for the trees they are harvesting for their products. Ask some of the following questions to continue a discussion:

    1. Would the children predict that companies in their area are or are not conserving trees and replanting as needed?

2. What kinds of information or evidence would they want to find about this?
3. Where do the children think they will find the information they want?
4. How will they find it?

In an area of the classroom, place three boxes labeled with the captions, "Favorite Informational Books about the Environment," "Favorite Stories about the Environment," and "Favorite Biographies about Environmentalists." Encourage the children to refer to these books as their "Inquiry Center." The center can be available for free-time reading, for help with spelling words, for finding information and ideas, and for finding models for drawing pictures and writing. After conducting research about tree harvesting and replanting with the books in the boxes (or during a library visit), have the children report on their findings and initiate a discussion about their reports with some of the following questions: "In what ways do you think your information is reliable (perhaps written by fair and disinterested writer)? In what way is some information similar to information offered by others in the class? In what way is some information different? How does this information compare to your predictions about local companies' policies?" After the discussion, have the children write statements about their original predictions, i.e., in what ways do they think their prediction was true (valid)? Encourage them to elaborate on their predictions and make any qualifications or modifications (perhaps only companies in the Northwest are conserving and harvesting on a regular basis) if some need to do so after hearing information from others in the group. Ask volunteers to read their statements aloud to the group.

**Home Activity**

Let your child make a tree poster and create a variety of shapes and figures related to trees and their value in a habitat by using "thumbprint" art—for instance, thumbprint whorls on tree trunks and branches and a thumbprint body for a bird, rabbit, spider, flowers, and so on. Fingerpaints or food coloring mixed with water make an inexpensive ink. Display the poster so others in the home can see it.

- **Koch, Michelle (1990). *World Water Watch.*** Illustrated by the author. New York: Greenwillow. Ages 5–8.

**Environmental context:** Plea to watch over the world and its water

Koch's book gives several reasons why some creatures in the world's oceans—sea otters, polar bears, whales, green sea turtles, seal, and penguins—may become endangered. Ecological problems such as pollution and abuse of the habitat are presented along with some of the steps that are currently being taken to help ensure the animals' survival. Muted watercolor illustrations.

**Activity: "Meaning from Pictures"**

**Language arts context:** To recognize story structure; to compose and read an original picture book

Invite the children to issue their own pleas about caring for the sea and sea creatures by making their own original picture books. Before they begin, help them understand the concept of what a book is by reading aloud excerpts from *Writing for Kids* by Lea Benjamin (Crowell, 1985, ages 6–9). The book is a helpful resource that shows how a story "works" and goes through the steps from the author's inspiration through publishing. Leave it on display for browsing and independent reading.

Mention to the children that they may select different features such as animation, use of decorative type, special dedications, and so on, to put in their books. If needed, guide them to some of the books that show these features in the list that follows. Encourage the children to use the ideas in these books as models:

1. **Animation.** Encourage the child interested in this feature to follow the directions in Patrick Jenkins's book, *Animation: How to Draw Your Own Flipbooks, and Other Fun Ways to Make Cartoons Move* (Addison-Wesley, 1991, ages 8–14) to make an original flipbook. For a child

interested further in motion on a book's pages, you could point out that the directions for making a zoetrope, a complicated eighteenth-century device for animation and motion, are at the end of Jenkins's book.

2. **Decorative Use of Type.** Show the child interested in this feature the use of unusual type with explanations at the end of each chapter in *Rainforests* and *Deserts* by Rodney Aldis (both Macmillan, 1991, ages 8–11). These books explain both sides of the conservation issues that relate to ecosystems.

3. **Dedications.** For the children interested in adding special dedications to their books, mention that authors tell readers who they acknowledge—their relatives, their readers, their friends—through the dedications in their books. Read aloud some of the dedications from different books and display them on a chart to show the children the authors' appreciation for the earth and their interest in protecting and preserving the environment. For example:

    From *Small Worlds: A Field Trip Guide* (Little, Brown, 1972, ages 6–8) by Helen Ross Russell: *"With memories of my first field trips, Sunday afternoon walks with my father who said, "Let's go see," "Look," "Listen," "Feel," "Smell," and "What do you think?"*
    (Others added by the children)

4. **Paper Engineering.** Show the children the fun and surprise that happens when objects move on pages of books in pop-up formats. For instance, *How to Make Pop-Ups* (Morrow, 1987, ages 7 up) by Joan Irvine, shows a child four different sections of directions labeled "Push and Pop Out," "Fold and Fit In," "Push, Pull and Turn," and "Combining Ideas." Following the directions, a child can construct an animal mouth that opens, a nose that pops out, or hands (paws) that reach forward.

**Home Activity**

Help your child bind a book that he or she is making about environmental awareness. Show your child how to make covers for the book out of cardboard covered with decorative adhesive paper or wrapping paper. The pages can be cut from blank sheets, inserted between the covers, and then taped inside, stapled, fastened with brads, or sewn with heavy yarn or thread. Take turns reading the pages aloud to each other. Discuss what you read.

### ■ Kroll, Virginia (1995). *Sweet Magnolia.* Illustrated by Laura Jacques. Watertown, MA: Charlesbridge. Ages 6–8.

**Environmental context:** Returning a creature to the wild

In Kroll's story, Denise visits her grandmother, a wildlife activist for creatures in the Louisiana bayou. There is a warm and affectionate relationship between the two as they explore the swamp and its wildlife and enjoy the taste of Cajun food. After Denise rescues a small bird, names it, and cares for it, she learns how hard it is to return a loved creature back to the wild. Full-color paintings.

**Activity: "Transforming Information"**

**Language arts focus:** To read information and convert it into another form or format

Show the children ways to change information they have gathered from one form into another, and tell them that they will have an opportunity to do this. Explain that the information they have read in *Sweet Magnolia* about the difficulty of returning a creature to the wild can be changed or converted into an advertisement, a chart, or a collage. Further, a crayon drawing, a dance, or a demonstration of what Denise did to care for the rescued bird could be ways to transform information from the book. Ask the children to select what project they want to work on to do this. Then have them show their projects to the whole group and read or tell about the information they included in their work.

**Home Activity**

Point out to your child that written information can be transformed into another form. Encourage your child, for example, to make a story mobile or paint a picture that shows what happens in a story about caring for the environment and its living things. Invite your child to suggest ideas and then choose one to create and display. Gather together as many family members as possible and ask your child to tell about the story transformed into art.

- **Norsgaard, E. Jaedicker (1988).** *How to Raise Butterflies.* Illustrated by the author. New York: Dodd Mead. Ages 8–9.

**Environmental context:** Raising butterflies

Norsgaard's book introduces ways to raise butterflies and then release them back into the environment. The text has step-by-step directions for collecting eggs, preparing them, and releasing butterflies back into their habitat. Along with an index, a list of butterflies, and the names of plants they need for food, some of the hibernation and migration patterns are included for reference use. Full-color paintings.

**Activity: "A Butterfly Habitat Map"**

**Language arts focus:** To explain; to write about a topic in a story

Ask each child to name his or her favorite butterfly from the book and to explain why. With partners in class, have the children write words about butterflies on a sheet of paper and draw ovals similar to the shape of cocoons around the words. Ask the children to choose three "cocoon words" and make them into a short story for someone in the class to read.

**Home Activity**

Take your child to a nature area, nearby park, zoo area (or a habitat that could become a butterfly garden or trail) and give your child a notebook, sketch pad, butterfly field guide, and pencil. Ask your child to sketch features of the environment—plants, trees, and so on—to make an environmental map. Have him or her look for a butterfly and make a series of *x*'s on the environmental map to note the distance and sequence the butterfly travels. With the guide, identify the butterfly and "read" some information from the environmental map to one another. Have your child tell what was learned about the butterfly from this activity.

## 132   Language Arts and Environmental Awareness

■ **Reynolds, Jan (1993).** *Amazon Basin.* Illustrated by the author. San Diego: Harcourt, Brace Jovanovich. Ages 8–10.

**Environmental concept:** Interdependence of humans, living creatures, and habitat

Reynolds's book is a photographic essay about the habitat of the vanishing Yanomama Indians, who live in the Amazon territory of Venezuela. This book emphasizes the importance of protecting any area that shelters a country's native people. In the rain forest, a young boy and his father, a shaman, show what they do during a day's activities of work and play. The two are seen closely linked to the ecosystem—especially for their food supply since they fish in the river, hunt in the jungle, and harvest plants for food. For recreation, they play in the water of the large Amazon river. Full-color photographs.

**Activity: "Ecology Quilt"**

**Language arts focus:** To identify a commonality with others; to read for information to make a quilt; to design ecological symbols

As a way of demonstrating environmental awareness, tell the children they will participate in making an ecology quilt to show their names as children who are serious about caring for the environment. Distribute to each child a square of white paper and ask them to write something on it about caring for the environment, then sign their name. Affix the squares to mural paper and have the children find and read the names of *three* others whose concerns are in common with theirs. Have the children with something in common get in small groups, and distribute to each child a square of white fabric. Then ask the four children to sign their names on each square, and design or draw symbols to represent their common ecological concern in the center of the square. Then, sew the squares together or paste them on a large sheet of butcher paper to make an ecological quilt design to display in the school.

**Home Activity**

Each time your child finishes reading a book related to caring for creatures and the environment, have him or her design a paper streamer and write the book's title on it to attach to the staff of an ecological flag or banner that your child has made. Let your child choose the colors, add the initial for the family name, and decorate the flag with ecological items. Each week or month, have your child carry the flag in the home to show other family members the streamers with book titles that he or she has read. Ask your child to describe one of the creatures in the book that he or she is currently reading. What would he or she like to do to help that creature? Why?

■ **Seymour, Tres (1996). *Black Sky River.*** Illustrated by Dan Andreasen. New York: Orchard Books. Ages 5–8.

**Environmental concept:** Decreasing numbers of birds

In Seymour's story, a father tells his son how he liked to watch the birds when they flew over his town in such numbers that they were called a "Black Sky River." He remembers that their migration flight was a "long, dark, endless ribbon" that sang "FWEET! FWEET!" Some of the inhabitants of the town, however, did not like the noise and the germs caused by the migrating birds and they fed the birds some poison seed. The number of migrating birds decreased to a few hundred and the "Black Sky River" was not seen again. The father is hopeful that someday their family will find a place where the birds will fly as a "Black Sky River" overhead again. Full-color paintings.

**Activity: "Environmental Balance"**

**Language arts focus:** To detect cause and effect relationships; to sketch and describe an environmental situation

To help the children see a cause and effect relationship, have them sketch a balance scale. First, show an illustration of this type of scale and point out that it weighs objects by putting them in balance with a known amount of weight. Have the children outline one container on each side of the scale. Ask them to sketch or draw several small black birds over one container on one side of their balance scale sketch. Continue:

1. In the container on the other side of the balance scale, have the children draw small sketches of plants that provide food and shelter

for the birds, and then above those sketches, draw some of the creatures (such as insects) that eat the plants.

2. Encourage the children to discuss what they have sketched on their balance scales with such questions as, "What do you think would happen to the balance in nature if people fed "poison seed" to birds that now are part of the habitat where you live?"

3. Ask the children to use a paper strip as a page mask and cover up the bird sketches on one side of the balance scale to simulate the loss of birds. Have them tell what would be missing from this balanced habitat if this took place. Discuss with them some of the following questions: "What would be out of balance? Why? What living things would be affected if birds were missing from the habitat? In what ways could these living things be affected?" Display the balance scale sketches in the room.

### Home Activity

Read aloud *Black Sky River*. Ask your child to listen to find out what happens to the birds and how the father feels about this. Ask your child to listen to parts of the story that tell the effect that people have on nature and on one another. Discuss these effects. Elicit your child's suggestions for changes that could be made to neutralize some of the negative effects that people have on nature. Ask your child to tell ways he or she can help to redress any harmful effects that he or she knows about.

### ■ Strete, Craig Kee (1996). *They Thought They Saw Him.* Illustrated by Jose Aruego and Ariane Dewey. New York: Greenwillow. Ages 5–7.

**Environmental concept:** Value of protective camouflage

Strete's story is set in the Southwest. In an adobe granary, a chameleon, along with many other creatures, wakes up from a winter nap and explores the warm day of spring. A hungry snake, also awake, sees the chameleon on a branch and thinks of food. When the snake slides closer to the chameleon, however, it seems to disappear. Through his natural ability to camouflage himself, the little creature outwits not only the snake, but also an owl, a fox, and a curious young Apache boy. Bright watercolor paintings.

**Activity: "Camouflage Search"**

**Language arts focus:** To read directions

Place several short tree branches together in the room in a container and ask the children to make replicas of the chameleon from pipe cleaners. Have them paint their chameleons in camouflage colors similar to the colors on the branches. Let them mix paints to get the camouflage colors they want. Ask the children to use their replicas in a camouflage activity by reading several directions from a chart, such as the following:

1. One at a time, hide your pipe cleaner chameleons on the branches while the other children close their eyes.

2. When the children open their eyes, invite a child to hunt for your replica while everyone listens to the story read aloud again.

3. When the replica is found, let the finder be the next child to hide his or her replica and invite someone else to search for it while the story continues.

**Home Activity**

With your child, read aloud some books about creature camouflage such as *Hidden Pictures: Find a Feast of Camouflaged Creatures* written by Audrey Woods and illustrated by Nicki Palin (Millbrook, 1996, all ages). You and your child can search for pictures of living creatures hidden by their protective coloring in the illustrations.

■ **Wolcott, Patty (1975). *Tunafish Sandwiches.*** Illustrated by Hans Zander. Reading, MA: Addison-Wesley. Ages 5–6.

**Environmental context:** Food chain in the ocean

Wolcott's concept book has a simple, limited text that explains the food chain to a child who is learning to read. The book points out how tiny phytoplankton (called "little, little plants") play their part in providing tuna for two children's tuna fish sandwiches. Full-color and line drawings.

**Activity: "Food Chain Story"**

**Language arts context:** To transform information from reading into a story; to read for details

Ask the children to divide into small groups. Have a child in each group start an ocean food chain story and then select a child to continue it. Give all the group members an opportunity to add to the story. If appropriate, ask one of the small groups to volunteer to retell their chain story to the whole group and copy their food chain on chart paper so it can be read aloud again. Display the charts in the room and let interested children re-read the completed versions throughout the school week.

**Home Activity**

With your child, discuss a food chain in an ocean habitat such as the one that follows:

>Little, little ocean plants are eaten by
>Little, little ocean animals who are eaten by
>Little fish who are eaten by
>Big fish who are eaten by
>Big, big fish like tuna who are caught,
>Processed, and become cans of tuna fish
>At the grocery store which people buy to make
>Tuna fish sandwiches. People eat big, big fish.

Invite your child to prepare a paper link chain to illustrate the words of the tuna fish food chain. The words can be written on narrow paper strips before the strips are encircled with one another and pasted together to make a chain. Display it in a place selected by your child and read it together the next time the two of you make tuna fish sandwiches.

# Involving Children in Reading: Ages 9–14

- **Arnosky, Jim (1992).** *Crinkleroot's Guide to Knowing the Birds.* Illustrated by the author. New York: Bradbury. Ages 9–12.

**Environmental concept:** Caring for birds

Through the character of a fictional naturalist named Crinkleroot, Arnosky's book gives basic information about what to look for when a reader observes birds, how birds live and grow, and tips on attracting birds. For example, a child can attract birds by planting shrubs and trees, providing water, hanging nesting boxes, installing a feeder with different foods to attract different birds, or by putting a bell on a cat that is keeping them away. Full-color drawings.

**Activity: "It's for the Birds"**

**Language arts context:** To read critically newspaper and magazine articles

Have the children divide into small groups and ask each group to make their own one-page newspaper about birds for others to read. They can select articles from the daily newspaper or from magazines, read them critically (asking questions in their minds as they read), and rewrite them. Additionally, they can write an editorial about ways to help birds stay in the area, i.e., putting up bird houses, writing letters to government officials about issues affecting birdlife, and getting involved in any local projects that help birds. Further, they can include controversies about birdlife in their newspaper's issue column entitled, "If I were in charge of this problem, I would. . . ." For each issue, have the children read material about the issue critically, consider both sides, and then write their own article about the concern. Have groups trade their newspapers for more critical reading and group discussion. If appropriate, duplicate the newspaper and have children take copies to read to someone in the home.

**Home Activity**

Ask each child to name his or her favorite butterfly from the book and to explain why. With partners in class, have the children write words about butterflies on a sheet of paper and draw ovals similar to the shape of cocoons around the words. Ask the children to choose three "cocoon words" and make them into a short story for someone in the class to read.

**Home Activity**

Ask your child to look for birds near your home and give your child sketching materials and a field guide about birds. Ask your child to sketch the environment to make a picture map. Have him or her look for birds and make check marks on the sketch to note where birds travel near your home. With the guide, identify any birds seen and "read" some information from the picture map. Have your child tell what was learned about birds from this activity.

- **Bailey, Linda (1996).** *How Come the Best Clues Are Always in the Garbage?* Illustrated by the author. Chicago: Albert Whitman. Ages 9–12.

    **Environmental context:** Plastic negatively affects the environment

    In Vancouver, Stevie and her mother, an employee of Garbage Busters, Inc., discover that the new owners of the Red Barn are selling their burgers in plastic containers. Although they hold the best burgers in town, the packages are gaudy, made of plastic, and definitely throwaway containers. This causes a local environmental group to announce that the Red Barn is negatively affecting the environment. Later, Stevie's mother leads a campaign against the fast-food business. Line drawings.

**Activity: "Overpackaging"**

**Language arts context:** To observe and read newspaper ads to look for evidence of overpackaging in environment; to read realistic fiction to build an understanding of human experience

When Stevie, an avid mystery reader, solves the mystery of her mother's apartment burglary in the story, a local newspaper headlines her as a girl wonder and Vancouver's answer to Nancy Drew. Ask the children, "In what ways do you think that Stevie's interest in reading mysteries might have helped her? Hindered her?" Invite the children to take the role of detective just as Stevie did and look for evidence of overpackaging of products in their environment. Have them read newspaper ads of food sales from grocery stores to give them a start at observing the packaging used by different companies. Ask the children to report their findings back to the whole group and tell what companies use plastic packaging and in what ways plastic packaging can negatively affect the environment. Continue the discussion: "In what ways do you see plastic as harmful for the environment? Overpackaging as harmful? Environmentally safe packaging that comes from trees as harmful? In what ways can you be "Garbage Busters" in your area and discourage the use of throwaway containers? What types of containers can be recycled? How can you set up recycling in your classroom?"

As a follow-up activity, have the children divide into small groups and imagine themselves in the role of city or county supervisors in charge of the disposal of solid waste. Ask them to write the available choices of disposal—landfill, incineration, ocean dumping, and recycling—as the headings for four columns on paper. Ask the children in each group to gather facts about the topics to determine the pros and cons of each disposal method. Have them list and discuss the advantages and disadvantages of choosing a particular method of waste disposal on note paper before their group decides on a final choice for their community. Perhaps some children will gather facts similar to the following: that landfill covers are often made of shredded material (some-

**140** Language Arts and Environmental Awareness

times shredded interiors of junk cars); that methane gas can be collected from decaying garbage, compressed and then used as fuel; and that many people wear clothing that is recycled from plastic products. Have a volunteer from each group announce the group's final decision about a method of waste disposal to the whole group.

**Home Activity**

Encourage your child to be a "Garbage Buster" and conserve resources around your home and use things again and again for more than one purpose. For instance, give your child a brown paper bag from a food store and ask him or her to think of some uses for the bag other than holding groceries. When your child accompanies someone to the store, invite him or her to take the paper bag and use it to pack the groceries so a new bag will not be needed.

- **Bang, Molly (1996). *Chattanooga Sludge.*** Illustrated by the author. New York: Harcourt. Ages 9–11.

    **Environmental context:** Cleaning up toxic waste

    Bang's book is about cleaning up industrial toxic waste in a waterway. It is the true story of Chattanooga Creek, polluted by years of industrial toxic waste dumping, and portrays the steps of how this problem was addressed. The city council hears about John Todd, a scientist from Massachusetts who uses plants in greenhouses to clean up sewage and transform the sludge into usable water. The council invites Todd to try out his process on samples taken from the creek's toxic water. He uses trial-and-error methods (shown with diagrams) to work on the large and complex cleanup problem. Collage artwork.

    **Activity: "Toxic Waste"**

    **Language arts context:** To read an informational book to build an understanding of human experience; to read word webs

    After discussing how John Todd helped clean up toxic water at Chattanooga Creek, show the children a video related to the effects of contaminants in the water cycle, such as one from the *Great Lakes Alive* series

(Films for the Humanities & Sciences, Box 2053, Princeton, NJ 08543). This series examines the role that water plays in life and the effects of contaminants in the water cycle. The videos show the interdependence of animals, humans, and their environments. They also illustrate the real-life applications of environmental science up through the international level where countries plan cooperative projects. Schedule a pre-video activity and a post-video activity, such as the following, with a related video of your choice:

1. **Pre-video activity:** Ask the children to record what they know or have learned from books about the effects of contaminants in water with a word web *before* seeing the video (see Word Web #1). For example, the children can record what they know about the contaminants and determine they are generated by individuals, by communities, by a state agency or statewide company, or by something that is happening nationally. The pre-video word web could look like this one:

### Word Web #1: Before Video
### What I Know about Contaminants in the Water Cycle

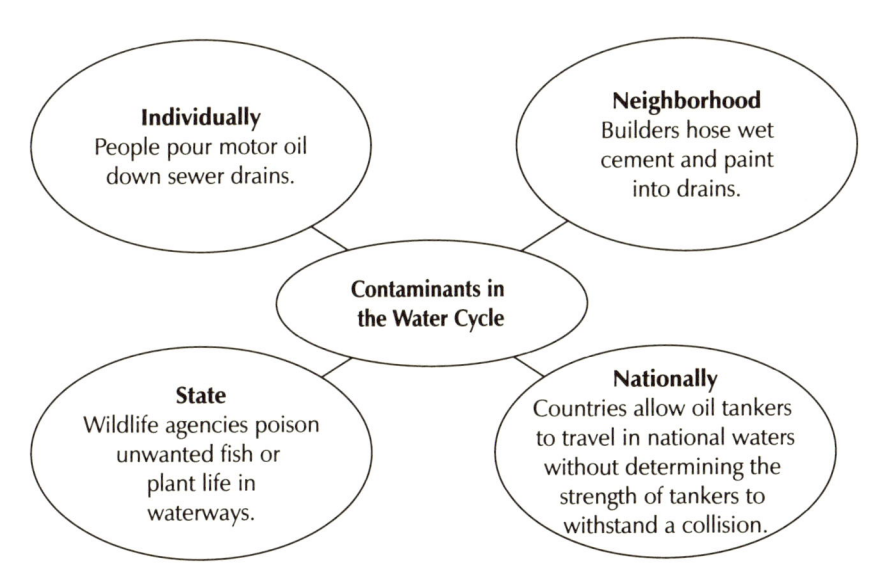

**Individually**
People pour motor oil down sewer drains.

**Neighborhood**
Builders hose wet cement and paint into drains.

**Contaminants in the Water Cycle**

**State**
Wildlife agencies poison unwanted fish or plant life in waterways.

**Nationally**
Countries allow oil tankers to travel in national waters without determining the strength of tankers to withstand a collision.

Now, show the video you have selected to provide the children with additional views of what is contaminating the water.

### 142  Language Arts and Environmental Awareness

2. **Post-video activity:** After seeing the video, have the children write their thoughts on another word map (see Word Web #2). Involve the children in a post-video discussion as a forum for the children to "read" their word maps and tell in what ways their ideas about the amount of contaminants in the water cycle *changed* after viewing the video. Encourage them to read their notes from their pre-video and post-video word maps during the discussion. This will allow them to make additional inferences about the effects of contaminants on living creatures and their way of life.

**Word Web #2: After Video**
**What I Know Now about Contaminants in the Water Cycle**

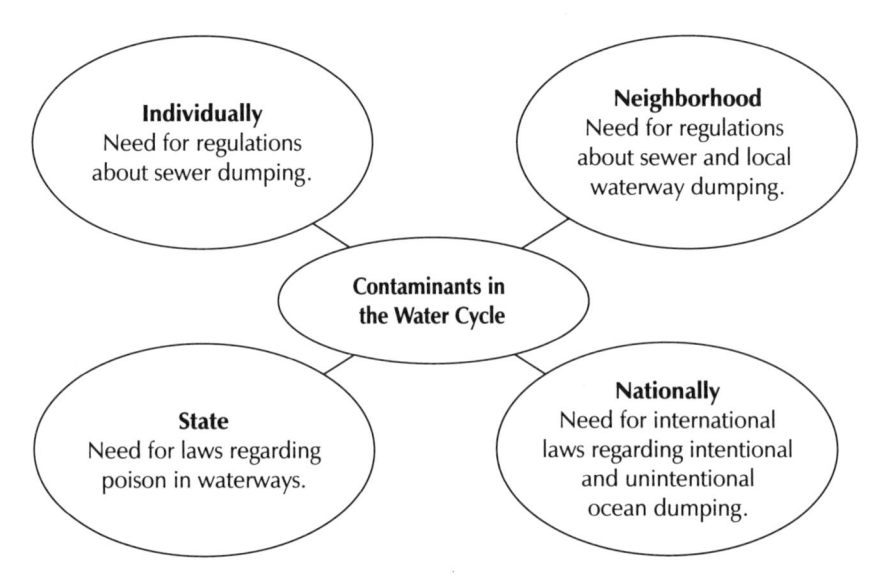

- **Individually**
  Need for regulations about sewer dumping.
- **Neighborhood**
  Need for regulations about sewer and local waterway dumping.
- **Contaminants in the Water Cycle**
- **State**
  Need for laws regarding poison in waterways.
- **Nationally**
  Need for international laws regarding intentional and unintentional ocean dumping.

3. **Additional activities:** Elicit suggestions from the children about ways to alert people to keeping the water cycle clean. Perhaps they could join with a city council, county supervisor, or youth group to stencil and spray paint a "Don't Contaminate" or "Keep Clean" message at the curb openings to storm drains in their area or put signs with similar messages along levees, jogging trails, and paths along waterways.

### Home Activity

Before reading a book (or showing a video) about cleaning up toxic waste in the water cycle, ask your child to dictate some items that he or she thinks would be important to have in a "good" book or video about cleaning up the water on earth. Write his or her ideas on a sheet of paper. Ask your child to listen to a book the two of you have selected (or watch a video you have checked out from your local library). Then, talk with your child about some of the following:

1. The items your child mentioned that *were* included in the book or video;
2. The items your child mentioned that were *not* in the book or video;
3. Any questions your child has *after* the book or video; and
4. Any ideas in the video that *conflicted* with your child's ideas about cleaning up toxic waste. Ask, "How can you discover more about these ideas?"

■ **Brown, Mary Barrett (1992).** *Wings Along the Waterway.* Illustrated by the author. New York: Orchard Books. Ages 9–12.

**Environmental context:** Protecting endangered wetland birds

In the introduction and the epilogue, the author states her message that humans and their way of life are the greatest threat to the continued existence of wetland birds. The author points out that the lives of the pelican, roseate spoonbill, and other wetland birds are entwined with nearby watery habitats—marshes, lagoons, swamps, rivers, ponds—and their very existence demands that these natural areas remain free from pollution and urban encroachment. As an example of the effect of pollution caused by humans, the brown pelican is facing extinction because its eggs fracture before the babies are mature enough to hatch. The shells are weakened by the bird's diet consisting of fish contaminated by the insecticide DDT. By contrast, in areas where DDT is banned, the pelican population has increased. Index and a bibliography for further reading are included. Watercolor paintings.

**Activity: "Survival Scenarios"**

**Language arts context:** To read critically and to skim for facts to answer questions; to read an informational book

Point out that humans and their way of life are not only the greatest threat to the wetlands, but also affect other habitats. Select situations from newspapers representing various environments and distribute them to small groups of children to conduct group research into each event. For group work, the children may participate in the following procedures:

1. Have each child ask any questions that he or she has about the situation and ask a group recorder to write the questions on chart paper.
2. Ask each child to conduct an individual or partnership inquiry about one of the questions and report what is found back to the small group.
3. Further, invite each group member or partnership to suggest an action to help resolve the situation. Ask each individual whether he or she is for or against what is going on in each scenario.

Have the small groups report on their findings and tell their decisions about their situation back to the whole group. Discuss with the children the agency and government officials or environmental groups to whom they could write as a way to express their points of view about what is going on in the different environments.

**Home Activity**

Have your child pollute a small paper cup of water with debris and then try to restore it to its clean original state. What ideas does your child have for the water's restoration? Encourage your child to write a letter to a newspaper editor or president of an industrial company to inquire about what is being done locally to help keep the water clean in your area. Have your child include a stamped, self-addressed envelope for a reply.

■ **Downer, Ann (1994).** *Spring Pool: A Guide to the Ecology of Temporary Ponds.* Illustrated with photographs. New York: Watts. Ages 9–12.

**Environmental context:** Effects of environmental hazards

The focus of Downer's book is on the formation of ponds by rain and melting snow, and as a result, the nature and growth of animal and plant life that occurs in and around the water. Environmental hazards such as acid rain and land development are discussed as well as people's efforts to protect pond life. As one unique example, the author mentions tunnels that have been built for toads and salamanders to help the creatures travel without crossing dangerous roads. An appendix includes information about plants and animals including physical description, food supply, and life cycle. Colorful photographs.

**Activity: "A Field Map and Guidelines"**

**Language arts context:** To read guidelines; to read an informational book

Demonstrate to the children how to draw a field map of a local pond (river, creek, waterway) and elicit their suggestions for one or two guidelines about protecting some of the things that live in or near the water. Engage the children in drawing their own field maps of a local pond of their choice and have them write their own guidelines about protecting the creatures there. Ask each child to trade the guidelines and map with another child to read and provide feedback for additions, changes, and deletions.

**Home Activity**

Tell your child that he or she will have an opportunity to see a way that acid rain can be a hazard to a pond and other areas in the environment. Point out that acid rain gets it name because it has a weak acid in it (similar to white vinegar) that it collects from polluted air. When acid rain falls, it can poison the lakes, rivers, and streams and even affect hard surfaces like rocks.

Since chalk is made of limestone similar to limestone rock, you can use it to simulate what happens to limestone when acid rain falls on it. Invite your child to pour one teaspoon of white vinegar over a piece of chalk in a container. Have your child observe what happens. (Limestone reacts to the acid vinegar and is eaten away as it gives off gas which your child sees as bubbles.) Ask your child to record what he or she did in this activity and read his or her writing aloud to another family member.

If your child is interested in additional activities about the environment, guide him or her to *Science Fair Projects: The Environment* (Sterling Publishing, 1995, ages 11 up) written by Bob Bonnet and Dan Keen and illustrated by Frances Zweifel. This book has projects that will encourage your child to find evidence, make predictions, use the senses, classify, determine patterns, compare and contrast, and so on. Several safety tips are included and adult supervision is emphasized. There is an index and a glossary with words such as *control group, density, hypothesis,* and others. Includes black-and-white diagrams and illustrations.

- **Facklam, Margery (1996).** *Creepy, Crawly Caterpillars.* Illustrated by Paul Facklam. Boston: Little, Brown. Ages 8–9.

**Environmental context:** Appreciation of contribution of butterflies and moths

Facklam's book discusses the anatomy of a caterpillar and some of its behaviors and then focuses on thirteen species of butterflies and moths including the monarch and the Hawaiian moth, *Eupithecia*. For each, the four stages of metamorphosis are shown in larger-than-life illustrations from egg to caterpillar, then to cocoon or chrysalis, and finally to butterfly or moth. For example, a reader sees that the eggs of the monarch butterfly are green and laid on milkweed leaves. The larvae are yellow with black cross marks and molts. The pupa is pale green, spotted with black and gold, and hangs from a branch. When the adult emerges, it can have a wing span of four inches and will migrate in large groups. A glossary is included. Oversize full-color illustrations.

**Activity: "Caterpillar Village"**

**Language arts focus:** To write and read captions of illustrations

Involve children in activities inside and outside the classroom where they can write and read captions with a partner. Inside the classroom:

1. Collect specimens in jars (no lids) and make a classroom caterpillar village. Label.
2. Make a caterpillar collection or paint a picture of a caterpillar village; Write captions.

3. Compare and contrast caterpillars. Have the children show their similarities and differences in sketches they make. Write captions.
4. Discuss, draw, and label body parts of a caterpillar. Make caterpillar-shaped pages for the drawings.
5. Make an alphabet book of caterpillars and read it aloud to others. The illustrations of caterpillars can be made by thumbprint art.
6. Find a picture of each of the four stages of butterfly metamorphosis (egg, caterpillar, cocoon or chrysalis, and butterfly or moth). Make a photocopy of each picture and cut the pictures into equally sized squares. Have the children divide into four groups, one for each stage, and distribute the squares to the children in the groups. Instruct the children to use rulers and graph paper to enlarge the piece they have by drawing it on a larger sheet of paper. If the piece measures one inch, have the children enlarge it to ten (or more) inches. Have the children cut out the enlarged pieces and assemble them on a class bulletin board to make enlarged illustrations of the four stages of metamorphosis. Have the children write captions for the illustrations and display the work in the room.

Outside the classroom:

1. Make a map of an area in which the children observe caterpillars. Label.
2. Observe caterpillars outdoors and have the children take notes and then read what they have written to another child.
3. Discuss vocabulary related to local caterpillars the children are familiar with in the area. Make word cards on index cards for a pocket chart.
    Elicit children's suggestions for ways to make caterpillar replicas from art paper, clay, and collage materials. Edible caterpillars can be made with marshmallows, adding cereal circles for eyes, licorice bits for legs, and so on. Write sentences on index cards to show how the replicas were made. Invite another class to see the display and read the cards as they walk by.

**Home Activity**

With your child, plant in a container or your yard some milkweed, day lilies, or other plants that attract butterflies. Observe them carefully throughout the year. With pencil and sketchbook handy, your child can observe the plants often and sketch any butterflies seen. Encourage your child to label his or her sketches with a caption that tells something about the season and the weather and how they could be affecting the plants and butterflies and their visits, i.e., "Sunny day in summer with temperature of _____; flowers in full bloom; lots of butterflies" or, "Rainy day in fall with temperature of _____; plants going to seed; not many butterflies to be found today."

■ **George, Jean Craighead (1996).** *The Case of the Missing Cutthroats: An Ecological Mystery.* New York: HarperCollins. Ages 9–14.

**Environmental context:** Importance of food chain

Visiting with her family at their cabin in Jackson Hole, Wyoming, thirteen-year-old Spinner Shatter tries to catch a fish so she can please her father and perhaps win back the family fishing medal in a local contest held at the Snake River. But Spinner would really rather be back in their home in New York City practicing her dance steps than fishing—though she knows her father wants her to like competitive fishing as much as he and his family does. While fishing, however, Spinner catches a record-breaking cutthroat trout, a rare large fish, and this surprises everyone. A fish like the one she catches has not been caught in this part of the Snake River in some time. This event leads her and her cousin, Alligator, to the mystery of how the trout came to live in a pool where, by all logical thinking, it never should have been. Spinner and her cousin backpack into the mountains to try to find out how Spinner's fish came to be in the pool and what has happened to the other cutthroats. As they try to solve the mystery, they find themselves confronting an ill-tempered grizzly bear, an electrical storm, and a dangerous descent into a narrow river gorge.

**Activity: "Environmental Awareness Survey"**

**Language arts focus:** To select reading passages pertinent to following directions for an activity; to conduct survey research

Distribute "Environmental Awareness Search Paper" I or II (following) to the children. Both papers are surveys of people who protect and care for the environment and living creatures. Ask the children to follow the directions on each search paper. Sample directions can include statements similar to the following:

> Find someone in our class or school who can answer one of the questions about environmental awareness. Look for a different person for each question. Write the answer to each question and then have that person initial the line.

**Environmental Awareness Search Paper I**

Find someone in our class or school who can answer one of these questions about environmental awareness.

1. Who has helped care for the environment this week? What did he or she do?
   Answer _____   Initial _____
2. Who likes to read about endangered animals? Which animal?
   Answer _____   Initial _____
3. Who knows how to build a birdhouse? What kind?
   Answer _____   Initial _____
4. Who likes to plant flowers and plants to attract butterflies? What kind of plants and flowers?
   Answer _____   Initial _____
5. Who has recycled and reused products this week? Which products?
   Answer _____   Initial _____
6. Who has helped keep water clean and unpolluted this week?
   Answer _____   Initial _____
7. Who knows something that he or she can teach to the group? What is it?
   Answer _____   Initial _____

**150   Language Arts and Environmental Awareness**

8. Who never litters?
   Answer _____ Initial _____

9. Who uses compost in a home garden? When was the garden planted?
   Answer _____ Initial _____

10. Who separates yard waste from household trash for recycling pick up?
    Answer _____ Initial _____.

11. Who has rescued a small bird or animal, named it, cared for it, and returned it to the wild?
    Answer _____ Initial _____

12. Who has raised butterflies and then released them back into the environment?
    Answer _____ Initial _____

13. Who has seen factories that emit toxic waste by releasing smoke, steam, and chemicals into the air?
    Answer _____ Initial _____

14. Who has conserved water and electricity this week?
    Answer _____ Initial _____

## Environmental Awareness Search Paper II

Find someone in our class or school who can answer one of these questions about environmental awareness.

1. Who has saved bottles, cans, and newspapers to be recycled this week?
   Answer _____ Initial _____

2. Who has caught and released fireflies?
   Answer _____ Initial _____

3. Who has prepared a butterfly garden?
   Answer _____ Initial _____

4. Who can explain the production of energy through solar radiation (or the power of the winds or the ebb and flow of tides)?
   Answer _____ Initial _____

**Involving Children in Reading: Ages 9–14**   151

5. Who knows that a rain forest affects the world's weather since it uses energy from the sun and gives it back (i.e., rainfall evaporates, carrying heat with it, and winds push warm air to cool parts of the globe)?
Answer _____ Initial _____

6. Who takes care of the earth's resources by knowing what garbage can be recycled, ways to reuse objects around the home, and how to be a wise shopper of recycled and biodegradable materials?
Answer _____ Initial _____

7. Who can tell you some effects of two environmental hazards—acid rain and land overdevelopment?
Answer _____ Initial _____

8. Who can tell you about people's efforts to protect pond life in their area?
Answer _____ Initial _____.

9. Who has alerted people to do something to keep the water cycle clean?
Answer _____ Initial _____

10. Who has joined with a city council, a county supervisor, or youth group to stencil and spray-paint a "Don't Contaminate" or "Keep Clean" message at the curb openings to storm drains or put similar signs along levees and jogging trails along waterways?
Answer _____ Initial _____.

11. Who knows ways plastic packaging can negatively affect the environment? Who knows ways to discourage the use of plastic throwaway containers?
Answer _____ Initial _____

12. Who attracted birds to their area in some way:
    a. by planting shrubs and trees
    b. by providing water
    c. by hanging nesting boxes
    d. by installing a feeder with different foods to attract different birds and

**152** Language Arts and Environmental Awareness

      e. by providing safe environment by putting a bell on a cat who stalks birds.

      Answer _____  Initial _____

13. Who has conserved energy by walking or biking this week?

      Answer _____  Initial _____

After the environmental searches are completed, have the children read the questions and answers in class. Recognize class members who have their initials on the papers.

**Home Activity**

Purchase or order pH paper from a biological supply company and invite your child to investigate amounts of acid rain that could damage the water cycle in your area. Encourage your child to collect and test water that is available, i.e., water caught in a container during a rainstorm or snowstorm, or water collected from a nearby puddle, pond, wetland area, community fountain, swimming pool, lake, or river. On a large sheet of paper, have your child make a chart to show the results seen from the pH paper your child inserts in the water. Show your child how to use the chart to make comparisons. For instance, discuss, "Which water is *most* acidic? *Least*? Why do you think this is so?"

■ **George, Jean Craighead (1990).** *One Day in the Tropical Rain Forest.* New York: Crowell. Ages 10 up.

**Environmental context:** Importance of rain forest to inhabitants

Set in a tropical rain forest in Venezuela along the Orinoco River, this story introduces a young boy named Tepui and his friend, a natural scientist. With Tepui's knowledge about a species of butterfly and the scientist's interest and dedication to saving its habitat, the two stop the bulldozers of the developers who are scheduled to tear down the rain forest for buildings. The ecosystem of the tropical rain forest is explained and the importance of its survival to humans and the world's air and water is emphasized.

**Activity: "Tepui's Success"**

**Language arts focus:** To record a viewpoint; to read silently

Ask the children to write a brief paragraph that tells their point of view about developers who want to tear down the rain forests that serve as habitats for living things. Have the children include their thoughts, feelings, and ideas about Tepui's success in stopping the bulldozers. For instance, ask if they agree or disagree that humans should not overdevelop the rain forests to extinction, as Tepui believed would happen. They also can include their beliefs that the destruction of a rain forest is justified or not justified and give their reasons. Have the children trade papers with one another to read silently. Encourage them to ask questions of one another so any unclear statement is elaborated and clarified. When the papers are returned, engage the children in using the "critiques" of their fellow students to do a written revision of their work, clarifying whatever was unclear. Have them draw a picture that illustrates their writing.

**Home Activity**

Discuss with your child the effect of the rain forests on the earth's atmosphere and water cycle as well as the survival of humans. Help your child see how erosion—the wearing away of the rock and soil—can be prevented by trees and plants whose roots anchor the soil. To do this, guide your child through the following procedure:

1. Have your child mix sand and soil together in the bottom of a glass pan (11" × 14") to make a mound that represents a small hill.

2. Ask your child to insert a plug of rooted weeds or grass that he or she has collected on *one* side of the mound/hill.

3. Give your child a small container of water or a sprinkling can and ask him or her to pour water on the top of the mound just as if rain were falling equally on both sides of it. Ask him or her to watch to see what happens to each side of the mound. Encourage your child to elaborate and tell you what he or she observes.

### ■ George, Jean Craighead (1995). *There's an Owl in the Shower.* New York: HarperCollins. Ages 9–11.

**Environmental context:** Efforts to save spotted owls

In George's story, Borden and his family face personal survival questions as they face the environmental issues surrounding efforts to save spotted owls. Borden's father has lost his job as a logger in the California forests, which generates many frustrations for the family. Borden's idea for revenge on the owls takes an unexpected turn when he discovers an abandoned owlet and takes it home. Only after the entire family falls in love with Brandy, the owl, do they realize the complicated issues surrounding the tensions between people who support the logging industry and those who support caring for the owl's habitat. The family gains a perspective on the spotted owl and discovers an important bond between nature, wildlife, and humans.

**Activity: "Reading with a Marker"**

**Language arts focus:** To respond to a story through crayon sketches; to read written descriptions to others; to select adjectives

Ask the children to react to the main idea of the story, the main character, relationships, conflicts, and mood of the story by reading with a marker (or crayon or colored pencil) in their hands. As the children read, have them make sketches to respond to the story and to express their feelings about what is going on. Have the children write descriptions of their sketches and then read their writing to one another in pairs.

Next, instruct the children as a whole group to observe how adjectives are used to describe the owl in the story. As you (or the children) reread excerpts aloud, have them select or read a dozen adjectives from the story and let volunteers write the words on the board. Involve the children further in a descriptive activity:

1. Distribute more paper and pencils so the children can sketch a picture to match each adjective (perhaps those on the board) that you read aloud.
2. Ask the children to draw sketches for a chart to show owls and other birds and elicit their suggestions for adjectives to describe each picture. Show a picture and let each child give one adjective

that might be used in telling about the picture. Display the children's artwork.

**Home Activity**

After reading George's story, invite your child to write a conversation between Borden and Brandy, the abandoned owlet, for others in the family to read. Point out the use of quotation marks in the dialogue. Suggest that your child tell how Brandy feels, how Borden feels, and what they both look like. Have your child include some advice that Borden would give Brandy before the owl is returned to the wild. Read the conversation aloud as your child listens. Encourage your child to make any additions, deletions, or other changes, and read aloud the revised conversation.

■ **George, Jean Craighead (1987). *Water Sky*.** New York: Harper & Row. Ages 9–11.

**Environmental context:** Importance of whaling to Eskimos

Lincoln Noah journeys from Massachusetts to Barrow, Alaska, to find his Uncle Jack James. Lincoln and his uncle plan to help save the bowhead whale from extinction. When Lincoln arrives, he realizes that the people of Barrow have been suffering in hunger, waiting for a whale for two years. Vincent Ologak, a whaling captain, talks of the importance of the large mammal to his people and predicts that one with a white tail will give itself to Lincoln, who has joined the whaling crew. Gathering at a camp, the crew is successful and the people celebrate the end of their hunger-time with a ceremonial sharing of food, knowledge, and love.

**Activity: "Lincoln's Alaskan Conflict"**

**Language arts focus:** To respond to issues related to protecting the whales; to participate in essay writing to inform, explain, and persuade a reader toward a point of view

Encourage the children to write their own brief essays telling their points of view about whaling. Everyone can read these at a later time in a classroom reading area. Ask them to express their thoughts about Lincoln's conflict over protecting the whales and providing food for the hungry people. Before the children write, you may model the process by writing a short essay on a transparency on the overhead projector. Elicit the children's responses about some of the following issues:

1. To what extent do the children agree or disagree that humans have no right to push the whales to extinction as Lincoln believed when he first arrived in Barrow?
2. Do they believe (or not believe) that the harpooning of a whale is justified?
3. Do they realize the importance of the bowhead whale to the Eskimos just as Lincoln did when he was ready to leave his friends at the whaling camp?

**Home Activity**

After reading together George's story about *Water Sky,* discuss the story's ending with your child: Lincoln finally realizes that the bowhead whale is like a hardware store to the Eskimos. He understands that a whale provides food for the people as well as material for houses, sleds, traps, fish lines, bows, artwork, and even brooms. Ask your child, "What compromises, if any, would be available to the native people if there was a zero-tolerance campaign that tried to save every whale or if there was a confrontation between native inhabitants and their opponents?" Draw a whale outline on paper and within the outline, write in the details of the compromises your child suggests. Display this in a place your child suggests.

■ **Goodman, Susan E. (1995).** ***Bats, Bugs and Biodiversity: Adventures in the Amazonian Rain Forest.*** Illustrated with photographs by Michael J. Doolittle. New York: Simon & Schuster. Ages 13–14.

**Environmental context:** Nature's cause and effect in rain-forest habitat

Goodman's book is a record of a trip taken by seventh and eighth graders from Michigan to the Peruvian rain forest to explore its habitat. They learn that a rain forest affects the world's weather since it uses energy from the sun and gives it back. Rainfall evaporates, carries heat with it, and winds push warm air to cool parts of the globe. The children also learn how to survive in the rain forest, to respect the needs of the people there, and to understand nature's give-and-take (cause and effect). Glossary, bibliography, and information notes are included. Full-color photographs.

**Activity: "An Inside Ecosystem"**

**Language arts focus:** To use language to interact with others while constructing an ecological system; to observe and write notes; to read observational notes and ask questions

Just as the Michigan children learned how an ecological system uses the sun's energy and returns it, tell the children they can learn about an ecological system they construct. Have them prepare an ecosystem with an aquarium of soil, sand, rocks, twigs, and plants to give food and oxygen for one or two insects. If appropriate, add some earthworms and beetles and caterpillars (to provide carbon dioxide and nutrients for the plants), and tape a screen on top with masking tape so it stays in place. Ask the children to watch what happens in the ecosystem for several days, write notes about what they see each day, and then trade notes with another child to read and ask questions about what was read. After a few days, have the children release the insects and earthworms in the ecosystem to the outside.

**Home Activity**

If your child is interested in environmental trips similar to the one the Michigan children took, encourage him or her to write for information to Jim Cronk, Children's Environmental Trust Foundation International, 572 Alice St., Zeeland, MI 49464. If your child is interested in learning more about another rain forest through an adventure story, suggest Malcolm Bosse's *Deep Dream of the Rain Forest* (Farrar, Straus & Giroux, 1993, ages 12 up). Set in post-World War I days, Bosse's story is about fifteen-year-old Harry Winston, an orphan, who visits his uncle in colonial Borneo and is captured by members of the Iban tribe. Harry learns that the native people are not simple and childlike as he has believed but that they are quite complex as they survive in their habitat. They take him along on a dangerous journey through the dense terrain to find an entity called "Big Fish," a vision that appears to one of the tribal members. Through confrontations with river pirates and war parties from other tribes, Harry learns to trust and respect the people who live in the rain forest as well as to appreciate the forest's ecosystem.

- **Henricksson, John (1991).** *Rachel Carson: The Environmental Movement.* Illustrated by the author. Brookfield, CT: Millbrook. Ages 10–14.

**Environmental context:** Gathering data about an environmentalist

Hendricksson's life story of Carson, a marine biologist, reviews the increased impetus of the environmental movement through a narrated table of events in Carson's life. The text chronicles Carson's respect for the environment beginning as a young child on her family's farm and continuing through her adult life, where highlights are the publication of her book *The Silent Spring*, and her important speech before the U.S. Senate against the use of DDT. In doing this, Carson brings the dangers of pesticides to the attention of America's legislators and gives an impetus to the environmental movement. Photographs.

**Activity: "Vignettes"**

**Language arts focus:** To portray contributions of a national figure; to read silently; to read aloud a report

Ask the children to locate a life story of Rachel Carson or another famous figure who has made positive contributions to the care of the environment and prepare a report as if they are these figures during their lives. To do this, encourage the children to use clothing or props to highlight the figure's life as they read aloud environmentally related events.

**Home Activity**

If your child is interested further in the contributions of Rachel Carson as a biologist and an environmentalist, suggest reading *Sounding the Alarm: A Biography of Rachel Carson* (Dillon Publishing, 1989, ages 10 up) by Judith Harlan or *Rachel Carson: Pioneer of Ecology* (Viking, 1988, ages 10 up) by Kathleen V. Kudlinski. After reading another biography about

Carson, invite your child to write some true or false statements about Rachel Carson's achievements for you to answer.

■ **Lavies, Bianca (1992). *Monarch Butterflies: Mysterious Travelers.*** Illustrated by the author. New York: Dutton. Ages 9–10.

**Environmental context:** Gathering scientific data about butterflies and habitat

The focus of this photographic essay is the importance of natural scientists to nature's creatures, particularly the monarch butterfly. The photographs show the monarch's winter home, only recently located by several scientists. The text discusses the eastern monarchs' wintering grounds in the Sierra Madre mountains of Mexico. Descriptions also are given about metamorphosis, how the butterflies are tagged, and ways scientific data are gathered to add to people's knowledge about the insect. Full-color photographs.

**Activity: "Butterfly Garden"**

**Language arts focus:** To read for identification purposes

Have the children read excerpts from nature guidebooks and other informational sources to identify the kinds of plants and shrubs that attract larvae of butterflies. Write the information on a class chart similar to the entries that follow:

| Butterfly | Food |
|---|---|
| Black swallowtail | Leaves of carrots, caraway, and related plants |
| Cabbage butterfly | Leaves of cabbage and related mustards |
| Monarch butterfly | Leaves of milkweed |
| Mourning cloak butterfly | Leaves of elm, poplar, willow, and hackberry |
| Tiger swallowtail | Leaves of birch, poplar, ash, and cherry |
| Viceroy butterfly | Leaves of willow, poplar, and aspen |

Use the children's suggestions and make arrangements to transform a small plot at your school into a garden for butterflies. Ask for help from parent volunteers to plant the shrubs, flowers, vegetables, and saplings that will attract butterflies to this new habitat. If appropriate, make a trail around the perimeter of the plot for children in future classes to use for nature walks in the area.

**Home Activity**

Ask your child to write his or her own descriptions of butterflies seen on strips of paper and put the strips in a container. Reach in and select a strip. Read the description aloud as your child listens—wings are yellow with a black border with some yellow spots, etc. Ask your child to guess the name of the butterfly being described (tiger swallowtail). Use a butterfly field guide if necessary. When a guess is correct, have your child tell you the clues or information he or she used to give the appropriate identification. Trade roles and have your child read several descriptions so you can identify the butterflies.

■ **Marzani, Carl (1972).** *The Wounded Earth: An Environmental Survey.* Reading, MA: Addison-Wesley. Ages 14 up.

**Environmental context:** Environment's health can be protected by current technology

The author, professor of economics at New York University, discusses how earth's ecosystem came to be what it is and how humans have the power to pollute their surroundings but also can create a better environment through the use of technology. For example, the author points out that the technology exists to eliminate practically all water pollution and air pollution in the United States. Technology also can be applied to agriculture, beginning with the use of artificial fertilizers and pesticides and continuing on to the production of energy through solar radiation, wind power, and tide flows. The text emphasizes that what is needed is money and human determination to help.

**Activity: "Concern, Inc."**

**Language arts focus:** To read for information and collect research tips to help consumers shop from an ecological point of view

Mention to the children that when Mrs. Richard Helms, wife of a former Central Intelligence Agency director, and Mrs. Paul Ignatius, wife of a former secretary of the navy, were living in Washington, DC, they organized a group called Concern, Inc. The group focused on consumer shopping from an ecological point of view. Today, the group sends out eco-tips which recommend or condemn consumer products. Some of the companies take notice and take remedial action on their products.

Have the children divide into small groups to role-play being a member of Concern, Inc. Ask the children to read informational material and research one or more eco-tips they select (i.e., use products wrapped in recycled materials) that could become a recommendation for a consumer product. With the class, have volunteers from each group read a report on the group's eco-tips and identify any consumer products that the group discussed. List the eco-tips on the board. After hearing the reports, ask the whole group to select one of the eco-tips as their first choice and have volunteers give the reasons *why* they voted as they did. Repeat the activity with a second choice, third choice, and so on. Encourage the children to prepare a one-page flyer of the eco-tips they have chosen as informative material to take home for other family members or neighborhood friends to read.

## Home Activity

With your child, discuss the idea of sending some eco-tip information on a one-page flyer to friends and relatives. Ask your child to prepare a one-page flyer with suggestions that recommend consumer products. Examples could include the following:

### Eco-Tip: Why You Should Use Recycled Paper

It's important to recycle to save our environment's resources—every ton of paper you reuse saves trees and helps keep pounds of garbage out of our landfills. It's also important to buy products made from the materials you recycle to let recycling companies know you support what they do. When you buy recycled paper products, you are saying "yes" to the recycling process and strengthening the recycling program in your area. **Say Yes to Recycling and Reusing!**

Ask your child to suggest names of people with whom to share his or her eco-tips. You child can distribute flyers in person or by mail, or call people up on the telephone.

■ **Milord, Susan (1989). *The Kids' Nature Book.*** Illustrated from various sources. Charlotte, VT: Williamson Publishing. Ages 9–12.

**Environmental context:** Appreciating and exploring nature throughout the year

Milord's book has an activity, poem, or story to help a child explore nature for every one of the 365 days of the year. Particularly suitable for a study of environmental awareness are the activities entitled "Endangered Species" and "Environment." In "Endangered Species" a child is encouraged to request information about animals from a conservation group, and in "Environment" a child is asked to conserve water and electricity, walk or bike short distances, and save bottles, cans, and newspapers to be recycled. A child also can catch and release fireflies, prepare a butterfly garden, hatch amphibian eggs, or make a snow gauge. A bibliography and index are included Black line drawings.

**Activity: "Become Famous Environmentalists"**

**Language arts focus:** To write interview questions; to write the results of an interview; to read interviews written by others

Create paper profiles of the children's faces as "famous environmentalists" to display in the class, hallway, or other area in the school. Trace the children's facial profiles on black paper taped on a wall or bulletin board. Trace the outline with a pencil. Have the children cut them out, glue the outlines on white paper, and write their name at the top. Next, have the children think of questions to ask one another about conserving water and electricity. For example, a child might ask another,"What do you do to conserve water and electricity, save energy, and recycle?" Have pairs of the children interview one another about the actions they take. Engage them in writing up their interviews in their best handwriting. Mount the interview results on construction paper and display the writing under the profiles for others to read.

**Home Activity**

Encourage your child to participate in an environmental action that helps save natural resources by recycling a small shopping bag. At the library, let your child photocopy and enlarge the cover of an ecological information book to fit the front of the bag. Let your child color the cover and then glue it to the bag. Your child can cover the front with wide clear tape to make the bag sturdy enough to use again and again.

■ **Montez, Michele (1994).** *50 Simple Things Kids Can Do to Recycle.* Illustrated by the author. New York: Earthworks. Ages 9–14.

**Environmental context:** Reducing, reusing, and recycling resources

Montez's focus in this book is the three R's of ecology—reducing, reusing, and recycling resources. There are suggestions about taking care of the earth's resources including what garbage can be recycled, ways to reuse objects around the home, and how to be a wise shopper. Black-and-white sketches.

**Activity: "Earthwise Circle: Reduce, Reuse, and Recycle"**

**Language arts focus:** To read to prepare for a panel discussion; to read an informational book to build understanding

Ask the children to read about conserving the earth's resources before they participate in a panel discussion to tell what they do or could do to reduce, reuse, and recycle the resources. Divide the children into groups of five for each panel. Mention that each child will be responsible for information on an aspect of the topic. When the whole group reconvenes, elicit suggestions from each panel about ways to organize reducing the use of materials, reusing them, and recycling in their very own classroom. Ask, "What would need to be done?" Write the children's suggestions around the circumference of a chalk circle on the board with a heading in the center, "The Earthwise Circle." Add the children's additional suggestions to the circle as shown:

**Recycle**
Use long-lasting rechargable batteries.
Recycle vegetable scraps for compost.
Recycle bottles, cans, newspapers, and tires.
Write to newspapers to support recycling.

**Reuse**
Reuse envelopes.
Use today's lunch bag for tomorrow.
Don't throw anything away that can be fixed. Fix it.
Reuse food containers.
Reuse your homework for notepaper.
Save your next package or box to reuse for another shipping and mailing.
Give your magazines to friends, charities, children's homes, youth shelters, and so on.

**The Earthwise Circle**

**Reduce**
Reduce the greenhouse effect by planting a tree to consume carbon dioxide.
Reduce water use by turning off the water when you brush your teeth.
Reduce water use by taking a short shower instead of a bath.
Reduce energy use by using cold water to wash your hands.
Reduce car pollution: bikes, skateboards, and roller skates can take you short distances.
Reduce energy use in your home. Put on a sweater when you are cold; heat your body, not your whole house.
Reduce electricity use by turning off lights and appliances when you are done.

For a display board activity, invite the children to write their names around the circumference of another "Earthwise" circle when they do some small things that can add up to conserving as a way of life. Have them draw stars by their names when they make some change in their actions at school or at home that shows they care about the environment.

**Home Activity**

Encourage your child to recycle and reuse earth's resources by carrying his or her own trash in an old backpack or hand tote for a day (week) to see how much is accumulated. Discuss the extent to which the child could change some habits by recycling and reusing resources instead of generating larger and larger amounts of trash.

- **Murphy, Jim (1995).** *Into the Deep Forest with Henry David Thoreau.* Illustrated by Karen Keisler. New York: Clarion. Ages 9–12.

**Environmental context:** Interrelationships between humans and nature

Murphy's book is an accounting documented from Thoreau's journal entries about his trip to the mountains in the Maine wilderness in the late 1800s. Thoreau portrays his genuine love of all things in nature (such as the mountain mist and the cries of the animals) and his need for peace and for an escape from busy humans rushing to do their many activities. Oil and pencil illustrations.

**Activity: "Predictions"**

**Language arts focus:** To read to make predictions

With book markers, divide a book about an environmentalist into four parts marked Part I, Part II, and so on. Tell the children that when they select this book to read they will have an opportunity to make predictions (guesses, hunches) about each one of the four parts of the book. You will give them a paper (similar to the following) and they should write on it their name and the title and author of the book and then follow the directions for making predictions:

## 166   Language Arts and Environmental Awareness

- **Part I:** Study the cover illustration and read the title and first page. Write down your predictions about the author's thoughts, feelings and any actions for later in the book after the first page and give reasons for your predictions using complete sentences.
- **Part II:** Read the second part in the book and then stop at the book marker. Write down what you predict will happen later in the book. Use what you have read to support your prediction.
- **Part III:** Read the third part in the book and stop at the book marker. Predict the outcome and offer reasons from your reading as support.
- **Part IV:** Finish reading the book and reread all of your predictions. Make any changes you want to your predictions on the paper. Give the paper to your teacher.

---

As you read the book, write your predictions below under Part I, Part II and so on. When you finish reading the book, reread all of your predictions. Rewrite any predictions you want to change on the paper (see below).

- **Predictions for Part I**
  Changes (rewrite your predictions, if necessary, after finishing the book):
- **Predictions for Part II**
  Changes:
- **Predictions for Part III**
  Changes:
- **Predictions for Part IV**
  Changes:

**Home Activity**

Invite your child to write a brief first-person report as an animal and tell about its life in a particular habitat—perhaps an ecosystem like that in the Maine wilderness that Thoreau visited. Have your child conduct research for information for the report. Share with your child an example of the beginning of a first-person report such as: I am a loon and live in the mountains in Maine. I call out cries that sound almost human in the night mists. When it's dark, l look for _____.


- **Pollock, Steve (1993).** *Ecology.* Illustrated by the author. New York: Dorling-Kindersley. Ages 9–12.

**Environmental context:** Effects of technology on environment

Pollock's book has a question-and-answer format beginning with the question "What is ecology?" and continuing with "What impact does ecology have on humans?" and "What is going on in ecology today?" The text discusses the price the environment has paid for many technological developments: factories that release smoke, steam, chemicals, and toxic waste; new and more intrusive ways to locate, catch, and process fish from the oceans; and dangerous non-biological methods of controlling crop pests. Colorful photographs.

**Activity: "Book Mark Message"**

**Language arts focus:** To read about or research a history of businesses and factories; to transform written information into another form

During a discussion about what technology has cost the earth and its inhabitants, encourage the children to talk about any "price" they see being "paid" today for factories in their area. Write on the board their suggestions about what it "costs" people in their area when there is an increased release of smoke, steam, chemicals, and toxic waste, or when factory owners show a lack of care of the waterways and other areas. List the children's ideas under two headings such as "Technolgy in Factories" and "Cost to the Environment."

Have the children suggest ways they can do further reading or research about the technological history of businesses and factories in their community and find out what the environment was like before the factories were built. Have them bring their findings back to the whole group and trade their notes with one another to read. Return the notes back to the original writers and encourage volunteers to present their information about how commerce has helped (or hindered) the people's quality of life in the community. Have the children transform their findings into messages written on book marks (4" × 11" paper strips) and trade them with one another.

**Home Activity**

Ask your child to locate the place where a factory now stands in your area and imagine that before any building was erected there, the land was a wetland or a prairie or a forest. Encourage your child to sketch the factory as it looks today, and then sketch a scene of what it might have looked like before any development took place. Talk about what scene your child likes best and why. Encourage your child to tell his or her point of view about what could have caused the changes in the area. Ask your child for a point of view: "Which changes do you think are positive ones? Negative? Why do you think this way?"

■ **Potter, Jean (1995).** *Nature in a Nutshell for Kids.* Illustrated by the author. New York: John Wiley. Ages 10 up.

**Environmental context:** Studying nature

In Potter's book, there are over 100 easy projects that a reader can accomplish in about fifteen minutes each, which makes the information suitable for nature study and activity programs. Topics include earth science, ecology, animals, and ponds, and the accompanying activities help a child learn about the environment and living things. Projects include making an ecosystem, observing how the sun warms a greenhouse, and observing the environment to get an appreciation of why people need to conserve and care for their surroundings. Adults should supervise young children who undertake the experiments and projects. Bibliographic references and an activity index with entries under the various categories are included. Black line drawings.

**Activity: "The Greenhouse Effect"**

**Language arts focus:** To read directions

On a chart or overhead transparency, copy the directions from Potter's book for a greenhouse effect project and place the materials nearby: timer, tape, four unbreakable thermometers, two cardboard pieces slightly larger than the thermometers, and a glass jar with lid. Have the children read the directions aloud before the group begins the activity. The steps of the activity are in the following sequence:

1. Tape two of the unbreakable thermometers to pieces of cardboard. Place them inside the room somewhere. Note: Do *not* let the sun shine *directly* on the thermometers.
2. Place one thermometer in the jar on a sunny windowsill and tighten the lid. Place the remaining thermometer against the window but facing inside to the room.
3. Turn a timer to three minutes (or five or six minutes) and then read the thermometers.
4. Record the temperature on a large chart. When the children discover the higher temperature in the jar, discuss what has happened: The sun's *short* heat waves warm things up and then warmed-up objects give off *long* heat waves. The sun's short heat waves can travel through glass but the longer heat waves cannot and stay trapped in the jar, making the temperature rise.
5. Write a brief paragraph explaining the temperature differences from your point of view. Include your interpretation of how the sun warms a greenhouse (refer to the temperature in the glass jar).

Have children trade paragraphs with others to read silently. Encourage them to ask questions of the writers that would help clarify or elaborate any parts in the paragraphs they read. When the paragraphs are returned to the original writers, have the children draw sketches of the activity in the margins.

**Home Activity**

Tell your child that the two of you can make it rain in the house. Encourage your child to do this by reading the directions for the activity "Water Cycle" in Potter's *Nature in a Nutshell for Kids*. Help your child collect the needed materials: soil, plastic zip-top bag, water, and tape. Have your child put soil in the bottom of the plastic bag and sprinkle the soil with water. Zip the bag closed and tape it to a sunny window. Encourage your child to observe what happens in the bag: your child will see a water cycle in miniature—the sun warms the soil enough to turn the sprinkled water into water vapor, which forms droplets at the top of the bag. When the water evaporates still more, it condenses until enough water is collected to become heavy and fall back down as "rain" on top of the soil.

If appropriate, invite your child to take close-up photographs of this mini- water cycle to show family members and friends or mail to the science editor of a local newspaper. Your child may be the first in your neighborhood to capture images of a water cycle in action and the editor of the children's section in the newspaper may want to publish it.

■ **Pryor, Bonnie (1987).** *The House on Maple Street.* Illustrated by the author. New York: Morrow. Ages 9–11.

**Environmental context:** Environmental changes take place over time

In Pryor's story, wild animals roam in a lush forest until a forest fire devastates the area. When the buffalo and other animals return as the grasses grow back, the Indians follow to hunt, and an Indian father shows his son how to make an arrowhead. The boy loses his arrowhead and the tribe moves on. Later, wagon trains come, a couple builds a log house, and their baby, Ruby, finds the lost arrowhead and puts it into one of her doll dishes to save it. However, a rabbit knocks the cup into its burrow and the arrowhead is lost again. Years later, the children of a new couple find the cup and arrowhead while digging for a garden and wonder who lost them. Full-color illustrations.

**Activity: "Story Circle"**

**Language arts focus:** To participate in a story circle; to read and conduct an inquiry; to read or write notes related to an inquiry

Have the children divide into groups for story circles and tell them they will have an opportunity to talk about situations/issues in their own lives that relate to the story. During a discussion of *The House on Maple Street*, encourage the children to talk about the land they live on and how it might have changed over the years. Have them suggest ways to research the environmental history of their community and imagine who first lived in their area many years ago as well as what the environment was like at the time. Ask, "What references would you read?"

Back together as a whole group, the children can list their suggestions on the board as a reference list before they search for related books in the room's reading area or school library. Ask, "In what ways could you take notes about what you read?" and introduce different ways to use adhesive-backed notes to help the children as they read books on the topic. Distribute sticky notes to the children and invite them to write notes to leave behind in a book for another child to read. Thus, other children can read the notes that tell where the book reminded the first reader of something that happened to the environment in his or her own life, or about the first reader's thoughts on caring for the environment, such as "I like the part on this page when. . . ." The children also can use the notes to communicate in other ways. Notes can also

1. Serve as place-holders or page marks for subsequent conversations the children have about the book or about caring for the environment;
2. Be the basis for a child's thoughts to be included in a daily ecological notebook;
3. Record what the children have noticed about the author's writing or artist's illustrations;
4. Be placed into groups or categories and then used as a basis for a child's short talk on ecology to others;
5. Be a record of the questions the book raises in a child's mind.

After time in the reading area or after a library visit, have the children show one of the books they selected as well as the sticky notes they wrote and then report their findings about a feature of the environmental history of their area to the group.

**Home Activity**

With your child, visit a library, museum, or newspaper office to locate old drawings or photographs of a place in your area. Photocopy what you find. When your child selects an old picture that he or she particularly likes, have your child make a drawing of the same place as it looks today. Encourage your child to talk about what might have caused the changes in the environment. Discuss changes that have helped or hindered the environment for living creatures in your area.

- **Rainis, Kenneth G. (1989).** *Nature Projects for Young Scientists.* New York: Franklin Watts. Ages 10 up.

**Environmental context:** Reading to participate in a nature experiment

Rainis's book has a collection of experiments that relate to fungi and plants (plant kingdom) as well as bacteria, one-celled organisms, and invertebrates and vertebrates (animal kingdom). The author encourages a child to be a nature detective. To do this, a child can observe, guess, test, and make a conclusion by participating in one of the suggested nature projects. Black-and-white illustrations.

**Activity: "Unseen Pollution"**

**Language arts focus:** To read a factual text before observing, guessing, testing, and concluding through ranking

After having the children read information related to pollution in earth's environment, elicit from them what dangers the pollution they see has for the environment. Tell the children that they can not always *see* pollution and they can create some *unseen* pollution in the classroom. To do this, first elicit suggestions from the children about kitchen ingredients that they have observed that could be unseen or invisible when mixed in water (perhaps white sugar, flour, salt, white pepper). They may use one of the ingredients as a "pollutant" and participate in the following experiment:

1. List the ingredients on the board and ask the children to read the list and then guess which ones might be the most unseen or invisible. Have the children take turns testing their guesses by placing small amounts of each ingredient in paper cups of water to observe them.

2. Ask the children to rank the ingredients with #1 being the most invisible, #2 being more visible, #3 still more visible, and so on.

3. Guide the children in making some unseen pollution by shaking a small amount of one ingredient (perhaps salt or white pepper or white vinegar) into a small glass container of water placed on the stage of an overhead projector. Turn on the light to magnify what is going on.

4. Ask a child to put a paper coffee filter over the top of an empty glass container and pour the polluted water through the filter and into the container. Let another child use a magnifying glass to see if the filter removed any small pieces of salt or pepper or signs of vinegar.

5. Ask the children to conclude if the water looks clear and clean and if so, have them taste the water when it is poured into small paper cups. Have the children describe how the clean-looking water tastes to them.

6. Encourage each child to write what was done and then read it to someone else in the classroom to retell the steps in making an example of invisible pollutants in water.

**Home Activity**

Invite your child to look through the daily newspaper to locate articles about water pollution and other damage to the environment. Read them with your child. Discuss what is happening to harm the earth. Encourage your child to suggest what he or she can do to affect some of the causes of damage—urban development, logging, grazing, soil erosion, water projects, mining, toxic waste, and air pollution. This type of family discussion adds current facts to your child's awareness about what is going on in the environment. As an example, information such as the following about the situation in the Sierra Nevada may be discussed when found in newspaper and magazine articles or heard on TV news:

1. In 1991, the Congress of the United States requested a thorough environmental study of the Sierra Nevada mountain range because of concerns about misguided land management practices, piecemeal environmental protection, worsening fire danger, and waning biodiversity—concerns that also affect other mountain ranges in the United States. The study, concluded in 1996, states that the moun-

tain range has been badly damaged by urban development, logging, grazing, soil erosion, water projects, mining, and air pollution. This will cause environmental conflicts among groups of people associated with the area.

2. More than any other recent human activity, logging actually makes forest fires worse (not larger but hotter) because the harvesting of timber affects the forest structure. Logging keeps the undergrowth dense and increases fuel accumulation in the local microclimate, making the fires more severe. Logging has simplified the forests, making them less hospitable to some wildlife species. Logging reduces the percentage of forests that have old-growth characteristics.

3. Grazing has had, in some places, irreversible ecological impacts. For example, in the Sierra Nevada in California, the oak woodlands in the western foothills are being damaged by overgrazing, woodcutting, and urban development.

4. Increased population has negatively affected and invaded habitats, brought in non-native plants and animals, caused changes in the stream flow and groundwater extraction, and increased septic effluent and waste water pollution. The human population in the Sierra Nevada area, now 650,000, doubled between 1970 and 1990, and this figure is expected to triple by 2040.

5. Sixty-nine species of Sierran wildlife, representing 17 percent of the mountain's fauna, are considered at risk. The species that are declining or already have dangerously low populations are the big mountain sheep, Yosemite toad, foothill yellow-legged frog, western pond turtle, California horned lizard, willow flycatcher, and olive-sided flycatcher.

6. Loss of habitat is the most identifiable cause of the decline of wildlife—especially in the Sierra foothill habitats.

Invite your child to visit the library or search the Internet with you to locate more information about any one of the topics in the previous list. Point out that solutions are not impossible and remedies for the forests include protecting old growth forests, reducing damaging air pollution, restoring forest structure, and recovering any degraded river channels, improved scientific monitoring, and collaboration among public and private groups in the area. Discuss with your child: "If interested, what can you do to help one of these groups?"

■ **Shedd, Warner (1994).** *The Kids' Wildlife Book: Exploring Animal Worlds through Indoor/Outdoor Experiences.* Illustrated by Loretta Trezzo Braren. New York: Williamson. Ages 9–11.

**Environmental context:** Interacting with wildlife

Shedd's book provides information about amphibians, birds, and mammals of North America along with suggested activities for interacting with animal life. One category, "Let's Talk," focuses on animal sounds and can start a reader's conversation with others about the different sounds various animals make. Other categories feature animal homes, what animals eat, and animal life. Animal tracks and range maps are included. Black line drawings.

**Activity: "Sketchbooks of Animal Life"**

**Language arts focus:** To do research; to write notes during a nature walk; to read notes and make predictions

Schedule a walk in the neighborhood with the children or go on a field trip to a nearby nature area to observe living creatures and to predict some animal homes that could be nearby. Have the children do some reseach on animal habitats in the area before the trip. Have the children carry sketchbooks (small notebooks) with them to record the names of the creatures they see, to make sketches, and to write their predictions about what animal homes the wildlife would need. Back in the classroom, engage the children in reading aloud their notes about the wildlife they saw and their predictions. Have them trade sketchbooks with friends, read one another's notes, and return the books. Among other questions about living creatures and their homes, ask, "What, if anything, did you see on the walk that could interfere with the shelter (or food) that wildlife would need? What was it and in what ways could it interfere? What could be done to intervene on behalf of the animals?"

Encourage the children to use their notes as a reference for the discussion.

### Home Activity

With your child, select a tree in your yard or neighborhood to "adopt"—preferably one with a bird's or squirrel's nest—and observe it carefully throughout the year. With pencils and sketchbooks, visit the tree often and draw any changes that you and your child see during the four seasons. Each day that you observe the tree, encourage your child to label his or her sketches with a caption that tells how the seasonal weather is affecting the tree, i.e., "Day of Wet Green Leaves," or "Day of Cold Bare Branches."

■ **Stone, Lynn M. (1989).** ***Wetlands.*** Illustrated with photographs by the author. Vero Beach, FL: Rourke Enterprises. Ages 9–12.

**Environmental context:** Wetlands habitat

Stone's book examines the wetlands as an ecological system and describes plants such as cattails, swamp lilies, and others as well as several wetland animals found there—snakes, water fowl, and fish. Reasons are given for conserving the wetlands since they help control flooding, filter pollutants, release oxygen, add water to the water table, and prevent invasion from the tides in coastal areas. Glossary and index are included. Full-color photographs.

### Activity: "Reading to Rank Importance"

**Language arts focus:** To read critically before ranking an article

Read aloud with the group a brief ecology article and discuss the main idea. Then, have the children divide into small groups and discuss the material in two additional articles you give them. Tell them that the purpose of reading the articles is to evaluate the importance of each attempt to care for the environment. Ask the children in the groups to rank these attempts in the following way: 1.) the most important attempt to care for the environment from their point of view; 2.) fairly important attempt; and 3.) not too important at this time.

Back together, ask a child from each small group to report on the group's rankings and the reasons for their decisions. Chart the children's rankings of the three articles on the board.

**Home Activity**

Visit a nearby nature area or wildlife sanctuary—some *do* feature wetlands—with your child to observe the living things in the area. Have your child take a camera to photograph living creatures in their natural habitat. Display the pictures after they are developed and ask your child to write captions for each one. Encourage your child to read the captions aloud to another member of the family. A sketchbook or notebook can replace a camera in this activity and captions can be written at the foot of each page.

■ **Van Cleave, Janice (1996).** *Janice Van Cleave's Earth Science for Every Kid: 101 Easy Experiments That Really Work.* Illustrated by Laurel Aiello. New York: John Wiley. Ages 9–14.

**Environmental context:** Observing what is happening to earth's resources

In Van Cleave's book, the experiments are grouped in sections labeled space, rocks and minerals, movement of the crust, erosion, weather, and oceans. Each experiment includes a purpose, list of materials, instructions, and an explanation of the results. Black line drawings.

**Activity: "From Sandwich to Sedimentary Formation"**

**Language arts focus:** To read and follow directions for an experiment

Read aloud the directions for an experiment which uses a peanut butter sandwich to demonstrate a sedimentary rock formation. Then, show the directions written on the board, an overhead transparency, or class chart so you can point to the words as you read them aloud again and ask the children to read along with you. Divide the children into small groups and have each group practice following the directions to make a replica of a rock formation by layering a peanut butter sandwich.

Back in the whole group, have volunteers from each group explain

## 178  Language Arts and Environmental Awareness

what happened as the members of their group followed the directions. Then, have the children write their own interpretation of the results. They should include an explanation of how a peanut butter sandwich demonstrates a sedimentary rock formation, as well as ways that living things might benefit from various layers of rock. After writing their thoughts, have each child pair up with a friend to read the writing aloud to one another and to give feedback about its clarity.

**Home Activity**

From a nearby library, introduce your child to other books in which he or she can read directions for self-selected activities and experiments. Let your child choose one book in which he or she is interested, select an activity, and read the directions aloud to you. Guide your child through the steps in the activity. Display the results for other family members to see.

■ **Van Cleave, Janice (1996).** *Janice Van Cleave's Oceans for Every Kid: Easy Activities That Make Learning Science Fun.* Illustrated by Laurel Aiello. New York: Macmillan. Ages 9–14.

**Environmental context:** Ocean pollution

In Van Cleave's book, activities related to the ocean habitat are arranged by topics and for each, the purpose is stated and materials are listed as needed. The procedures for the activities are given clearly. For example, there is information about ocean pollution and the related activities include observing what run-off does around a waterway and the effect that oil has on a bird's feathers. Maps, a bibliography for further reading, and a glossary are included. Black line drawings.

**Activity: "Effect of Oil on Feathers"**

**Language arts focus:** To read directions; to write or read a paragraph

Tell the children that they will have an opportunity to read the directions to an activity about how useful a bird's feathers are and see what happens when oil gets on a feather. Have children read each of the following directions aloud before they begin:

1. Collect three or four goose or duck feathers from a pillow and fill one eyedropper with water and another with cooking oil. Place a piece of plastic wrap on the stage of the overhead projector to keep the stage clean before feathers, oil, and water are added.
2. Turn on the projector light so everyone can see that a feather has barbs. Mention that each barb is covered with an oily substance made in the bird's body that keeps water away from the bird.
3. On the plastic wrap, place more feathers and have someone put a few drops of water on the feathers. Ask someone to tell what he or she observes from the magnified projection of the feathers and water drops (water will roll off).
4. Put the feathers in a shallow container and pass them around with a magnifying glass so everyone can see close up what happens to feathers when the water gets on them.
5. Repeat the activity with feathers and oil drops. Have the children summarize what they learned.

**Home Activity**

Ask your child to put a few drops of oil on different types of feathers. Put the oiled feathers in a shallow container and look at them with a magnifying glass. Let your child observe and explain what happens when oil is put on the feathers. Supervise for safety and let your child experiment with a variety of soaps or detergents or cleaners to observe which are the best in removing the oil. Encourage your child to tell someone in the home or neighborhood what he or she learned from this activity.

■ **Walsh, Jill Paton (1982).** *The Green Book.* New York: Farrar, Straus & Giroux. Ages 10–11.

**Environmental context:** Life in a futuristic environment

A future time period in Earth's history is part of the setting in this story about a group of Britons who leave the dying Earth for a new planet. After years of space travel, they land on a planet and establish a new

## 180 Language Arts and Environmental Awareness

settlement called Shine. In Shine, everything is like crystal and all the plants shatter like glass except wheat, the only crop from Earth that grows well. Patti, the youngest settler, keeps a record of what is going on in her notebook (called *The Green Book*) and her record is the beginning of the history and literature of the settlers' new culture in Shine.

**Activity: "Settlers and Newcomers in Shine"**

**Language arts focus:** To read notes related to role-playing

Ask the children to divide into groups of eight. Half of the children in each group can take the roles of the first settlers in Shine and the other half can take the roles of newcomers to the planet. Invite the two subgroups to create a brief drama scene together. Ask the subgroups to consider what they could act out in the following situation:

> In a futuristic settlement called Shine on a new planet, one of the settlers returns from a long walk and says that he has seen a large space ship with newly arrived people who are trekking toward the settlers' homes. The newcomers appear at the top of a nearby hill and four of them approach the Shine inhabitants. Four settlers walk out to meet the newcomers. The newcomers say that they, too, have left the dying planet and they want to join the Shine settlement. The settlers tell about how most plants grown on the planet shatter like crystal and how they have overcome the problem by growing wheat, the one food plant from their home planet that survives in Shine. The settlers also tell the newcomers how they have added the word "Shine" to the end of each of their names (Patti-Shine) and about their favorite "Shine" sayings (such as "A ditch in Shine grows wheat so fine"). They also talk about what they had to do to adapt to the new planet's environment and to care for the wheat crop so important to their lives.

Have the two subgroups meet and write notes to decide what to say to one another to create the scene. Ask the children to decide about the following:

1. What do you imagine about the environment? What would you say in a "think-out-loud experience" about the planet Shine? What contributions would you make about the following?

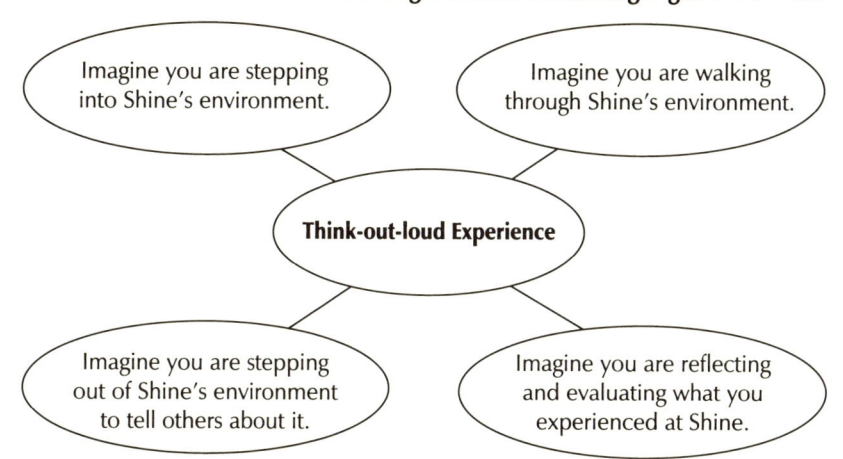

```
┌─────────────────────────┐         ┌─────────────────────────┐
│ Imagine you are stepping│         │  Imagine you are walking│
│ into Shine's environment.│        │ through Shine's environment.│
└─────────────────────────┘         └─────────────────────────┘
              \                     /
               ┌─────────────────────────┐
               │  Think-out-loud Experience │
               └─────────────────────────┘
              /                     \
┌─────────────────────────┐         ┌─────────────────────────┐
│ Imagine you are stepping│         │ Imagine you are reflecting│
│ out of Shine's environment│       │ and evaluating what you │
│ to tell others about it.│         │ experienced at Shine.   │
└─────────────────────────┘         └─────────────────────────┘
```

2. What questions will you ask? What would you feel, say, and do as a person in the situation?
3. What "Shine" sayings based on well-known proverbs do you want to include? Perhaps "Still waters . . . will get you wheat" or "When there's wheat, there's food." What will you say about the growing and harvesting of wheat that they have to do in Shine?
4. Who will play the role of the authority figure (mayor, leader) for the Shine settlement? Role of the newcomers?
5. Which children will be settlers in Shine to accept or oppose the arrival of the newcomers? What reasons could they have for accepting the newcomers? Opposing them?

After the first role-playing, ask the subgroups to trade roles and recreate another scene so both groups can play the roles of the newcomers. Invite subgroups to volunteer to present one of their scenes to the whole class.

As a follow-up activity, have the children transform one of their role-playing situations into writing just as young Patti did in *The Green Book* and describe the settler–newcomers' encounter from their point of view. Ask the children to trade their writing with one another to read silently. Invite volunteers to read their writing aloud and discuss the various encounters that were acted out in the dramas.

**Home Activity**

With your child, designate a spiral-bound notebook as a "Green Book" and encourage your child to keep a record about caring for the environment in a manner similar to young Patti. As a follow-up activity, invite your child to read his or her writing out loud using a futuristic voice. For example, by speaking through a clean comb covered with plastic wrap or mimicking a space voice, your child can create the voice he or she wants.

■ **Wong, Ovid K. *Hands-On Ecology.*** Illustrated by the author. Chicago: Childrens, 1991. Ages 9–11.

**Environmental context:** Effect of resources on humans

Wong's book offers learning activities related to the earth's resources—subjects include air, water, and land pollution, recycling, and energy conservation. Each activity is organized in steps and fully illustrated. There is a "Think and Explore" section for further inquiry. Drawings for illustrations.

**Activity: "Taking Role of Naturalist"**

**Language arts focus:** To conduct research; to read messages about the earth's available resources

In this activity the children will take the roles of naturalists interested in the availability of resources on our planet. Elicit from children the names of environmentalists from around the world and have the children determine which people are from countries other than the United States. If appropriate, suggest names such as Rachel Carson and others. Before choosing and playing the roles, have children list some questions they want answered about the person and what he or she has done and then have them search further for information in bibliographies. Some of the their questions might be:

1. In what ways is this person interested in environmental science/ecology?
2. What has this person said or done in the field of environmental science/ecology?
3. What has this person done to back up what he or she has said about caring for the environment?

Let the children search for facts about their selected naturalists before they take their roles. Have them write notes about the person, read and reread the information they have, and then talk to one another in partnerships in the persona of their naturalists. Encourage them to tell about the person's contributions and achievements in conserving earth's resources.

**Home Activity**

With your child, design an illustration of a naturalist on posterboard (8½ " × 11"). Encourage your child to write some facts about the figure on the back of the card—name, birthplace, and contributions. Display.

# V · Involving Children in Speaking

# Involving Children in Speaking: Ages 5–8

- **Baker, Jennie (1991). *Window*.** Illustrated by the author. New York: Greenwillow. Ages 7–8.

  **Environmental context:** Changes caused by city growth

  Baker's book introduces the concept of changes in the environment. Each page in the story shows two-year intervals going by through different views from a bedroom window where a mother holds her infant son, Sam. Birthday cards on the window sill indicate that time is passing by as the changes in the environment are seen through the window. The green environment changes to tall buildings, graffiti, busy traffic, and smog. After Sam becomes an adult and moves away with his wife, a final illustration shows Sam holding his baby son and looking from his window to see birds and trees. On the horizon is a city and across the road, Sam reads a sign, "House Blocks for Sale." Rapid city growth has taken place and replaced most of the green environment during Sam's lifetime. Full-color illustrations.

  **Activity: "Rapid Growth"**

  **Language arts focus:** To discuss topics related to the story; to participate in one-to-one conversations; to tell others a point of view

  Show the children pictures of their area from years ago and have them compare those scenes with what is found in the same area today. Elicit from them any reasons they have for the changes they see and the effects of the changes on the environment. Follow up by asking the children to use a ruler and draw two-inch squares on sheets of paper in the form of a game of tic-tac-toe. Distribute unpopped popcorn kernels to the children and have them place one kernel in each square to represent the population in their community years ago. Ask them to double the kernels of popcorn in each square to represent the population growth in their community as yearly intervals go by. Repeat this activity until there is no longer enough space in each square to double the kernels again. Discuss any or all of the following questions:

1. How many kernels (population numbers) did you place in each square?
2. What meaning does this have for the growth of the population in your school, community, town, state? What additional services and resources from the earth are needed to take care of this growth?
3. What problems, for instance, might be caused by having twice as many children in their classroom (lack of desk and chair space, lack of supplies, computer use, textbooks)? In their school (at lunch, on the playground, getting a seat on the school bus, sharing school supplies, drinking fountains, and athletic equipment)? In their community (more traffic and pollution, longer lines at the grocery stores, gas stations, medical and dental services)? In what ways could these problems be resolved?

Distribute newspapers and magazines to the children and ask them to cut out pictures that indicate growth of cities and some effects of city growth or misuse of resources such as air, land, and water. Have the children show the pictures they have found and suggest any remedies for improved use of earth's resources or what could be done by city planners to prevent misuse of resources. Ask the children to give their points of view to partners about any detrimental effects of city growth on resources they know about just as the man in Baker's story saw a green environment turn into fast-moving traffic generating smog and tall office buildings covered with graffiti.

With the whole group, ask the children how they could individually affect some positive changes, and how *both* children and grown-ups could make a difference in coping with the effects of urban development. Perhaps they could take part in a door-to-door walk to encourage drivers to ride their bikes one or two days a week to cut down on pollution and traffic congestion; or participate in a cleanup or an improvement project at a school, children's home, park, roadside, or rest area. Record the children's ideas on a class chart, "Ways We Could Help," and invite them to tell how they could implement their suggestions.

**Home Activity**

Invite your child to determine the traffic pattern in your neighborhood. Have your child count and tally the number of cars that go by at a certain time in the morning and again at a certain time in the evening. Ask your child to determine when there were more cars, morning or evening, and if appropriate, the number of cars during an evening on a weekday compared with a day on the weekend. Ask your child if he or she can think of something near the house that could increase or decrease the traffic in some way.

■ **Cherry, Lynne (1992). *A River Ran Wild.*** Illustrated by the author. San Diego: Harcourt Brace Jovanovich. Ages 7 up.

**Environmental context:** Monitoring a waterway

Before Christopher Columbus and other explorers land in the "new" world of the Americas, Native Americans know of a beautiful fast-moving river that they call the River of the Pebbled Bottom—*Nash-a-way* (the present-day Nashua River). The water is so clean that someone looking at the river can see the pebbles on the bottom. This waterway is very important to the native people but white settlers eventually populate the land and force the native people away. The settlers use the river for transportation, food, and for power for running machinery. More and more manufacturing plants are built beside the river to use its water power, and later, to use it as a disposal system for factory waste. The increase in cities, factories, and dump sites leads to heavy pollution of the water. Marion Stoddart, an environmentalist, sees what is happening and works hard to clean up the Nashua River so people today can enjoy the beauty just as the early Native Americans did. Author's note, maps, and timeline of events are included. Full-color illustrations.

**Activity: "Monitoring a Waterway"**

**Language arts focus:** To conduct research; to communicate by designing a map; to engage in a telephone conversation; to participate in a class discussion

Have the children research a body of water that is no longer available for recreation or other use because of contamination. Help them make a map of the area and talk to an official in the Water Resources Department over the telephone to find out how polluted the water is and what is happening to resolve the situation. Ask the children to think of ways they could help monitor the situation to help preserve the integrity of the waterways. At a later time, invite a representative from your state's department of natural resources or local water agency to talk to the children about improvements to this body of water and some waterways in the area. Ask, "What clean-up has been done? What still needs to be done?"

**Home Activity**

Have your child suggest ways to tell people in your neighborhood about water pollution and persuade them to support a cleanup project in your area. If appropriate, help your child discover some of the sources that affect the water. Engage your child in making a chart to show the sources and present the chart first to neighbors and then to a local government representative.

■ **Cone, Molly (1992). *Come Back, Salmon.*** Illustrated by Sidnee Wheelwright. San Francisco: Sierra Club. Ages 7 up.

**Environmental context:** Water pollution

In Everett, Washington, the children from Jackson Elementary School clean up a polluted stream that runs past their school and raise Coho salmon from eggs in a school fish tank. They restock the creek, and wait for the salmon to return. The children study the life cycle of the salmon, who go from eggs to fry to smolts in freshwater and then journey to the ocean, where they mature. Finally, the mature fish return to their freshwater origin to spawn and die. This record is based on taped interviews with the children. Photographs.

**Activity: "Action Groups"**

**Language arts focus:** To participate in discussion groups or action groups

Identify a pollution or littering problem with the children's input. Emphasize that the problem should be a critical one related to their neighborhood or school. Ask the children to brainstorm what steps to take and what will be needed to help resolve the problem. Ask, for example, "Is there a local waterway that needs to be monitored to preserve its integrity? If so, which one? Should a business letter be written to an official? Will a proposal need to be drafted? Should a news item be written? Should we lobby someone about the problem? If so, whom should we lobby?" Write the children's suggestions on the board and ask the children to get in discussion groups to talk about what each could do related to the list of suggestions. Back in the whole group, invite the children to volunteer as participants and write their names beside the steps written on the board. Arrange a time when everyone can do something to help in resolving the problem and report what happened to the class.

**Home Activity**

Mention to your child that just as it is important to monitor a water way to see that it is pure and clean for wildlife, so it is important to notice if your drinking water is clean. Ask your child to put a coffee filter over the mouth of a clear plastic glass or cup and put a rubber band around the filter to keep it in place. Place the container under the faucet to collect some tap water and then remove and examine the filter. What does your child see with his or her eyes? With a magnifying glass?

■ **Edwards, Hazel.** *Stickybeak.* Illustrated by the author. New York: Nelson. Ages 5–8.

**Environmental context:** Caring for nature's creatures

Edwards's story is about Stickybeak, an animal companion in a classroom, who thinks some of the school students are its parents. Each weekend, Stickybeak the duck becomes the companion of one of the children, who cares for the duck at home. During the week, he lives in a box at school. In the classroom, Stickybeak quacks a lot, which delights the young listeners. He rides home in a car with a seatbelt around him, eats a breakfast of cornflakes, and swims in the bathtub; but Stickybeak becomes afraid of some other ducks in the water at a recreational area and runs away. Full-color illustrations.

**Activity: "Speakerphone Conversation"**

**Language arts focus:** To participate in a speakerphone conversation.

Read aloud excerpts from *Stickybeak* to the children and present Stickybeak's problem to the group—he is frightened of the other ducks at the lake and runs away. Ask the children to try to understand his problem and ask some who, what, when, where, and how questions such as:

- What could be done to help the duck?
- Who could be helpful?
- When and where could others be of assistance to a frightened animal?
- How could people help an animal feel safe and not be afraid?
- How could people assure an animal's safety near a large body of water?

Invite the children to talk about their ideas on caring for a domesticated animal in a speakerphone conversation with a local veterinarian. Place the phone so the whole group can hear and talk with the vet on the other end. Try to reach a common agreement about ways to help a frightened animal and distinguish between an animal companion and an animal in the wild. If appropriate, have the children contact other resource people about other issues such as:

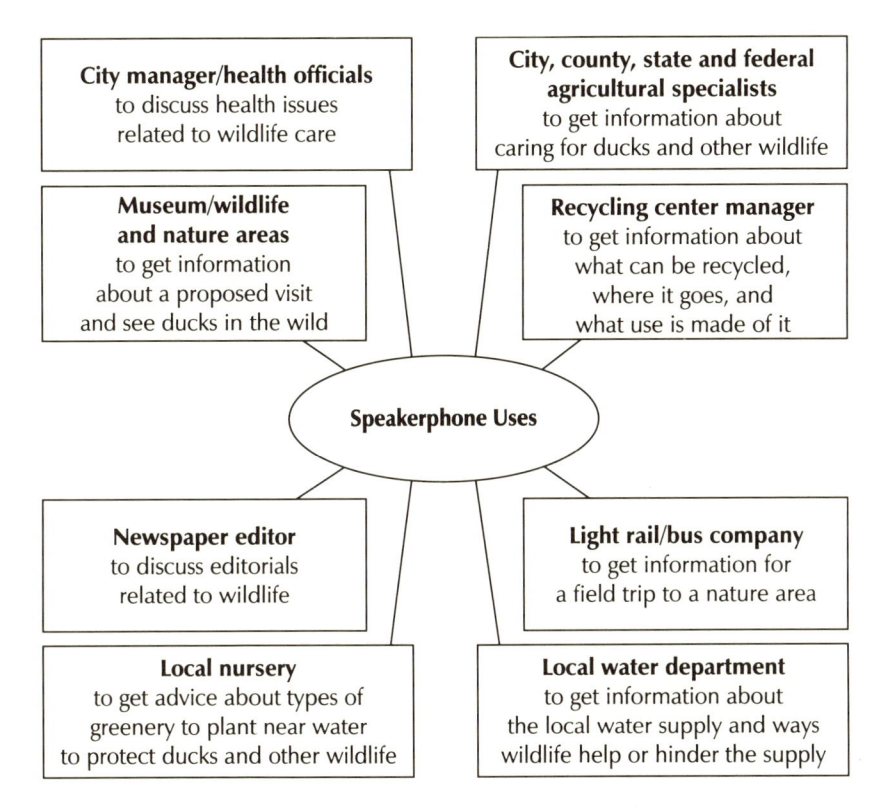

| City manager/health officials<br>to discuss health issues<br>related to wildlife care | City, county, state and federal<br>agricultural specialists<br>to get information about<br>caring for ducks and other wildlife |
|---|---|
| Museum/wildlife<br>and nature areas<br>to get information<br>about a proposed visit<br>and see ducks in the wild | Recycling center manager<br>to get information about<br>what can be recycled,<br>where it goes, and<br>what use is made of it |

**Speakerphone Uses**

| Newspaper editor<br>to discuss editorials<br>related to wildlife | Light rail/bus company<br>to get information for<br>a field trip to a nature area |
|---|---|
| Local nursery<br>to get advice about types of<br>greenery to plant near water<br>to protect ducks and other wildlife | Local water department<br>to get information about<br>the local water supply and ways<br>wildlife help or hinder the supply |

Help the children realize that there is always someone within telephone reach who can give them valuable information about environmental topics and additional help when they need it.

**Home Activity**

Mention to your child that valuable information about animals and the environment is available in story form from several government agencies for independent reading. Let your child write to inquire about the information. Examples of children's material that can be ordered from government agencies include the following:

*Chessie: A Chesapeake Bay Story* (Wildlife Services Publication Office, 1986) emphasizes the importance of the ecology of the bay, and has illustrations and a poem by Chessie, the cousin of the Loch Ness Monster.

*Let's Reduce and Recycle* (Environmental Protection Agency, 1995) has curriculum ideas and introduces children to the Garbage Gremlin, a symbol of wastefulness who teaches concepts and vocabulary of waste disposal. The booklet also introduces older children to renewable versus nonrenewable resources, composting, and the impact of bottle recycling bill legislation.

*The Processing and Recovery of Jon Thomas—Cool Cat!* (Environmental Protection Agency/Macmillan, 1989) is a coloring book story of Jon Thomas who is picked up with the trash and almost becomes part of a landfill.

*There Lived a Wicked Dragon: An Environmental Coloring Book for Children and Adults* (Environmental Protection Agency, 1973/Macmillan, 1989) is the story of a dragon who sleeps most of the time and feeds and grows on pollution.

- **Fisher, Aileen (1975).** ***Once We Went on a Picnic.*** Illustrated by the author. New York: Crowell. Ages 5–8.

**Environmental context:** Observing living creatures

In Fisher's story, four children decide to have a picnic in the park and stop along the way to comment on the plants, insects, and animals they see and to give away their food. They have a wonderful morning as they enjoy one another's company and the company of the living creatures they meet. By the time they reach the park, the children are ready to eat since it is noon-time but their lunches are all gone. Full-color drawings.

**Activity: "Character Dialogue"**

**Language arts focus:** To participate in a character dialogue and role-playing

Read aloud the following role-play anecdotes and let children select which story they want to read or listen to for the activity "Caring for Creatures." In small story circles, let the children read the story and dictate what actions and dialogue can be included as they take turns role-playing the main character for their group. Here are some stories suitable for this activity:

- **Role-play anecdote 1:** In *My Father Doesn't Know about the Woods and Me* (Atheneum, 1988, ages 6–8) by Dennis Haseley, you are going to read (hear) a story about a young boy who runs ahead of his father as they walk together in the woods. In his mind, the boy becomes the animals he sees and he mimics what they do. Read (listen) to find out what he does when he sees the eagle, fish, and wolf. Think of ideas to act out the boy's animal movements and give him words to say.

- **Role-play anecdote 2:** In *A Package for Miss Marshwater* (Dial, 1987, ages 7–8) by Effie Donnelly, you are going to read (listen to) a story about Miss Marshwater, a proper lady who wears elegant clothes but experiences a change in her life when her cousin Everett in Australia sends her two duckbill platypuses named A and Bea. Read (listen) to find out how this change takes place and what happens when A and Bea become parents of two babies named Cee and Dee. Think of ideas to perform Miss Marshwater's actions and give her words to say.

- **Role-play anecdote 3:** In *The Mammoth, the Owl, and the Crab* (Macmillan, 1975, ages 5–7) by Claudia Fregosi, you will read (hear) a story about a young girl who cares about living creatures and one morning when she does not want to get out of bed, she imagines herself to be a woolly mammoth frozen in ice, an owl that sleeps in the daytime, a hibernating fox, and others. Read (listen) to find out some of the ways the girl shows that she is sensitive to the feelings of the animals. Think of ways for you to pose to show the girl when she sleeps as an owl, hibernates as a fox, and so on, and give her words to say about each experience.

### Home Activity

Read aloud to your child one of the stories and invite him or her to suggest pantomiming actions to show sensitivity for the animals in the story. Write your child's suggestions on a sheet of paper, and with your hand signal as a cue, let your child respond in pantomime at selected places when you reread the story aloud.

■ **Lasky, Kathryn (1995).** *Pond Buddies.* Illustrated by Mike Bostock. New York: Candlewick. Ages 6–8.

**Environmental context:** Pond life and ecosystem

Lasky's story is about two curious six-year-old girls who play together around the pond in their neighborhood. They learn a great deal about life in the pond water and not only discover tadpoles (and how they grow) but also dragonflies and other inhabitants that live in and near water. Full-color illustrations.

**Activity: "Closing a Pond"**

**Language arts focus:** To conduct research about views of others; to participate in creative drama

Ask the children to imagine that they are going to attend a public meeting with other neighbors—some protesters, some supporters—about the closing of a nearby pond in their community. A state biologist arrives to explain why the pond has to be closed to the public: It is a habitat for small endangered creatures and is environmentally fragile. Have the children research informational books to discover what they think the biologist (and the neighbors) could say. Ask for volunteers to take the role of the biologist (and a team of specialists) with the rest of the children playing the role of neighbors at the meeting. Include the protesters' discussion as part of the drama. Repeat the activity by having different children take the roles of the biologist and the specialists.

**Home Activity**

Further introduce the topic of birds and other animals that live in the wetlands to your child by reading aloud *Squishy, Misty, Damp and Muddy: The In-between World of Wetlands* (Sierra Club, 1996, ages 5–8) by Molly Cone. The book emphasizes the value of the wetland environment and the need to preserve the different habitats. The text explains the various kinds of wetlands—bogs, marshes and swamps—as well as the different types of animals that live there. Talk together with your child about the importance of this environment as well as what is going on that destroys it.

- **Lasky, Kathryn (1995).** *She's Wearing a Dead Bird on Her Head!* Illustrated by David Catrow. New York: Hyperion. Ages 5–9.

**Environmental context:** Impact of fashions on wildlife

Lasky's story is a fictionalized account of two energetic ladies, Harriet Hemenway and her cousin, Minna Hall, who are outraged at the then-popular fashion in the late 1800s of killing birds to decorate women's hats. In Boston in 1896, the women protest the slaughter of huge populations of birds for the decorations. They speak out against putting dead birds on top of the latest ladies' headwear. The two are quite vocal about this and through their determination and hard work, they are instrumental in forming a group that becomes the first Audubon Society in Massachusetts, whose members help pass and enforce laws to protect birds. An author's note is included about the environmental protection work of the Audubon Society today. Watercolor-and-ink illustrations.

**Activity: "Alphabetical Conversation"**

**Language arts focus:** To speak out on an issue; to converse with others with sentences in ABC order

Tell the children they will have an opportunity to divide into small groups and participate in a conversation about Lasky's story by saying their sentences in alphabetical order. This means every sentence in the conversation will begin with a subsequent letter of the alphabet and each child gets a turn. Group members can help one another if appropriate. Here is an example of a conversation that begins in ABC order:

> *A*ll right, here is an alphabetical conversation about the story.
> *B*ut what's it about?
> *C*ould it be about endangered birds used to decorate ladies' hats?
> *D*on't know.

## 198  Language Arts and Environmental Awareness

*Everyone's* waiting.
*First*, let me say . . .
*Good*, I want to say something about wearing dead birds on hats.
*I* have another thing to say.
*Just* tell me more about . . .
(Other sentences suggested by the children. For example, subsequent ones can begin with *Kid, Look, Many, Now, Oh, Predict, Queue, Repeat, State, Tell, Understood, Verify, Watch, Xerox, Yell, and Zip.*)

As a follow-up activity, distribute pages of fashions from newspapers and catalogs to the children and ask them to look at the now-popular fashions and determine what impact, if any, the fashions have on wildlife. Ask, "Is there a fashion that is harmful to birds and animals that you want to speak out against? What is the fashion? In what way do you think the fashion is harmful?" Have the children meet with partners to speak out to one another about what they observed related to any particular fashion trend and its impact on wild creatures.

Discuss any ways the children are interested in forming a group in their class to protect wildlife from being harmed by current fashions. Ask, "What name do you want to call your group? In what ways could you speak out against a harmful practice?" List the children's suggestions on the board and set aside a time for them to begin to plan to implement their actions.

**Home Activity**

If your child is interested in speaking out against a fashion trend that negatively impacts wild birds and animals (or speaking out on another environmental issue), help your child think through his or her initial decision by talking about the following steps in decision-making shown in "My Decision Circle":

## My Decision Circle

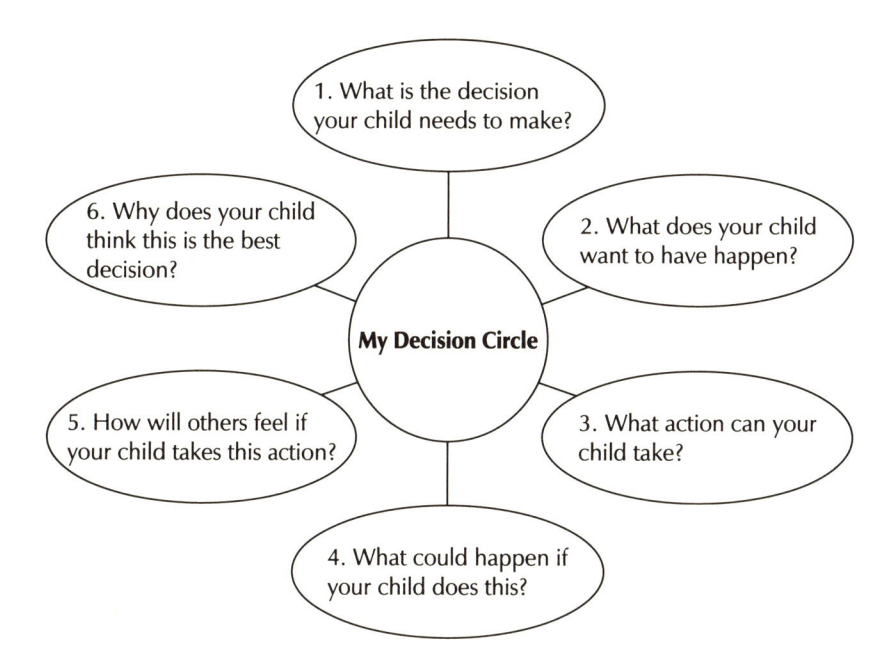

1. What is the decision your child needs to make?
2. What does your child want to have happen?
3. What action can your child take?
4. What could happen if your child does this?
5. How will others feel if your child takes this action?
6. Why does your child think this is the best decision?

- **Seltzer, Meyer (1992)** *Here Comes the Recycling Truck!* Illustrated by the author. Chicago: Whitman. Ages 5–8.

**Environmental context:** Importance of recycling

Seltzer's book shows how a recycling center operates and focuses on the actions of Elisa, a truck driver in Ann Arbor, Michigan. Through the driver's daily activities, the text gives information about what children can do to recycle glass, metal, paper, and plastic. Color photographs.

**Activity: "Panel Discussion: Recycling"**

**Language arts focus:** To conduct research; to participate in a panel discussion

Mention to the children that they will have an opportunity to take part in a panel discussion on recycling by dividing into small groups, with each group becoming a panel. Each child in a panel will be responsible for information on an aspect of the topic of recycling. Elicit the children's questions on the topic of recycling and write them on the board.

Examples of their questions might be "What happens to trash and garbage? What happens when there is no more land for landfills?" Provide time for the children to search for answers to their questions. After the children research their information, have each group elect a leader for the panel and let the leader introduce the other group members before they share their ideas about recycling. The leader sums up the group's discussion.

**Home Activity**

Invite your child to make a fact-filled poster (about 11" × 22") that gives other people practical ideas about how they can recycle. Distribute copies of the poster to friends and relatives. Here are some suggestions your child can illustrate:

1. Write to newspapers and local officials; talk to friends and neighbors and help get your community into recycling.
2. Use long-lasting rechargable batteries and fewer hazardous chemicals will end up in our waste dumps.
3. Recycle glass bottles; glass can be transformed into carpet material, sleeping bag linings, ski jackets, and other items.
4. Make a compost pile that will turn your organic garbage into fertilizer for next year's garden.
5. Recycle the family's bike and car tires; these items can be used to make road asphalt.
6. Turn in your old newspapers; they can be used to make cardboard boxes.
7. Collect and recycle aluminum cans; you'll collect cash for your favorite environmental charity.

■ **Swinburne, Stephen R. (1996)** *Swallows in the Birdhouse.*
Illustrated by Robin Brickman. Brookfield, CT: Millbrook. Ages 5–8.

**Environmental context:** Bird habitat

When two children put up a birdhouse in the spring, two swallows take it over as a home. Inside the house, the female builds a nest of grass and feathers, lays her eggs, and sits on them for two weeks. The male guards the nest. When the eggs hatch, the parents collect bugs for the baby birds until they are ready to leave the nest. The swallow family joins hundreds of other swallows in early autumn for a migratory flight to the south. Facts about swallows, tips on attracting them, field guide information, and directions for making a birdhouse are included. Watercolor objects are used for collages in the photographs.

**Activity: "Round Table Discussion: Building a Birdhouse"**

**Language arts focus:** To participate in a round table or round-the-group discussion with moderator and panelists; to summarize

Have the children divide into groups of six, a moderator and five other participants, to have a round table or round-the-group conversation. Ask them to share ideas about a way to build a suitable birdhouse for birds that inhabit the local area. Encourage the children to discuss the following:

1. What features would be needed (height, width, size of openings, etc.) for the birdhouse?
2. What materials could be used?

After the members of each round table informally make their suggestions among themselves, ask the moderator to sum up the discussion for the group. With the whole group, ask the moderators to report on the summaries so everyone can hear what ideas were presented. Elicit suggestions from the group about implementing some of their ideas for building a birdhouse to attract local birds in the area.

**Home Activity**

Introduce owls and other forest dwellers to your child by reading aloud *In the Forest* written by Ann Cooper and illustrated by Dorothy Emerling (Roberts, Rinehart, 1996, ages 6–8). Help your child measure the life-size paw prints that are imposed over the book's words, and together, sketch a forest "hamburger" to show each layer of the forest and the creatures that live in each: tree top or canopy layer instead of top bun; shrub layer or understory instead of meat; floor layer instead of condiments; and the fourth level is the subfloor (i.e., underground where roots and insects are) instead of the bottom bun.

■ **Udry, Janice May (1956). *A Tree Is Nice.*** Illustrated by Marc Simont. New York: Harper & Brothers. Ages 5–7.

**Environmental context:** Value of trees and conservation

Udry's informational book explains the value of trees through the seasons and tells how trees make a landscape beautiful, cool a home in the summer, and protect a home from chilling winds in the winter. Trees also drop leaves for children's play, grow limbs to climb, grow apples and other fruit to eat, and give shade to those who want it. The final page suggests that a reader *do* something—plant a tree—to show appreciation for all trees do for us. Black-and-white sketches and colored watercolors are included.

**Activity: "A Taped Interview with a Nursery Worker"**

**Language arts focus:** To develop interview skills; to take notes; to role-play an interview

Before an invited visitor from the local nursery arrives in the classroom, have the children role-play situations where they practice asking their questions about planting trees and familiarize themselves with the right buttons on the tape recorder for stop, record, rewind, and so on. They can practice taking notes and role-playing an interview so things can go smoothly for all.

During an interview practice, suggest to the children that they incorporate different interviewing techniques to get ready for their real interview. Several examples follow:

1. Elaborate on a specific event, such as a fund-raiser to purchase trees to plant, and say something such as: "I understand that every year you visit classrooms to talk about the care and planting of trees. . . . What kind of trees do you recommend (or not recommend) for planting in this area? If we had a fund-raiser to purchase trees to

plant behind our school, how much money would we need to buy one tree? Two trees?"

2. Ask for a time line or a chronology about planting a tree and say, "And then what happens after we do that?"

3. Thank the interviewee when a question is answered. They can repeat a question when it isn't answered the first time. Say, "But that wasn't my question," or, "Let me repeat my question; I'm not sure I made myself clear"; or, "I don't think you are answering my question; my question is. . . ."

**Home Activity**

Invite your child to carry a magnifying glass and go on a neighborhood walk with you to look for a tree with wounds (signs of damage such as scars or knots on the surface, sap leaking from a wound, a callus at the edges of an opening, jagged edges around an opening, tree growth moving inward in an opening). Have the child inspect the damages under the lens and discuss, "How do you think the tree was damaged?" and, "What do you see that shows the tree heals itself?"

# Involving Children in Speaking: Ages 9–14

- **Alvin, Virginia, and Robert Silverstein (1991).** *Recycling: Meeting the Challenge of the Trash Crisis.* Illustrated by the authors. New York: Putnam Group. Ages 10 up.

**Environmental context:** Importance of recycling

For a reader interested in recycling, this book discusses the importance of keeping discarded items and using them again. The point is emphasized that finding another use for an item generates less garbage and helps people use the earth's resources more carefully. Black line drawings.

**Activity: "Partner Views: Recycling"**

**Language arts focus:** To write a news article collaboratively; to speak about one's views; to read a class newspaper to someone in the home

Read aloud to the children a news article about recycling. Discuss the importance of the information in the article. Talk about the idea that the facts were meaningful enough and important enough for reporters to write and by implication, important enough for the children to know about, too. Have the children work with partners and write their own news articles for a class newspaper about what they know and believe about recycling. Encourage them to use their news articles as references and ask them to speak up for their views about recycling with partners in the classroom. Paste their articles on a large chart to compose the class newspaper. If appropriate, type it, duplicate it, and send copies home with the children to read to a family member or a neighbor.

**Home Activity**

Encourage your child to use and say words about the environment that he or she collects from various sources such as the radio, television, computer programs, newspapers, and magazines. Help your child write words about the environment—recycling words, animal words, insect words—and then write the words that go together (classifying) on a sheet of paper. Later, help your child make a small "Environmental Reference Word" notebook in alphabetical order from the words he or she has selected. Encourage your child to make sketches to illustrate the words and to refer to the words in future writing experiences.

- **Amon, Aline, adapter (1981).** *The Earth Is Sore: Native Americans on Nature.* Illustrated by the adapter. New York: Atheneum. Ages 10 up.

**Environmental context:** Protecting the environment

Amon's book presents points of view about protecting the environment. The text celebrates nature and mourns the abuse of earth and what the abuse does to its inhabitants. There are songs, invocations, prayers, and explanations, and all are documented to show the source and its tribe of origin. Black line drawings.

**Activity: "One-Quote Note"**

**Language arts focus:** To read verses; to describe images

Help the children examine a poet's tribute to earth by reading aloud verses from *Earth Songs* by Myra Cohn Livingston (Holiday House, 1986, all ages). Have the children imagine their own pictures about the words and tell their images to others in the group before selecting and copying one direct quote from the verses and telling an interpretation in their own words. Have them write their interpretations as "One-Quote Notes." Ask the children to sketch or draw a picture that represents the feelings or understandings they received from the words. Encourage them to show the beauty of the earth and reflect geographic features in such phrases as "round hills that rise to bluffs"; "towering mountain peaks"; and "hot volcanoes whose red mouth and throat burn."

Have the children discuss their "One-Quote Note" with a partner in class. Display the illustrations, then collect them and place them into a class notebook so the children can browse through the pages at a later time.

**Home Activity**

For a creative activity, encourage your child to sketch a fanciful supercreature that would be able to survive all the environmental threats that affect the beauty of the earth. The threats can include the shrinking of various creatures' habitats, the falling of acid rain, and the proliferation of litter. Have your child write a short story to tell about what the creature would eat for food and what its habitat would have to be like in a threatened habitat. Let your child select a name for it and describe the creature's physical features, i.e., extra pads on fingers as eye-wipers to wipe off acid rain, teeth arranged as filters to drink polluted water, a nose with a mask for breathing polluted air, an appetite for plastic containers, an ability to go without drinking clean water for a long period of time, and an ability to smell the overpackaging in a fast-food place from miles away. Ask your child to read his or her short story aloud to you.

■ **Faber, Doris, and Harold Faber (1991).** *Nature and the Environment.* Illustrated. New York: Scribner's. Ages 10 up.

**Environmental context:** Recognizing conservationists and environmentalists

The Fabers' book contains brief biographies of people who have made a difference in earth's environment—early conservationists as well as recent environmentalists. Over twenty people are mentioned, including some outside the United States, and selected entries include such figures as Henry David Thoreau (American author), Rachel Carson (American author), Charles Darwin (English scientist who developed the theory of evolution), and Theodore Roosevelt (American conservationist). Black-and-white drawings and photographs.

**Activity: "Defining and Debating: Environmentalists Versus Opponents"**

**Language arts focus:** To read definitions; to demonstrate and describe a term; to relate an illustration to a selected word; to participate in a debate.

Mention to the children that they will have an opportunity to define the word *environmentalist* (or *conservationist*) in four different ways—by reading, by demonstrating, by describing something about the word, and by displaying an illustration about the word. Write the four ways of defining a word on the board in the following manner:

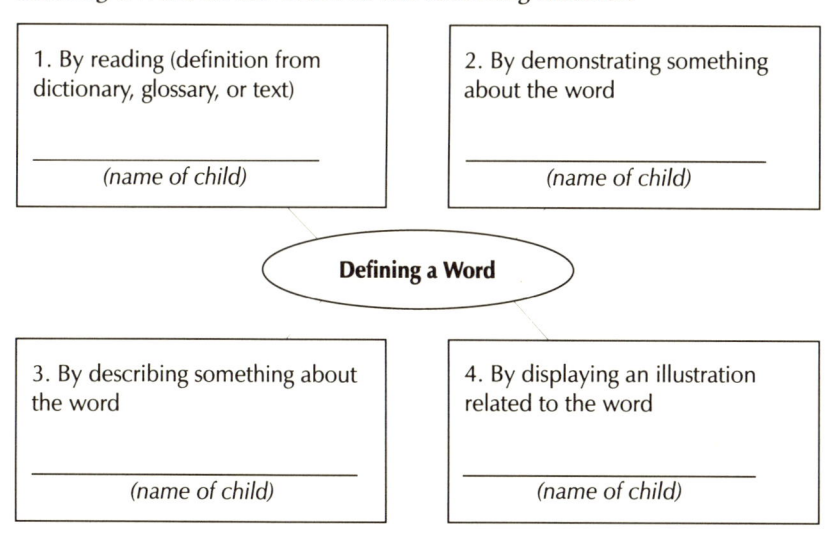

| 1. By reading (definition from dictionary, glossary, or text) <br><br> _____ <br> (name of child) | 2. By demonstrating something about the word <br><br> _____ <br> (name of child) |
|---|---|
| **Defining a Word** ||
| 3. By describing something about the word <br><br> _____ <br> (name of child) | 4. By displaying an illustration related to the word <br><br> _____ <br> (name of child) |

Have different children participate in defining the word *environmentalist* in each of the four ways. Write their names on the board after you ask the following questions:

1. Who will read a written definition of *environmentalist* from a dictionary? a glossary? a textbook?

2. Who will demonstrate something that an environmentalist does, to help define the word?

3. Who will describe an environmentalist they know about?
4. Who will show us a picture that is related to the word *environmentalist*?

After the four children define the word *environmentalist*, tell the whole group that they will be reading biographies about leading conservationists and environmentalists from *Nature and the Environment* or another source they select. After they have read (or heard) one or more of the biographies, lead a discussion with questions similar to the following:

1. Why did the figure become a conservationist or environmentalist?
2. What influence, if any, did the figure's view on the environment have in America?
3. In what way do you think that this figure's attitudes are important today?

Tell the children they will have the opportunity to represent the ideals of the environmentalist they read about to a partner when they discuss a current environmental issue. Distribute copies of newspapers and ask the children to locate an issue, concern, or controversy related to the environment or living things. Have them divide into partnerships and debate the issue as if one child were representing the ideals of the environmentalist he or she read about and the other child representing the ideas of an opponent. Have the partners trade sides of the debate so each one can argue the point of view of an environmentalist/conservationist.

**Home Activity**

Mention to your child that in Hong Kong harbor on Sunday, May 3, 1992, a nearly 150-foot-tall figure of a man, made of bamboo, was displayed with lights and towed through the water. It was created by the Australian artist Andre Heller to represent environmental unity. Together, think of ways the bamboo environmental man symbolizes this theme and represents the interdependence and the oneness of people and the environment. To make a comparison, have your child write down what is alike between the two concepts in a T-diagram similar to the one that follows. Talk together about what your child writes on the diagram:

|  | Similarities of |
| --- | --- |
| **Environmental Unity** | **Environmental Figure of Bamboo Man** |
| Habitats are interrelated. | Respiratory and circulation system of a human are interrelated. |

■ **Friedman, Judi (1992).** *The Siberian Crane.* Illustrated by the author. New York: Dillon. Ages 10 up.

**Environmental context:** Endangered species

Friedman's book offers information about ways that scientists and others gather information, work together in a scientific community, and go public with their work. As an example, the cooperation between American and Russian scientists in protecting the Siberian crane, now an endangered species, is examined with this text. Photographs.

**Activity: "Reporting Aloud: Endangered Species"**

**Language arts focus:** To prepare a transparency related to a report; to conduct research in small groups; to report on an endangered species

Ask the children to report on an endangered species of their choice and include an overhead transparency they have prepared to illustrate their report. Discuss various possibilities of the use of transparencies with the children. Examples include the following:

1. **Environmental transparency story.** Use felt-tipped pen lines and colored acetate sheets to create a background habitat for the endangered animal. Make drawings of endangered living creatures on heavy strips of clear acetate. Have the child manipulate the drawings while discussing the endangered animals' diet, place in a food chain, habits, predators, and so on.

2. **Species growth.** Use three overlays to show the growth of an endangered species. Overlays can show (1) the young, (2) the adolescent, and (3) the adult.

3. **Species tracks.** Use the overhead to compare the shape and size of an endangered animal's tracks. If appropriate, use this approach for a game or quiz and ask others to identify the endangered animal by its track.

4. **Species observations.** Place small snails, earthworms, polliwogs, tadpoles, or small fish in a glass bowl or dish. Place a sheet of colored acetate on the projector stage to cut down the glare for the creatures in the dish. Have the children observe their actions on the screen and remove the dish quickly to protect the creatures from the heat. Turn off the light several times during the report to cut down on the heat generated by the light.

**Home Activity**

Take a nature walk with your child and collect leaves of different colors. Back at home, encourage your child to tell you something about the collection to encourage language use, i.e., your child may describe the leaves as pretty, colorful, speckled, smooth, prickly, and so on. Have your child write the words on a sheet of paper and refer to them in sentences. Encourage your child to use some of the descriptive words as he or she talks to you during the day.

■ **Fritz, Jean (1974).** *Theodore Roosevelt.* Illustrated by Margot Tomes. New York: Putnam Group. Ages 9–12.

**Environmental context:** Protector of environment

Fritz's book is the life story of Roosevelt beginning with his early childhood in New York as "Teedie," the second of four children of a prosperous New York family. As a child, Theodore develops an interest in nature. He collects butterflies, birds, mice, and other animals. As the president of the United States in 1901, one of his presidential crusades is the conservation of the nation's natural resources. He tells Congress that the forest and water problems are the most vital internal problems of the United States. To discourage the squandering of forests and mineral resources, Roosevelt sets aside many acres of government timberland as national forest reserves and transfers control of the national

## Involving Children in Speaking: Ages 9–14

forests to the Department of Agriculture. He supports the passage of the Reclamation Act in 1902 which provides for the reclamation and irrigation of the arid lands of the West. He calls the National Conservation Conference in 1908 to publicize the conservation movement and give the movement prestige. Black-and-white illustrations.

**Activity: "Pantomime and Interpretation: Roosevelt's Life"**

**Language arts focus:** To listen to or read a biography; to report on a biographee through drama in small groups

After listening to or reading the book about Roosevelt, have the children suggest some of the scenes from his life story that they can depict through drama. Write their suggestions on index cards—one suggestion per card—and put the cards in chronological sequence. Some of the children's suggestions might include the following situations:

1. You are a young Theodore Roosevelt, the second of four children, trying to look at a butterfly though your eyes are weak. You also are coughing because you have asthma.
2. You are a college-aged Theodore Roosevelt and your clothes smell of mice and other animals that you collect. You are looking at your butterfly collection and arranging and labeling some of the entries.
3. You are a middle-aged Theodore Roosevelt dressed in colorful western clothes. Ranching in the West is now your business and you ride the range and hunt buffalo.
4. You are a middle-aged Theodore Roosevelt and a member of the "Roughriders," a calvary unit based in New York. You are dressed in Calvary clothes along with the other members of the unit—some are polo players, and some western cowboys.
5. You are the president of the United States, dressed appropriately to speak to the members of Congress, and known for your expression, "Speak softly but carry a big stick." Explain what you mean by this statement to others.
6. You are the president of the United States and you try to educate people about waste and pollution. Also, you create national forest

reserves and establish over one hundred national forests, over fifty bird and game preserves, and five national parks.

7. You are the president and you sign the passage of the Reclamation Act which provides for the reclamation and irrigation of the arid lands of the West. You also sign the National Monuments Act to set aside the first eighteen national monuments in the United States. Tell what you know about any of these monuments—Arizona's Petrified Forest, California's Muir Woods, Washington's Mount Olympus, and Wyoming's Devil's Tower.

8. You are the president and you organize a national conservation conference in the early 1900s to publicize the conservation movement and give it prestige. You are known as the conservation president because you teach people to respect what nature is all about.

Number the cards so the events stay in order. Distribute the cards and ask the children to divide into small groups, where each child dramatizes their scene from Roosevelt's life. Then, have the children in the whole group tell what they observed and interpreted about Roosevelt's life from the drama.

**Home Activity**

Invite your child to create life-size figures of two or three people who are known for their dedication to caring for the earth. Your child can have a family member trace his or her body on large sheets of paper. Then your child can cut out the silhouettes and draw faces and clothing on the figures. Hang the figures on a large wall and have your child write a brief biographical paragraph for each. Paste the writing in each figure's hands. Have your child guide family members past the figures and say if he or she agrees or disagrees with the actions each figure took. Examples of dedicated people who protected the environment include the following:

1. Chico Mendes is the biographee in *Chico Mendes: Fight for the Forest* (Twenty-first Century Books, ages 9–11) by Susan De Stefano. Government policies and business interests threaten the existence of the tropical rain forest and Chico Mendes, a Brazilian rubber tapper,

loses his life in the harsh conflict between conservationists and advocates of industry.

2. Gaylord Nelson is the central figure in *Gaylord Nelson: A Day for the Earth* (Twenty-first Century Books, 1992, ages 9–11) by Jeffrey Shulman and Teresa Rogers. Nelson's early boyhood days in Clear Lake, Wisconsin, are described as well as his fights to protect the natural resources as the governor of Wisconsin and later, as U.S. senator.

3. Franklin D. Roosevelt and the effect of some of his actions are found in *When the Whippoorwill Calls* ( New York: Tambourine, 1995) written by Candice F. Ransom and illustrated by Kimberly Bulcken Root. Roosevelt dedicated the Shenandoah National Park in 1936 and this new park forced families to be relocated from the Blue Ridge Mountains in Virginia when land owners sold their land to the United States government. In Ransom's story, Polly's family, with others, is moved to the flatlands to make way for the park.

### ■ George, Jean Craighead (1995). *Everglades.* Illustrated by Wendell Minor. New York: HarperCollins. Ages 9 up.

**Environmental context:** Ecosystem of the Everglades

In this story, George describes one of the earth's unique environments, the Florida Everglades, through a storyteller and five children from different cultural heritages. They glide through the water in their long, narrow canoe and observe the setting around them. On their trip, the children learn about how the area evolved from a sea with a limestone bottom into Lake Okeechobee, which eventually flooded and formed the Everglades as it is known today. They see some evidence of this in small seashells. Plant life is described—the children notice not only tiny plants but an abundance of towering grass. They learn that this is the home of alligators, egrets, frogs, flamingoes, and turtles. They learn, too, that deer, otters, panthers, and raccoons are some of the other creatures which coexist in this environment. The storyteller tells the children about the Seminole Indians who lived here and the people who conquered them, the effect of increasing industrialization on the area, and the disappearance of much of the original Everglades. Full-page paintings.

**Activity: "Everglades Ecosystem"**

**Language arts focus:** To listen to or read excerpts; to ask questions related to the topic; to participate in discussion groups

Have the children listen to excerpts read aloud from George's book about the Florida Everglades. Ask the children to write at least two questions about the environment that they want to discuss. Have the children meet in small groups and discuss their questions during a set time period (twenty to thirty minutes). Let them take turns being the group leader—they can change leaders each time the question is changed. Have copies of the book available so each group can use a copy as a reference. Ask the children to return as a whole group and ask a volunteer from each group to report on the one question that generated the most discussion in the group.

**Home Activity**

Mention to your child that not only is there a delicate ecosystem in the Everglades' waterways, there is also a balance of living things in the watery habitat of a pond near your home. Visit a nearby pond with your child, and together, watch for creatures living near or in the pond. As a follow-up activity, suggest that your child read about two friends and their wonderful times together at a pond in *Pond Year* (Cambridge, MA: Candlewick, 1995, ages 8 up) written by Kathryn Lasky and illustrated by Marian Bostock. The author and her childhood friend, Carole, watch frogs' eggs grow under the pond scum, make slides from mud, and race crawdads down the inclines. As a further sign of their friendship, the two girls braid scum into friendship rings and promise to be "scum chums" forever.

■ **Keene, Ann T. (1993).** *Earthkeepers: Observers and Protectors of Nature.* New York: Oxford. Ages 9 up.

**Environmental context:** Preservers of the environment

The biographical profiles in Keene's book, along with anecdotes, introduce a reader to over forty contributors who preserved the environment or contributed to ecology. For an example from the 1700s, there is a profile of John Bartram, a self-taught botanist, and from contemporary times, a profile of John Muir. Diagrams, full color illustrations, and photographs complement the accounts of the naturalists' important work. Black-and-white photographs.

**Activity: "Members of Conservation Hall of Fame"**

**Language arts focus:** To conduct research on the contributions of a selected conservationist; to participate in role-playing

Mention to the children that when the National Wildlife Federation established a Conservation Hall of Fame in 1965 to recognize people who protected the environment, the committee voted for John Muir along with John James Aubudon, Theodore Roosevelt, and Henry David Thoreau. Ask the children to divide into small groups and pretend that each group is the nominating committee for the Conservation Hall of Fame in the 60s. Ask the children in each small group to select one of the people who was recognized in the Hall of Fame and do research on the contributions of that person. Back in the whole group, have volunteers from each group use their research to argue for their candidates and cite the person's contributions to conservation. After hearing the arguments, ask the whole group to vote for one of the individuals as first choice and have volunteers give the reasons why they voted as they did. Repeat the activity with a second choice, third choice, and so on.

**Home Activity**

Relate the previous activity to what is going on currently in your area and ask your child for the name of a person protecting the environment today that he or she would nominate for a current Conservation Hall of Fame. Ask your child to defend the choice by citing some of the nominee's contributions.

As a follow-up activity, help your child learn more about what is happening today to keep the earth healthy and encourage your child to contact one or more of the following through a long distance telephone operator and request information about the organization's founder before making a nomination for a contemporary Hall of Fame choice:

Air Quality Clearinghouse (*nonpolluted air*)
Biodynamic Farming and Gardening Association (*compost*)
Environmental Action (*toxic waste*)
Environmental Protection Agency (*dangers of chlorine and dioxins*) 401 M Street, SW, Washington, DC 20460
Greenpeace USA (*dangers of chlorine and dioxins*) 1436 U Street, NW, Washington, DC 20009
Human Ecology Action League (*home environment*)
Pesticide Action Network (*organic growing*)
Sustainable Cotton Project (*organic growing*)

■ **Lauber, Patricia (1986). *Volcano.*** Illustrated by the author. New York: Bradbury Press. Ages 9–14.

**Environmental context:** How nature rebuilds

Lauber's book is a photographic essay about Mount St. Helens, its eruption on May 18, 1980, and its rebuilding. The eruption creates a mountain-side laboratory for natural scientists who are interested in seeing how life returns to the land. The first summer, scientists notice that fireweed survives the eruption and other plants, such as sedge, are alive below ground and take time to sprout. They see ants and mites come back first. Some fish, frogs, snakes and water insects are found alive under nearby ice-covered lakes. Animals—chipmunks, red squirrels, and pocket gophers—return later. The scientists see that bacteria, fungi, and cottonwood seeds are blown in by the winds, and spiders fly in on wind-blown web threads. The scientists study the links among these forms of life, for each form is linked to another living thing and its surroundings for food and habitat. Full-color photographs.

**Activity: "Future Environmental Technology"**

**Language arts focus:** To participate in small group discussion; to participate in creative thinking and sharing ideas aloud; to consider possibilities of future technology for natural scientists

Divide the children in small groups of three or four to discuss the technology that might be used in the future by natural scientists as they study in an outside laboratory similar to the side of Mount St. Helens. Ask the students to envision what the technology might be like twenty years from now. Have them consider possibilities for this by introducing the concept of "ramblings." In the word *ramblings*, each letter stands for a possible change in technology that scientists might use and that the students can use to think creatively in their small group discussions. For example, the letter R stands for the idea of rearranging something about present technology to make life better for users. Children can consider, "What items in our current technology could be rearranged to be more efficient or economical or useful?" For example, could a miniature TV screen and cellular phone be rearranged together to become a TV telephone a scientist could wear as a watch?

The other letters in *ramblings* have the following meanings:

**A** stands for additions. What could be added to current technology?
**M** stands for magnification or miniaturization. What could be magnified or miniaturized?
**B** stands for bolstering something. In what way could strength or improved efficiency be used to bolster something a scientist might use?
**L** stands for linking. What could current technology be linked to or combined with in the future?
**I** stands for improvements. What improvements in equipment are needed for scientists?
**N** stands for novelty. What new and unusual ways could there be to use current technology or future technology?
**G** stands for gadgets. What small tools or machines could be developed to attract a scientist's attention?
**S** stands for substitutions. What substitutions could be used in this technology? (An example could be substituting waterproof coating for existing coating on equipment so it could be used underwater).

### Home Activity

If your child is interested in technology, he or she can follow the interest and enter an annual technology awards contest co-sponsored by the National Science Teachers Association and Toshiba Corporation. First place winners receive $10,000 U.S. savings bonds. Encourage your child to write for information to: Toshiba/NSTA Exploravision Awards Program, 1940 Wilson Blvd., Arlington, VA 22201–3000. Phone: 703-243-7100.

- **Pringle, Laurence (1996).** *Taking Care of the Earth.* Illustrated by Bobbie Moore. New York: Boyds Mills. Ages 9–14.

**Environmental context:** Earth-friendly activities

In this book, Pringle assures a reader that he or she can make a difference and influence the decision-makers in our country to help take care of the earth. An interested reader can plant a tree, take part in preserving wild places, protect birds and other wildlife, and support conservation of the rain forests. Environmental organizations are listed. Black-and-white pencil drawings.

**Activity: "Barter the Word"**

**Language arts focus:** To participate in discussions; to choose a favorite topic-related word

After listening to or reading Pringle's book, have the children select a word related to the environment that they like best (i.e., *rain forest, wildlife,* or *preserving*) and write a paragraph telling why they chose that word. Ask the children to divide into small groups, take turns, and use their paragraphs as references to speak out about a word's meaning and importance and persuade others to barter their words for the offered word. Reconvene as a whole group and ask a child from each group to tell which word generated the most discussion and why they think this happened.

**Home Activity**

With your child, visit a nearby library to inquire of the librarian for sources of free and inexpensive materials related to caring for birds or other creatures in the environment. Your child can then write and request some of the free materials. Ask to see any of the following:

*A Guide to Print and Nonprint Materials Available from Organizations, Industry, Governmental Agencies and Specialized Publishers.* New York: Neal Schuman, 1996.

*Freebies for Kids and Parents Too!* Chicago, IL: Probus, 1991.

*Freebies: The Magazine with Something for Nothing.* 1991. PO Box 5025, Carpenteria, CA 93014–5025.

- **Reeder, Carolyn (1991).** ***Grandpa's Mountain.*** Illustrated by the author. New York: Macmillan. Ages 9–14.

**Environmental context:** Productive land used for other purposes

Set in Depression days in the United States in the 1900s, Reeder's story is about the battle that eleven-year-old Carrie faces when she visits her grandparents' home in the Blue Ridge Mountains one summer. Carrie finds her grandpa is a changed man because he is fighting some government men who want to turn his land (and that of other landowners) into the Shenandoah National Park. In the ensuing fight, he becomes as firm, stern-faced, and unmoving as the men he opposes, a behavior which shocks Carrie. Full-color illustrations.

**Activity: "Actions, Beliefs, and Consequences"**

**Language arts focus:** To state a point of view; to participate in small group or whole group discussions

Encourage the children to offer their views about the various actions of the government, the beliefs and actions of Carrie's grandpa and the other people living in the Blue Ridge Mountains, and the consequences of the actions on both sides. Write headings on the board and organize the children's comments underneath:

| Government actions | Consequences |
|---|---|
| Acquiring land of owners for national use | National park established |
| **People's actions** | **Consequences** |
| Government men try to enforce action | Landowners fight government men |

Guide the children to see that this set of events and its consequences has relevance for situations today in which the government still weighs projected benefits for the many against the disruption of the lives of a few. Encourage the children to tell about someone that they know in their lives today who is arguing with the government about an environmental issue. Write the issues on the board.

Ask the children to select one of the issues and join in small groups to talk about it from their point of view. Further, encourage them to consider other problems that might have resulted if the Shenandoah National Park had been stopped and no recreational area had been set aside in the mountains. Back in the whole group, have volunteers from each group report on what might have resulted if the park had been stopped.

**Home Activity**

Invite your child to tell of a time when he or she visited a nature area, an environmental center, or a national park. Ask your child to tell what he or she might have missed if there had been no nature area or park to visit.

■ **Seuss, Dr. (pseud., Theodore Geisel) (1971).** *The Lorax.* Illustrated by the author. New York: Random House. All ages.

**Environmental context:** Humans' effect on the environment

In this story, the Once-ler deforests the land of Truffula trees and the Lorax sends a warning message about what is happening to the forest. The Once-ler replies he is doing something useful and is making a Thneed—something that all people need. He chops additional trees, builds factories, and knits more and more Thneeds. To do this faster, he invents a Super-Axe-Hacker to chop down trees more quickly. The Lorax snaps back that bad things are happening: The Brown Bar-ba-loots have no Truffula fruits to eat now that the trees have decreased and the smoke from the Thneed factories is affecting another species, the Swomee-Swans. He says that the leftover factory glue (the Gluppity-Glupp and Schollity-Schlopp) is glumping the pond where the Humming-Fish once hummed. Their gills are all gummed. Finally, the last Truffula tree is chopped and there are no more Thneeds and factories—just a bad-smelling sky. With a change of heart, the Once-ler realizes that someone needs to care a lot to make the environment better and he gives the last Truffula seed to a person who will plant it, care for it, grow a new tree, and protect it from axes that hack. This story is a metaphor for government and business policies that permit certain actions detrimental to the environment. Full-color cartoon-style drawings.

**Activity: "Silent Speaking: Yea or Boo"**

**Language arts focus:** To share a message of support or lack of support for story actions; to critically analyze printed material; to gather data for a class survey; to state a point of view

Ask the children to print the words "Yea!" and "Boo!" on a pair of index cards, and as the story is read (or the corresponding film is viewed) a second time, ask them to select one of the printed cards and hold it up to send their message about what is happening each time you ask, "What do *you* think about what's going on?" If you are using the film version of the book, you can repeat the activity with the sound off to allow the children to focus on the actions of the characters.

During a rereading of the story, collect information for a class survey and select different points in the plot to stop to ask questions similar to the following:

1. "How many of you liked what just happened here? Hold up the 'Yea!' card if you did." Ask the children to give their reasons for their support for the action(s). Tally this information, and the information from the questions that follow, on a chart on the board for a class survey.

2. "How many did *not* like what just happened? Hold up the 'Boo!' card if you did not like what was going on." Again, ask the children for their reasons for their decisions.

3. Record the message that the children are sending and ask a volunteer to tally the "Yea!" or "Boo!" messages on the board to determine the majority vote. For example, if the children approve when

the entrepreneurial Once-ler knits Thneeds, builds a factory, and invents the Super-Axe-Hacker, let the volunteer tally the "Yea!" votes.

4. If the majority of children do *not* like it when the Once-ler sends the Bar-ba-loots away because there is no food in the trees, emits smog and smoke into the air, drives the singing Swomee-Swans away, and "glumps" the ponds with garbage, let the volunteer tally the "Boo!" votes.

5. After the tally, ask the children to work with partners and use the backs of their index cards to sketch selected actions from the story. For instance, the back of the "Yea!" card will have sketches of actions the children liked and the back of the "Boo!" card will have actions the children did *not* like. Invite them to talk about their drawings with the whole group and give their reasons why they liked or did not like the actions they selected.

**Home Activity**

With your child, read *The Lorax* aloud together and then view the video of the same title. Invite your child to watch and listen to determine if the story is interpreted on the video as it is written in the book by Dr. Seuss. Discuss, "In what ways is the message the same? Different?" Have your child note any additions, changes, and omissions in the video compared to the story in the book. Together, talk about the current government and business policies that permit certain actions harmful or helpful to the environment.

If your child is interested further, suggest another story to read, *Jan and the Great One* written by Peter Evyndson and illustrated by Rhian Brynjolson (Winnipeg: Pemmican,1990, ages 9 up). Jan, a young girl, sits and listens to the last ancient pine called the Great One as it tells her its life story. With the wind as its voice, the tree talks to Businessman, Politician, and Road Builder. They are only interested in making money by cutting down trees, which eventually destroys the forest and leaves only the Great One who tries to survive in spite of environmental pollution. Jan understands what is happening and so she and her friends plant seeds from the tree's pine cones to restock the forest. The Great

One understands something, too: it will be the children who will nurture the seeds of hope for the earth's future.

- **Simon, Hilda (1976).** *Snails of Land and Sea.* Illustrated by the author. New York: Vanguard. Ages 9–14.

**Environmental context:** Protecting endangered species of snails

In Simon's text, over eighty species of snails are depicted along with information on the snail's life cycle from egg-laying to hatching of the young to the growth of the shell. Several endangered species are discussed. For example, the beautiful North American arboreal snail, a native creature of Florida that climbs trees and feeds on mosses and lichens, is threatened by land development that has destroyed much of its native habitat. To save the snail, national park rangers, biologists, and conservationists have banded together to transplant small snail colonies into areas of the Everglades National Park. Full-color drawings.

**Activity: "Conservationists' Meeting"**

**Language arts focus:** To conduct research; to create dialogue for drama; to participate in creative drama

Have the children meet in small groups and conduct a drama on the topic of conservationists at a meeting to save an endangered species. Here's a scene to consider for one situation:

> A meeting of conservationists is held to save the endangered arboreal snail. A park ranger and a biologist explain to the conservationists who come to the meeting why the snail is endangered, and how they propose to transplant the snails to a new habitat.

Ask the children to research information to discover what the park ranger and biologist could say about the threatened species, and then conduct the drama. In the drama, encourage the children to include the conversation of the conservationists, who have suggestions for collecting and transporting the snail to its new habitat in the Everglades. Let the children exchange roles and repeat the drama.

### Home Activity

Ask your child if he or she knows of any endangered species in the area. If so, which ones? Discuss, "What is being done to protect the species that you know about? How could you find out more about what is going on? How could you help protect the species too?"

# VI ▪ Involving Children in Writing

# Involving Children in Writing: Ages 5–8

- **Arnold, Tim (1992).** *Natural History from A to Z: A Terrestrial Sampler.* Illustrated by the author. New York: McElderry/Macmillan. Ages 8 up.

**Environmental context:** Habits and habitats of selected animals

In Arnold's alphabet book, familiar and unfamiliar animals from anteater to zebra finch introduce the letters of the alphabet and demonstrate a biological concept such as adaptation, evolution, extinction, migration, etc. For instance, the yak introduces the letter Y and the accompanying informative text relates that the yak's hooves are suitable for walking in snowy mountain habitat as well as in low marshes and are an example of the animal's adaptation to the wide range of its environment. Black-and-white and full-color illustrations.

**Activity: "Writing Patterns"**

**Language arts focus:** To develop and expand spelling, capitalization, and punctuation skills by identifying key words

Mention to the children that writers use the mechanics of writing to help them send their message so others can read it clearly. Display several alphabet books that can be used as spelling resource books and show the children where to find key words naming living creatures and their traits on the pages. Here are some examples of patterns of writing that you may want the children to complete to involve them in spelling words and in using capitals and punctuation:

1. A is for *(adjective & animal name)*. B is for *(adjective & animal name)*.
2. People should care for the environment because _____.
3. My name is _____ and my friend's name is _____. We care for the environment and we _____.
4. One _____ Sunday morning, I protected the environment and I _____. On a _____ Monday morning, I protected the environment and I _____. *(Continue through the days of the week or months of the year)*.
5. Grizzly bear, grizzly bear *(select state animal)*, what do you see? I see a *(something in environment)* looking at me.
6. If I found a *(something in enviroment)*, I would *(action)*.
7. Write Environmental ABCs such as, T is for toxic waste, terrible, and troubling.
   Pattern for other letters:
   *(letter)* is for *(noun)*, *(adjective)*, and *(adjective)*.

**Home Activity**

Together with your child, write "The Environmental Pollution Monster" poem. Encourage your child to think of similes and metaphors (comparisons) to write in the blanks below. Point out that to write a comparison, your child should try to think how the two things would be most alike in various situations. Suggestions are in the following sentences:

I am the Environmental Pollution Monster.
My hair is like smoke *(air pollution)* because they are both gray and smelly;
My ears are like_____ *(noise pollutants)*;
I am the Environmental Pollution Monster.

I am the Environmental Pollution Monster.
My nose is like_____ *(dangerous chemicals)*;
My eyes are like_____ *(water pollutants)*;
I am the Environmental Pollution Monster.

I am the Environmental Pollution Monster.
My teeth are like _____ *(plastic litter)*;
My fingers are like _____ *(endangered species)*;
I am the Environmental Pollution Monster.

Ask your child to draw a picture of his or her pollution creature and copy the verses below the sketch. Have your child write a list of adjectives to describe the monster. Display the work in your home.

■ **Bash, Barbara (1996).** *In the Heart of the Village: The World of the Indian Banyan Tree.* Illustrated by the author. San Francisco: Sierra Club. Ages 6–10.

**Environmental context:** A tree's relationship with other living things

In a small village in India, a sacred banyan tree is the center of the villagers' lives and it is protected and worshipped by the people as a reminder of nature and the interconnectedness of life. Under the tree during the day, traders barter for goods, students sit through their classes, various people rest from the heat, children swing from vines, and conversations take place in the shade. Birds and monkeys chase one another in the branches. In the evenings, the tree becomes a shelter under which dancers and storytellers perform. Later in the dark night, the flying foxes come out. The text summarizes an entire day in the life of the tree and how it contributes to the lives of living things. The text is hand-lettered. Full-page watercolor illustrations.

**Activity: "A Tree's Relationship with Others"**

**Language arts focus:** To dictate or write a paragraph

Tell the children that they can bring their senses into play as they put themselves in a scene in the book. Urge them to imagine that they are there under the banyan tree in the village during the day and write about the sounds that they hear (sense of hearing). They can tell what they see (sense of vision), the tastes they would experience (sense of taste), smells in the air (sense of smell), and textures in the objects around them (sense of touch), especially the texture of the tree, protective coverings of living creatures, and people's clothing. Additionally, they can write about the patterns in nature they notice and tell how they would act if they were in the scene. Have them meet with partners to read their writing aloud to one another.

**Home Activity**

After reading Bash's book together with your child, ask your child to imagine being there under the banyan tree in the coolness of the evening and tell you about what he or she would see, hear, feel, taste, and touch. Emphasize the senses that your child would use to experience being in this scene under the huge tree watching the animals.

■ **Brinkloe, Julie (1974).** *The Spider Web.* Illustrated by the author. New York: Doubleday. Ages 9–10.

**Environmental context:** Humans' effect on nature's creatures

At dawn, one early morning, a spider spins a silk thread between the tallest blades of grass. The spider works hard and drops and climbs repeatedly to create the web. When the beautiful web is finally complete, it glistens and shimmers as a work of art but meets its fate when a human decides to mow the lawn. Pen-and-ink drawings.

**Activity: "Words for a Wordless Book"**

**Language arts focus:** To dictate a story's beginning; to write sentence strips; to write a story that complements the illustrations in a wordless book

Look at the illustrations in Brinkloe's wordless book with the children and encourage them to dictate the beginning of a story about the spider and its web and point out the setting, main character, and the setup of the problem. Write words to describe the story's setting, character, and problem on separate strips of tagboard. Have the children arrange the tagboard strips on the chalk rail in different ways to guide them in composing the story's beginning in various ways. Once the children have arranged the strips in a sequence they want, let them suggest sentences to show the sequence they have arranged. For example, if the children arrange the strips in the order of setting, main character, and problem, then encourage them to compose the story's beginning in that way, i.e., in the yard's grass (setting), the spider's (character) web was right in the path of the lawn mower (problem). Examples of other ways to begin a story that the children can use are in the list that follows and are based on the illustrations in *The Spider Web*:

- **Setting + problem + character:** In the yard *(setting)*, a churning lawn mower moved toward *(problem)* the web of an unsuspecting spider *(main character)*.
- **Character + problem + setting:** A spider, unaware of the danger of lawnmowers, spun its web in the grassy lawn.
- **Character + setting + problem:** A spider, who made its home in the family's yard, spun its web in a place where the man always mowed.
- **Problem + setting + character:** Unaware of what humans do with lawnmowers, sitting in its web in the yard, directly in the path of the machine, was a spider.
- **Problem + character + setting:** Unable to understand the use of a human's lawnmower, a spider placed its web in the lawn.

**Home Activity**

Ask your child to sketch at least five spiders and their web arrangements on large chart paper. Encourage your child to make the drawings large enough so that two or more siblings or other children can color in parts of the drawings. Ask your child to write captions to tell about a spider in its environment. Encourage your child to donate the drawings to his or her younger siblings, to a family with young children in the neighborhood, to a dentist or doctor who treats young children, or to a younger class of children at school.

■ **Burton, Virginia Lee (1942).** *The Little House.* Illustrated by the author. Boston: Houghton Mifflin. Ages 5–6.

**Environmental context:** City growth impacts countryside

In a country environment, a little house eventually is surrounded by growth from a nearby city. The quiet country surroundings of trees, hills, and landscape change to a noisy city setting of streets and subways, tall buildings, and crowds of people. In time, the great-great granddaughter of the house's original owner makes arrangements for the little house to be returned to the country. Full-color illustrations.

**Activity: "Writing a Request: A Family's Home"**

**Language arts focus:** To participate in role-play; to dictate or write a letter of request

Have the children meet with partners and imagine that they are the great-great grandchildren of an old house's original owner and need to arrange for the family's house to be returned to the country. To do this, they will write a business letter to a city official explaining what they want to do. The following is an example of a brief business letter that can be shown to the children on a transparency:

Nancy Smith<br>
123 Sunny Street<br>
Our Town, CA 01234<br>
<br>
January 1, 2000

Ms. Dione Cordero
Office of the Mayor
123 Main Street
Our Town, CA 01234

Dear Ms. Cordero:
I am writing this letter to ask that _____.

Sincerely,<br>
<br>
_____<br>
Nancy Smith

**Home Activity**

When your child is going on a trip with others, give your child a copy of an "Environmental Journal Entry" to take along on the trip. Mention that when the child returns, others in the family can learn something about the environment from the child's trip. Ask your child to write in some of the information requested on the journal sheet. If appropriate, someone else on the trip can help the child write in the information. Your child can take as many journal entry sheets as the days he or she plans to be away and of course, add anything extra that will be of interest to the family.

**Environmental Journal Entry**
for _____(child's name)

**Date:**

When you go on a trip, please take one of these environmental journal entry sheets with you. Take as many sheets as the days you plan to be away. When you get back, we all will learn from your trip. If needed, have someone else fill in some of the information with you. Add anything extra that will be of interest to your friends and relatives.

> The way I traveled was:
> The weather was:
> What I wore was:
> The best activity we did today was:
> After breakfast, what I saw about caring or not caring for the environment was:
> After lunch, what I saw was:
> After dinner, what I saw was:
> My sketches to show someone cared for the environment are:
> Other:

■ **Cameron, Elizabeth (1984). *A Wildflower Alphabet.*** Illustrated by the author. New York: Morrow. Ages 9–14.

**Environmental context:** Protection of wildflowers

Cameron's purpose in writing this book is to inform her grandchildren about wildflowers, for she feels that they know too little about the world of nature. She selects wildflowers from anemone to zigzag clover that are native to her home in Scotland to illustrate each letter of the alphabet, and annotates each with a hand-lettered passage about the flower's name(s), habitat, and uses. She advocates protection, care, and respect for flowers. For example, she mentions that the mountain avens is the rarest of all the avens and cautions her grandchildren, ". . . so do not pick it if you ever find it." Point out to the children the author's use of manuscript print in the guiding alphabet letters that begin the names of the wildflowers at the tops of the pages, in the marginalia, in the captions for the illustrations, and in the author's note at the end of the book. Watercolor illustrations.

**Activity: "Manuscript Writing"**

**Language arts focus:** To examine others' handwriting; to improve manuscript writing skills

Have the children look again at Cameron's handwritten compositions as examples, and then write their own brief compositions in manuscript (printing). If appropriate, have the children get into groups and take part in a classroom manuscript handwriting contest. Ask the children to use the environment as the topic for writing short compositions in their best manuscript style. Ask parents or older students or teachers from other classes to be judges to select *all* of the writing samples in each group that represent legible manuscript writing. Everyone can be a winner in this contest! Display all of the writing samples in a class book.

**Home Activity**

Mention to your child that there are annual handwriting contests and invite your child to use the environment as a topic for writing in his or her best cursive (script) style as an entry. If your child is interested in entering a contest, he or she can contact one of the following:

1. The yearly National Handwriting Contest at Zaner-Bloser Educational Publishers/Parker Pens. Call for an informational packet: 1-800-924-9233.

2. The annual National Cursive Handwriting Contest at Peterson Handwriting. A winner receives a U.S. savings bond and is elected to the National Cursive Handwriting Honor Society. Your child can write for an entry form by sending a stamped, self-addressed envelope to Peterson Handwriting, 315 S. Maple Ave., PO Box 249, Greensburg, PA 15601–0249; or call 1–800–541–6328; fax: 412–836–4110.

- **London, Jonathan (1996).** *Jackrabbit.* Illustrated by Deborah Kogan Ray. New York: Crown. Ages 5–8.

**Environmental context:** Wildlife in natural habitat

In London's story, a little lost jackrabbit is rescued by a woman and later released back into its natural environment. Named "Jackie" by the woman, the jackrabbit is cared for by the family until she is ready to be released to run with the wind, to chase shadows, and to leap like a jackrabbit should leap. The text has brief and clear to-the-point sentences such as "A dog barks," and "A light flashes," and "Jackrabbit freezes." Pastel illustrations.

**Activity: "Invisible Environmentalist Kid"**

**Language arts focus:** To write and answer questions in the role of an imaginary friend; to write legibly so others can read a traded paper

Tell the children, "There is an invisible environmentalist kid in the room (a "pretend" kid) and nobody can see the kid but you. Anything you ask about the environment, the kid will answer. What questions would you like to ask?" Elicit the children's questions and write them on the board. Ask the children to copy the questions legibly on lined paper and trade them with one another. Give the children a week to answer the questions from the point of view of the environmentalist kid. Ask them to draw sketches of this imaginary pen pal and attach the sketches to the questions and answers. Trade the papers back to the ones who wrote the questions. In a group arrangement, have volunteers read aloud their questions and the answers from the "Environmentalist Kid."

**Home Activity**

Help your child write the dialogue for a scene in a book about caring for a creature and releasing it back into its habitat. Talk with your child about what was written. Then, encourage your child to sketch or draw three things your child learned about wildlife from this activity. Have your child tell the one thing he or she considered to be the most important in caring for a living creature.

## 236  Language Arts and Environmental Awareness

■ **McDonald, Megan (1995).** *Insects Are My Life.* Illustrated by Paul Brett Johnson. New York: Orchard Books. Ages 7–9.

**Environmental context:** Interest in bugs

In McDonald's story, Amanda, a young girl, has a personal passion for bugs. Wearing safari-type clothes, she follows her interest in a determined and preoccupied way and shows her love for bugs in spite of what anyone else thinks. For example, she makes signs for a "Bug Crossing" on a well-worn path. She stubbornly shows that she wants to be different and realizes that nobody else she knows cares for her outdoor interest. Full-color illustrations.

**Activity: "Partner Paragraphs"**

**Language arts focus:** To dictate descriptive words; to write a paragraph; to collaborate with a writing partner

Discuss with the children a variety of words (synonyms) to use in writing a paragraph about a selected insect. Have the children suggest different words (and ways) to write about an insect. For example, the word *insect* can be replaced with other words such as *it, he* or *him, she* or *her, that roly-poly (busy, coffee-colored, flying) creature, that creepy bug, that small thing*. Write their suggestions in a synonym list on the board. Suggest the children meet with partners and together write a brief paragraph on paper sheets cut in the shape of a particular insect (ladybug, for instance) and use the words they thought of about the insect in their writing.

**Home Activity**

On a sheet of paper, write the main heading "Insect: _____" and have your child suggest the name of an insect to write in the blank. Ask your child to dictate words that describe the looks, feel, or if appropriate, the smell of the insect. Discuss the words your child suggested and ask your child to sketch a scene of the insect in an upper left-hand corner of another sheet of paper and then use some of the words on the first paper to dictate or write sentences about the creature.

■ **Newton, James R. (1980).** *Forest Log.* Illustrated by Irene Brady. New York: N. Y. Crowell. Ages 8 up.

**Environmental context:** Value of a fallen tree

Newton's book describes plant and animal life surrounding a fallen tree in a Pacific Coast forest. A Douglas fir, over 250 feet long, becomes a "nurse log" and provides nourishment and homes to plants and animals such as squirrels, beetles, woodpeckers, fungi, termites, ants, shrews, a black-tailed deer, and moss. The text shows that the life cycle of a tree in a forest adds to the richness of the soil. Full-color illustrations.

**Activity: "A Log's Point of View"**

**Language arts focus:** To participate in discussion; to write from a new perspective

Discuss with the children the idea that a log at the end of its life cycle adds to the richness of the soil and provides homes and nourishment to living things. This is why a fallen tree is called a "nurse log." Have the children take the point of view of a fallen log and write a brief perspective about what happens to it. Tell the children to imagine being the fallen log and what happens when animals come to the log. Here is an example of a beginning to read aloud to the children. Ask them to help fill in the blanks as you read:

> I feel myself fall. I hit the ground and there is a sound of a crash. This is like the sound of _____. My roots are in the air. My tree top is on the ground. I feel _____. My branches touch something flat, brown, and crunchy. Crashing to the ground is like _____. My life as a tree standing tall was better because I _____. Now, on the ground, I _____.

Encourage the children to mention which animals make their homes *on* and *in* the log and which plants get nourishment from the tree's bark and other nutrients. Have the children make tree-shaped pages on which to write their perspectives. Invite them to illustrate their writing. Ask volunteers to read their pages aloud. Collect the children's work to make a tree-shaped class book and place it in a reading area for the children's independent reading.

### Home Activity

Invite your child to make an environmental panorama by taping cardboard together to make hinged sections for a scenic mural that stands alone. Encourage your child to sketch/draw/paint one side to show his/her residential area. And on the other, draw and write (or dictate) a description of a scene of plant and animal life surrounding a fallen tree in a forest that once might have grown in the residential area years ago.

■ **Rood, Ronald (1994). *Wetlands*.** Illustrated by Marlene Hill Donnelley. New York: HarperCollins. Ages 7–8.

**Environmental context:** Value of wetlands

Rood's book is a description of the inhabitants that live in a wetland pond, such as caddisworms, dragonfly nymphs, salamanders, and snails, as well as those that live nearby out of the water (birds, frogs, insects, raccoons, and turtles). The book includes directions for activities such as making a simple microscope and experimenting with surface tension of water. Full-color illustrations.

**Activity: "Word Webs and Letters"**

**Language arts focus:** To design a word web; to engage in writing a letter to others

After the children listen to excerpts from *Wetlands*, show them how to draw a word web on the board about the wetland habitat and the creatures that live there. Suggest that the children select their own topics for the word web to show what they learned. Have them create their own word webs on paper and use the webs to write several letters to others to tell what they have learned about this environment.

1. Invite children to write several letters about what they have learned to different people—themselves, their friends and peers, their acquaintances at school, teachers, parents, or other adults in the home.
2. Show them an example of a personal letter on the board or overhead transparency. Example:

Pat Jones
123 Sunny Street
Our Town, CA 01234

January 1, 2000

Ms. Dione Noriega
Teacher, Fourth Grade Class
Our Town School
Our Town, CA 01234

Dear Ms. Noriega:
Recently I studied the wetland habitat in my class at school. One of the most exciting things I learned about the value of the wetlands and wetland creatures was _____.

Your friend,

Pat Jones

**Home Activity**

Clip several photographs depicting caring for living things and the environment from daily newspapers and paste the captions on the back. Ask the child to guess what is happening in each picture. Then read the caption on the back together to find out what really happened. Encourage your child to make his or her own set of photographs and captions for you to guess what is going on in the scenes.

■ **Schmid, Elenore (1994).** *The Living Earth.* Illustrated by the author. New York: North-South Books. Ages 8–9.

**Environmental context:** Ecosystem of the earth

Schmid's book introduces concerns about the world's environment and reveals ways people depend on the living earth. The informative text points out that the earth is changing like a precious living thing and there is particular value in topsoil as it provides nutrients to grow plants. The idea that nature is a cycle that renews itself also is discussed with

### 240  Language Arts and Environmental Awareness

the view that all living things die and return to earth and break down into new nutrients for new seeds and plants. Full-color paintings.

**Activity: "A Handful of Soil"**

**Language arts focus:** To make predictions; to work collaboratively with others while studying; to write a brief essay about what was learned

Tell the children they will have an activity to study soil on the schoolground and write about what they find. Ask them to predict:

1. What a handful of soil will feel like, smell like, and look like
2. What living organisms will be in the soil

With the children outside, have them take handfuls of soil, look at the material, and let it slip through their fingers. Encourage the children to notice its texture (delicate or crumbly), how it smells, and what is found in the handful (pebbles, twigs, bugs).

Back in the classroom, have the children look at another handful of soil under a magnifying glass or microscope. Mention that some scientists say there are more living things in a handful of soil than there are people on the entire earth and challenge the children to find some of these living things. Ask, "Who can see grass roots, evidence of fungi, soil worms, etc.?" Have the children each write a brief essay about this experience to tell what they learned from the activity. Have the children take their writing home to read to a family member and tell what they learned.

**Home Activity**

Help your child become aware of organisms that live in the soil, and display a photocopy of a picture of one of the soil organisms (algae, bacteria) that you find illustrated in an information book. Tell your child this is a mystery photo that he/she can investigate by looking in other books, interviewing others, going to the library, or using computer information. Give your child one week to find out what it is. Give your child some clues about the picture and have him/her listen and write them down. At the end of the week, ask for your child for the name of the soil organism and discuss your child's response. Place the photocopy in a binder for future browsing together to see how many photos of soil organisms your child can remember through the year.

- **Wegen, Ronald (1977).** *Sand Castle.* Illustrated by the author. New York: Greenwillow. Ages 5–6.

**Environmental context:** Changes in nature

Wegen's book is a wordless story about a turtle that comes out of the sea, digs three holes, lays eggs, and covers them up with sand mounds. In the pictures, a reader will see the author's creative idea that other sea creatures add to the original mounds and build a larger sand castle, which later is destroyed when the tide comes in. Small watercolor illustrations.

**Activity: "A Group Chart Story"**

**Language arts focus:** To participate in discussion; to express feelings; to dictate events for a group story

Look with the children at Wegen's illustrations again on an opaque projector and discuss the idea of environmental change—the sand castle is destroyed by the sea when it is washed away at high tide. Invite the children to make their own original sand castles in a tub or in a small plastic wading pool filled with sand. Encourage them to add to one another's original castles to build a larger sand castle just as the sea creatures did in the story. Have them demonstrate the effect of water (tides) on the sand castle by pouring different amounts of water over their castles to see the sand structures wash away and encourage them to tell others in the group what changes occurred in the activity as well as their feelings about what happened. Engage children in dictating what was done and write their sentences on a class chart. Read the writing aloud as a group story.

**Home Activity**

Invite your child to write a description of an imaginary walk on the beach. Instruct your child: "Imagine you are taking a barefoot walk along a sandy beach. It is night and is so dark that you cannot see anything. You have to use your feet to feel, your nose to smell, and your ears to hear. Write (or dictate) a description about your walk along the beach and what happens when your feet feel a large mound of sand and your toes sense the cold tide water swirling around."

# Involving Children in Writing: Ages 9–14

■ **Barron, T. A. (1993).** *To Walk in Wilderness: A Rocky Mountain Journal.* Photographs by John Fielder. New York: Westcliffe Publishers. Ages 9–14.

**Environmental context:** Protecting a wilderness habitat

For thirty days, author Barron and photographer Fielder walk with three llamas that carry their food, gear, and photography equipment to explore the Maroon Bells-Snowmass Wilderness near Aspen, Colorado. Fielder takes pictures of the terrain—eye-catching flowers in alpine meadows, craggy rock outcroppings and cliffs of varied colors, and towering mountain peaks. Both men write entries in their journals which show their sensitivity to environmental concerns. Their words reflect how they value wildlife and what they think of the environment they are in—whether sweltering heat or bone-chilling cold—as well as how they see the area as a microcosm of all parks, wildlife refuges, and nature areas that are protected. Photographs for illustrations.

**Activity: "Environmental Journal Entries"**

**Language arts focus:** To participate in a nature walk; to work collaboratively in small groups; to compose a list

Discuss with the children the idea that journal entries can explain the attraction that nature and the wilderness has for the writer to others who read the journal. To have the children determine what attracts them in the environment, go on a walk in the neighborhood or a nearby wildlife area to observe nature and its creatures. Have the children write notes and make sketches on paper about what interests them. If appropriate, focus on a particular creature on the walk. For example, you can suggest that the children imagine they have been hired by a spider to locate a new spot for a larger web or hired by a local bird to locate a new spot for a nest. Have them divide into small groups as they walk and decide what to look for.

Back in the classroom, have the groups report on the creature they selected (bird or spider), their reasons for selecting the new nest or web site (near food, sheltered by weather, hidden from predators, away from traffic), as well as the location of the site they selected for the creature. List the sites. Ask the class to vote on the best site for each creature after the children have considered all of the reasons for the site selections. Have the children use their nature walk notes and transform them into complete sentences with capitalization and punctuation.

**Home Activity**

Help your child make a community bird book entitled "My Neighborhood Bird Book." Suggest that the book feature your child's sketches, drawings, or snapshots, as well as handwritten descriptions of the birds your child notices. Your child also can add special pages of information that reflect the following:

- A list of birds' names in order according to the syllables in the names—such as wren (one syllable), bluejay (two syllables), and whippoorwill (three syllables);
- A line graph to show the number of birds in the yard on Monday, Tuesday, and so on.

| Number of Birds | Mon. | Tues. | Wed. | Thur. | Fri. |
|---|---|---|---|---|---|
| More than 5 | | | | | |
| 5 | | | | | |
| 4 | | | | | |
| 3 | | | | | |
| 2 | | | | | |
| 1 | | | | | |

- A hand-drawn map that shows where each bird was seen in the yard or neighborhood;
- Full-color drawings to help identify the birds.

Invite your child to put out food for the birds in an area where they can be seen easily.

■ **Butterfield, Moira (1995).** *Richard Orr's Cross-Sections.* Illustrated by Richard Orr. New York: Dorling Kindersley. Ages 10 up.

**Environmental context:** Characteristics of habitats

Butterfield's book is a collection of Richard Orr's cross-sectioned illustrations of habitats found in nature. A reader sees a desert in the United States, as well as scenes in other countries—a rain forest, a tropical river bank, and life in the Arctic and Antarctic. Additionally, smaller habitats are presented through a termite community and a beehive. Each environment's characteristics are presented in brief factual paragraphs. Colorful oversize paintings for illustrations.

**Activity: "ROPE to Summarize"**

**Language arts focus:** To read for information; to organize information in writing; to summarize characteristics

Tell the children that they will learn how to summarize information from an environmental awareness book, such as Butterfield's, and that they can use this kind of information as part of a report about ecology. Point out that the steps to take to summarize information in this activity are the same ones they can use when they write a summary on their own. Thus, they will be learning skills to help them in their future writing. Mention that the letters R, O, P, E, represent the steps to summarize information and write the letters on the board. Tell them the meaning of the letters:

**R** stands for reading and rereading for information;
**O** stands for organizing information;
**P** stands for presenting information; and
**E** stands for elaborating on the knowledge about the subject/topic.

Guide the children through the following procedures related to the ROPE letters:

1. **Reading.** Have the children read a description of the characteristics of a selected habitat from Butterfield's book and ask them to remember all that they can. If appropriate, distribute copies of the description to the children and have them read it silently. Have them tell all they remember about what they read. Write their recollections on the left side of the writing board.

2. **Rereading.** Have the children reread the description silently to add more information about details. Ask them to tell any additional information they have. Write their recollections on the right side of the board. Point out what information was gained from the children's rereading and what value rereading has in getting information.

3. **Organizing.** Discuss the information from both sides of the board with the children. Ask them to dictate complete sentences about the information and write the sentences on the board. Revise any sentences as needed. Point out to the children that the sentences that are revised can combine details, sum things up, include additional words for coherence, and have more elaboration. Have the children write their own summarizing sentence(s) about a part of the description at the same time you are writing a sentence to summarize the same material on the writing board. Ask volunteers to read their sentences aloud. Include any sentence parts from the children that you consider better than yours into your sentence on the board. Repeat with other material related to the description of the habitat.

4. **Presenting.** With the children's help, put the sentences in order (number them 1, 2, 3, and so on) to make a paragraph that summarizes the reading.

5. **Elaborating.** To elaborate, have the children copy their group paragraph and revise any sentence they want so they can show their additional knowledge about the topic. Perhaps some of the children will want to add information to their sentences to make them more meaningful to each individual writer.
6. Have the children meet with partners and read their ROPE summaries aloud to one another. Encourage them to make revisions and to use these same steps in writing summaries on their own about other topics.

**Home Activity**

Invite your child to make a "summary web." To do this, ask your child to let his or her mind wander from word to word when thinking about a key word. For example, when your child hears the key word *rain forest*, he or she might think of wetness. Ask, "What other words does *rain forest* make you think of? Can you choose a word that is different from the word *wetness*?" Have your child write the words to make a brief "summary web" similar to the one that follows.

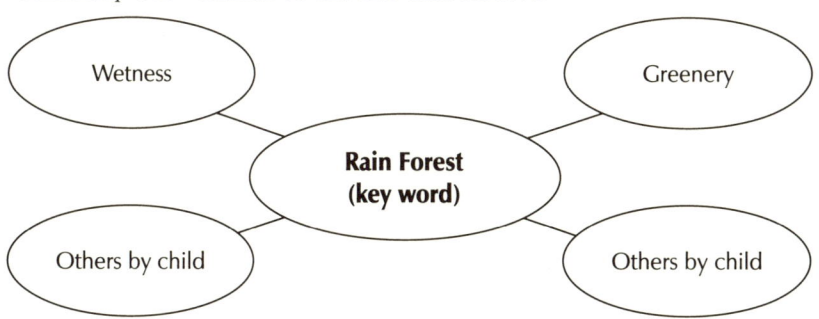

```
    Wetness              Greenery

            Rain Forest
            (key word)

  Others by child      Others by child
```

■ **Carson, Rachel (1962). *The Silent Spring.*** New York: Macmillan. Ages 14 up.

**Environmental context:** Damage chemicals do to the environment

The author, a marine biologist, calls attention to the damage that DDT (now banned in the U.S.) and other chemicals can do to the environment. Evidence is presented about pesticides that kill more than pests.

It seems that creature-consumers eat sprayed insects and retain the pesticides in their bodies. Thus, the concentrated chemicals eventually become dangerous to creatures at the top of the food chain, including humans. The author emphasizes the point that with the continued use of pesticides, humans threaten their own existence. Black-and-white photographs for illustrations.

**Activity: "Environmental Hero/Heroine"**

**Language arts focus:** To write expressively about one's point of view in a personal letter; to read a partner's writing and provide feedback

Invite the children to write their own individual letters of no more than a thousand words to an environmentally concerned person who has made a positive difference in their lives in the form of a "Who's Your Environmental Hero?" letter. Have them review the form for a friendly letter (see page 239) and trade the first drafts of their letters to partners to read and provide feedback about spelling, capitalization, and punctuation. Encourage them to make additions, deletions, or other changes, before mailing the letters.

**Home Activity**

If your child is interested in entering a letter in the Who's Your Hero National Essay Contest co-sponsored by Conari Press and the National Collaboration of Youth, invite your child to write for information from Conari Press, 2550 Ninth Street, Suite 101, Berkeley, CA 947710 or call 1-800-685-9595. There is one condition: the entrants must be affiliated with agencies affiliated with the National Collaboration of Youth, i.e., Scouts, 4-H, the Salvation Army.

■ **Dekker, Midas (1988). *The Nature Book: Discovering, Exploring, Observing, Experimenting with Plants and Animals at Home and Outdoors.*** Illustrated by the author. New York: Macmillan. Ages 10–11.

**Environmental context:** Observations of plants and animals

With this book, a child is introduced to ways to observe living things as well as ways to keep a notebook of observations. Results of experiments with food in the home can be kept after doing the activities on the pages labeled "Food Is Nature, Too." Black line drawings for illustrations.

**Activity: "Writing Observations"**

**Language arts focus:** To take notes; to compose lists related to a topic

Have the children prepare a notebook about bird, animal, and plant observations that they see on several nature walks. For each living thing chosen as a subject, ask them to list on a page ways that the creature helps the environment or humans and ways that the creature might be in danger. For example, if the subject "bird" is selected, the children might write that birds provide food (chickens lay eggs), clothing (down for vests, bed mattresses, pillows, quilts), recreation (feeding, pets, pigeon racing, photography, watching), symbols (state, national, in sayings, in business ads), and topics in literature (poems, tales, myths).

Have the children list on another page the ways that the creature is in trouble. Using the subject "bird" again as an example, they could list some of the following:

Birds are in trouble because:

1. Some have lost or are losing their habitat;
2. Some bird feathers are used and sold for crafts and fashion;
3. Some exotic birds are used as pets and brought into U.S. illegally at times;
4. Some birds are poisoned by pollutants found in water
5. Some birds are affected by pesticides and the pollution of water by oil spills and chemicals.

To complete their nature notebooks, have the children repeat this activity with other plants and animals that they saw on their nature walks.

**Home Activity**

Select an inexpensive visor, baseball cap, or cotton painter's hat and invite your child to use tubes of textile paints on the headgear and create his or her own custom slogans, messages, and designs about caring for plants and animals in the environment.

- **Fraser, Mary Ann (1994).** *Sanctuary: The Story of Three Arch Rocks.* Illustrated by the author. New York: Holt. Ages 9–10.

**Environmental context:** Establishing islands as a game preserve

Off the coast of Oregon in 1901, William Finley and Herman Bohlman, nature photographers, discover local hunters killing the seals and birds that they want to photograph on the islands of Three Arch Rocks. To show President Teddy Roosevelt the value of establishing the islands as a protective game preserve, the two men camp on the islands for two weeks. They keep daily diaries and photograph the wildlife as they confront the hunters. Glossary, maps, and photographs of the photographers are included. Photographs for illustrations.

**Activity: "Diary Entries"**

**Language arts focus:** To prepare a simulated diary; to write entries in a diary in another's persona

Have the children who have read or heard this wildlife-activist story take the persona of one of the photographers and keep a diary (fold writing paper in half, add a cover of art paper, and staple the pages) and record the events of the two-week camp-out on the islands as they happen in the story. Encourage the children to sketch what the photographers see and then write about some of the sights, sounds, and smells of the islands. Also, invite the children to write about the wildlife that is photographed and about the men's impressions of the events that take place, as well as about their reason for being there.

**Home Activity**

Encourage your child to prepare a "My Ecology Activities" chart as a record and reminder of daily and weekly activities related to caring for the environment that your child does each day. Make a simple grid with spaces for names of jobs to be done from "separate trash for recycling" to "pick up litter." The jobs that are completed can be acknowledged with a gold star in the Sunday through Saturday spaces.

- **George, Jean Craighead (1973).** *Who Really Killed Cock Robin: An Ecological Mystery.* New York: E. P. Dutton. Ages 9–12.

**Environmental context:** Food chain

In the pollution-fighting town of Saddleboro, hundreds of bass and sunfish float on the surface of the marsh, yellow ants appear in the trillions, and a red robin dies—signs that something is wrong in the ecology of the town's environment. One of the young people, Tony, works for the local newspaper, the *Patent Reader*, and thinks that these signs mean some animal is missing in the food chain for some mysterious reason. Tony's friend Mary Ann helps him investigate and search for the reason: Is the cause detergents with arsenic or dyes that are dumped into the town's waterways? The two children prove the extent to which detergent and dyes affect the wildlife.

**Activity: "News Articles"**

**Language arts focus:** To prepare a class newspaper about the food chain and other ecological topics

Encourage the children to prepare a classroom ecological newspaper. Elicit suggestions from them about what news articles and feature articles could be included. Write their ideas on the board, a chart, or overhead transparency. The sections could include ads for new books about environmental awareness, ecological book reviews, columns on gardening, birdwatching, and so on, articles about the student-authors who write the feature articles, editorials on an ecological point of view, as well as cartoons that feature an original ecological character. Additionally, some children can imagine that they are environmental reporters and write accounts of what is going on locally. Collect the children's contributions and affix them to a class chart to make an oversize class newspaper. Display in the room.

**Home Activity**

Encourage your child to ask if a local newspaper editor would print an occasional child-written editorial, feature article, or a review of a book on the environment in its weekend edition and engage your child in preparing the material the newspaper editor wants.

- **Gibbons, Gail (1994).** *Nature's Green Umbrella: Tropical Rain Forests.* Illustrated by the author. New York: Morrow. Ages 9–11.

**Environmental context:** Ecology of a rain forest

Gibbons's book discusses the importance of forests to the world's climate since the trees balance gases in the air by taking in carbon dioxide and giving off oxygen. The text explains the climatic conditions of a rain forest as well as the layers of plants and animals that comprise the ecosystem—tall trees form the canopy layers, below that is the understory, and then the forest floor is the home of decomposing leaves that send nutrients into the soil (the subfloor). The author points out that currently trees are harvested for farming and grazing and roads, and, as forests disappear, so do plants and animals. Flooding also appears from erosion and an increased global warming is developing. The warming effect is clarified: with fewer trees, the earth's warmth is trapped inside a layer of gases and our climate becomes warmer. To protect against this, the author calls for areas of protected plants called extraction reserves, where only a limited amount of fruit, plants, nuts, rubber, and other products can be taken out of the area. The author also suggests that trees should be cut down only selectively. Full-color maps included. Part of the royalties are donated to tropical forest preservation agencies. Watercolor paintings for illustrations.

**Activity: "Essay Grid"**

**Language arts focus:** To participate in discussion; to research information on an essay grid; to write an essay emphasizing a point of view

Discuss with the children some of the benefits people receive from a rain forest and list them on the board. Have children refer to the list and write a brief essay about ways to protect a rain forest from further depletion. These can include establishing reserved areas for living things to protect them; encouraging selective cutting of trees; and establishing rain forest extraction policies which could limit the amount of fruit, plants, nuts, and rubber products that could be taken out of a rain forest area.

To assist the children in writing a short essay about the rain forest, draw as essay grid (see the one that follows) on large mural paper. Tell the children they will fill out the spaces in this essay grid as a whole group. First, have the children suggest topics related to the rain forest and list the topics across the top of the grid.

| Sources | Topic 1 | Topic 2 | Topic 3 | Topic 4 |
| --- | --- | --- | --- | --- |
| Dictionary | | | | |
| Encyclopedia | | | | |
| Others suggested by children | | | | |

Next, elicit from the children their suggestions about information resources—encyclopedia, Internet web sites, informational books—and write the titles down the left-hand side of the grid. Have the children research information about the topics and write any related information they find on adhesive-backed sticky notes and place the notes in the squares. Show the children how to refer to the notes for one of the topics to write a paragraph for a demonstration essay on an overhead transparency.

Repeat the activity with another topic and use the children's notes to write another paragraph on the overhead related to the rain forest. Then give the children blank copies of the grid and ask them to write in their own topics on the subject of the rain forest and start their research with informational sources as the basis for writing their papers. When their research is finished, ask the children to meet with partners and to read aloud what they have written. Encourage them to make revisions if they wish. Collect the papers and display them in a class book.

### Home Activity

Encourage your child to keep a journal titled "My Ecology Days." Ask your child to show others in the family/neighborhood what he or she does to help protect the environment by recording something daily in the journal. This can be your child's log to keep through the week/month/school year. Envelopes can be added to hold magazine articles, clippings, sketches, drawings or photos, and records of friends who care for the environment. If needed, add extra pages for place names, dates, and comments about what your child does.

- ■ **Gonick, Larry, and Alice Outwater (1996).** *The Cartoon Guide to the Environment.* Illustrations by Larry Gonick. New York: Harper-Perennial. Ages 13 up.

**Environmental context:** Challenges to earth's ecosystems

In this book, there is a contrast between the light cartoon-style format and the sober message about what is happening to the earth. The authors make a reader aware of the destructive actions of humans and present the history and related science research for several environmental challenges facing humans today. As one example, they discuss the collapse of Easter Island. Terms, events, and situations are further explained in cartoons. Authors' notes and bibliography included. Black-and-white cartoons for illustrations.

**Activity: "Sense of Hope"**

**Language arts focus:** To participate in discussion; to record one's thoughts; to use appropriate capitalization and punctuation

Discuss the book's message (the fate of life on earth depends on people's actions) with the children and ask them to what extent they agree or disagree with the authors that there is a sense of hope for our planet's future. Ask them to do more research through informational sources about what is happening to the environment—its protection, its destruction—and then write their findings for others in the class to read. Have the children trade their writing papers with one another and read what others have written. Encourage the children to insert any missing capitals or punctuation marks in what they read. Have the papers returned and encourage the original writers to make any changes that they want to make. Collect the papers for a class book entitled "Sense of Hope" and place it in a reading area so children can read and browse through it as they wish.

**Home Activity**

Ask your child to write entries for a one-page reflection on the future of earth's environment and living creatures. Encourage your child to use capitals and punctuation in the sentences in this activity. You can suggest that it be a one-time only activity or that daily entries be made. An example of a possible format follows:

**My Hope for the Future for the Environment**

_____

(*name of child*)

**Date**    **What I Hope for:**

_____   _____
          _____
          _____
          _____
          _____

Display your child's writing on the refrigerator or other prominent place in the home.

■ **Heinrich, Berne (1990).** *An Owl in the House: A Naturalist Diary.* Illustrated by the author. Boston: Little, Brown. Ages 9–11.

**Environmental context:** Caring for nature's creatures

Heinrich's diary makes a realistic comment about a naturalist's interest in wildlife. The author adopts a great horned owlet that he finds in the Vermont woods and keeps a record of the changes in the owl's appearance and its growing interest in food. Black line drawings for illustrations.

## Language Arts and Environmental Awareness

**Activity: "Transformations"**

**Language arts focus:** To list reasons and transform them into descriptive sentences; to transform written information into an art product

Have the children divide into teams to list at least five reasons why birds, including owls, are important, and conduct further research and inquiry into the topic. Examples of reasons for the importance of birds include the following: They (1) provide food for the food chain; (2) spread seeds of plants; (3) eat pests and insects; (4) eat decaying plants and animals; (5) offer viewers a sense of beauty in their own right; and (6) provide a variety of recreation and career opportunities for humans. Suggest that each team make an environmental quilt to show the value of birds and present the information they gain from their research and inquiry. Steps for making a "Value of Birds" environmental quilt are:

1. Have the children divide into teams. Ask each team of children to show in quilt form what each member does to help protect the birds and their environment.

2. Have the children talk to one another and find out what each does to care for the habitat. Let each team take notes and use information from the members' interviews to sketch quilt squares on paper. The children may represent what they do, or what they want to do in the future.

3. Ask the children to create final sketches of themselves caring for the birds in the environment on broadcloth quilt squares and use fabric markers, textile paints, fabric scraps, or even embroidery thread to make their scenes.

4. Invite classroom volunteers and parents to help sew each team's quilt together. When the quilts are ready to display, have the children write paragraphs telling about their squares and display the writing near the quilt.

**Home Activity**

Encourage your child to have some sidewalk fun by using non-toxic chunky chalk to write some ecology messages about the value of birds or other topics on your part of a sidewalk or driveway.

■ **Hirschi, Ron (1993).** *Save Our Oceans and Coasts.* Illustrated by Erwin and Peggy Bauer, et al. New York: Delacorte. Ages 9–12.

**Environmental context:** Protecting ocean and coastal habitats

Hirschi's book discusses the characteristics of animal life and the importance of oceans and coastal areas as well as ways to protect these habitats for animals. The text mentions that the threats to the areas are oil spills, plastic pollution, disposal habits, sewage, toxic waste, and harvesting too many fish. The author includes a case study of how the beach at Bowerman Basin in Aberdeen, Washington, was saved and turned into a life refuge. Index included. Full-color wildlife photographs.

**Activity: "I Can Join the Fight"**

**Language arts focus:** To participate in discussion; to give reasons and transform them into descriptive sentences; to write a brief essay

After reading excerpts from the book aloud, point out to the children that the author makes a plea to join the fight to help save endangered species and help the fragile, valuable coastal areas. Elicit the children's ideas about what they can do to help protect ocean and coastal animals and their habitat and write their ideas on the board. The children's suggestions might be similar to the following:

1. I can pick up/clean up a river bank or beach area.
2. I can recycle plastic that could become an ocean pollutant.
3. I can support groups that care for the needs of animals in coastal areas.
4. I can let people know about vanishing species such as sharks, endangered tuna, or threatened coastal habitats that I know about in my area.
5. I can write letters to companies who pollute the environment stating my point of view.
6. I can write letters to local, state, and national officials about the way they handle problems in the environment.

Ask the children to use the ideas on the board as a reference and write a brief essay to tell others what they can do to help. Have the children read their essays to others in the class and make revisions in their writing if they wish to do so. Collect their papers for a class book and display it in a reading area.

**Home Activity**

Encourage your child to use a shoebox to make an "Endangered Species Fan" box. Have your child select several favorite endangered species and do research about each one. The findings can be recorded on index cards placed in alphabetical order in the shoebox. Put the box on display so other family members can read and browse through the index cards as they discover one another's favorites among the endangered creatures.

■ **Jennings, Gary (1974).** *The Earth Book.* Illustrated by the author, Reagan Bradshaw, Jim Olive, and Blair Pitman. New York: Lippincott. Ages 9–12.

**Environmental context:** Changes caused by rapid growth

The author points out that air, water, and soil give our planet the ability to support life, and discusses the long-range effects of pollution caused by overcrowding in the environment. There is an emphasis on everyone doing what they can to help save the earth from the damage that humans have caused. Suggestions include helping organized groups in their pickup and cleanup campaigns, writing letters as a customer of the future to companies who pollute the environment, and making suggestions to the mayor, governor, or congressman about their handling of the environment's problems. Full-color photographs.

**Activity: "Population Growth"**

**Language arts focus:** To write information on a class chart; to record one's thoughts about population growth

Demonstrate to the children how to use a copy of the U.S. Census. Compare the latest population of the largest major city in your area with its previous population in ten-year intervals: 1980, 1970, and so on. Have the children make a chart to show the current population of the city with its population ten years ago or make a chart showing the present birth and death rates with the birth and death rates from ten years ago. As a follow-up activity to verify population growth, ask for volunteers to compare a telephone directory from 1980 with a current one to look for growth in selected services such as day care, clothing stores, dentists, fast-food outlets, motels, service stations, and other businesses. Have the children show what they found on charts to display in the room and explain their findings to the group. Engage the children in writing a paragraph to explain the information on the charts. Have them trade paragraphs and give feedback to one another. Encourage them to make revisions—additions, deletions, changes—that improve their writing.

**Home Activity**

Ask your child to list/dictate the needs of people that impinge directly on the natural environment and write them in a list under the heading, "Wants of People." Ask your child, "in what ways would *you* be willing to change your life to protect for and care for the environment?" List your child's suggestions in a second list entitled, "What I Would Do."

| Wants of People | What I Would Do |
| --- | --- |
| 1. Houses with windows, doors | 1. Check for air leaks around doors and windows. Caulk or add weather strips. |
| 2. Shopping centers, roads | 2. Take public transportation |
| 3. Money from land sales | 3. Support nature areas |
| 4. More energy for heating, cooling, etc. Consume natural resources | 4. Be energy efficient by using insulated curtains or drapes; close drapes at night and open drapes on sunny days; replace furnace filters on a regular basis; use cold water to wash clothes in full loads only to save on gas, electricity, and water heating costs Save water by fixing leaky faucets; use solar water heater |

| Wants of People | What I Would Do |
|---|---|
| 5. Gas for transportation | 5. Bike when possible, car pool, support solar vehicles |
| 6. Others by child | 6. Others by child |

Encourage your child to implement as many of the suggestions in the second list as possible. For example, if your child is interested in how a solar water heater works, invite him/her to write to James Dulley (mechanical engineer and syndicated columnist), 6906 Royalgreen Drive, Cincinnati, OH 45244, for more information and a guide to solar water heaters. Display your child's lists in an appropriate place in the home.

- **McHargue, Georgess (1992).** *Beastie.* New York: Delacorte. Ages 9 up.

**Environmental context:** Studying the environment/living creatures carefully

McHargue's story is about three kids who call themselves "moles"—Mary, Scott, and Theo—who try to catch an elusive "Beastie" in a remote Scottish loch. They monitor a scientific expedition, make secret boating excursions and notice things that indicate that someone is trying to stop them. Tayze, a local girl, tells them that she has seen the "Beastie" with its long neck, olive brown stripes, and fat flippers—and it is endangered. When the scientific expedition leaves without discovering the "Beastie," Tayze and the others are relieved. The children fly home to London, where they agree they are interested in a trip down under to Australia to find another water monster—a bunyip. This ending sets the stage for a sequel.

**Activity: "Sloppy Writer, Keeper Writer, and Chief Writer"**

**Language arts focus:** To identify favorite excerpts from a story; to identify characteristics of narrative writing found in a selected story; to engage in narrative writing in the roles of "sloppy writer, keeper writer, and chief writer"

Have the children read aloud excerpts from *Beastie* as examples of narrative writing that moves the story along. Example: "It was while she was still staring out across the water that Mary first had the uneasy feeling of being watched." If appropriate, show some examples of the text on an overhead transparency and elicit from the children any of the characteristics of narrative writing that *they* notice from the examples. Write their findings on a class chart with the heading "Narrative Writing: Characteristics We Saw." Mention to the children that they will have an opportunity to use some of these characteristics in a story.

Tell the children they also will use the approach of "Sloppy Writer, Keeper Writer, Chief Writer" to write the story. To do this, they will write in the personae of the roles in sequence and write first as Sloppy Writer, then as Keeper Writer and finally as Chief Writer to tell their stories. They can identify each role with a name tag made of adhesive-backed paper and learn to use these three roles to draft their writing, polish it, and refine it. These are the steps to follow:

1. Have children take the role of *Sloppy Writer* by writing the words *Sloppy Writer* on a name tag and putting it on. Encourage the children to write in a sloppy, crazy way—either mechanically with messy penmanship or careless in the way they write their thoughts. They can write about things that their main character is enthused, unhappy, or concerned about.

2. Have the children switch to the role of Keeper Writer and put on a name tag with the words *Keeper Writer* on it. Ask them to read what they wrote in the role of Sloppy Writer, and then as Keeper Writer, find and select only the parts that they think are worth keeping. They may add more words and thoughts for the development of the story.

3. Have the children change next to the role of Chief Writer and put on a name tag with the words *Chief Writer* on it, Ask them in the Chief writer role to rearrange the ideas they wrote as Keeper Writer and put them together in a logical way (just as a chief or a leader of a group would do) and make sure that the sentences are written clearly and go into the appropriate paragraphs.

## 262   Language Arts and Environmental Awareness

4. Have the children trade papers with friends who will check to see that the transitions in the story are smooth and that thoughts have been put together in sequence. Finally, have the children return the papers to the original authors and ask them to consider their classmates' suggestions, to reflect about what they read, and then rewrite and polish any unclear parts of the story. Invite volunteers to read parts of their stories aloud.

**Home Activity**

Explain to your child that the first ten words of his/her writing can be the eye-catcher—the "hot spot" lead that attracts and interests others. Show your child some of the first-sentence eye-catchers that authors use when they write about caring for the environment. Read some examples aloud from children's books, especially titles selected by your child when you visit the library, and encourage your child to write some "hot spot" leads that he/she could use in future writing.

■ **McLaughlin, Molly (1986).** *Earthworms, Dirt and Rotten Leaves: An Exploration in Ecology.* Illustrated by Robert Shetterly. New York: Atheneum. Ages 9 up.

**Environmental context:** Importance of earthworms

This is a chapter book about the earthworm's digging, eating, digesting role in making soil, in improving the humus condition of the soil, and in recycling nutrients through plants, water, soil, and air. The text emphasizes the earthworm's contributions. Plant nutrients are taken from the environment and returned to it through decomposition in the worm's body in the digestion of rotted leaves. Soil is loosened by these subterranean strong men when they budge soil particles that weigh fifty times as much as they do. Experiments in earthworm behavior are focused around questions such as: "How do earthworms react to light and dark? To damp and dry areas? How do different colors of light affect the earthworm?" and, "How do different parts of the earthworm react to touch?" Ways to make up one's own experiments are suggested. Pen-and-ink sketches.

**Activity: "Earthworms"**

**Language arts focus:** To read and follow directions for a project; to engage in procedural writing to tell how to do something or perform an experiment

Engage the children in performing a simple experiment to determine ways that earthworms react to the light of a flashlight. After the activity, have them write their version of the procedure. Some of the steps in the activity include the following:

1. Cover a flashlight with dark paper that has a small hole in it to let light through.
2. Put an earthworm on a moist paper towel and darken the room, or use a large box to darken the area around the worm.
3. Aim the beam of light at the worm's tail. How does it react?

After the experiment, mention to the children that authors sometimes use procedural writing (discussing the steps in an experiment) when writing about creatures and the environment. If appropriate, read aloud some examples of procedural writing that are found in fiction, informational books, and textbooks, and show some examples of the text on an overhead transparency. Elicit from the children some of the characteristics of procedural writing that they notice from the examples and write their findings on a class chart with the heading "Procedural Writing: Characteristics We Saw." Have the children compose a paragraph or more of procedural writing to explain what they did during the earthworm experiment. Give each child two colorful gummy worms (one to eat and one to glue to the header of the page or to the margin of the writing) and encourage the children to display their writing in one of the several ways listed in the following Earthologue:

**Earthologue: 30+ Ways to Go Public with Writing**

1. Arrange an environmental display in the classroom, a school office, or a district office.
2. Author a beginning-of-the-year or end-of-the-year environmental letter to friends at school.

3. Author a "caring for the environment" letter to a newcomer at school or a friend who is leaving.

4. Collect writings for a class anthology that shows each writer's self-selected "environmental" writing of the month.

5. Collect writings and illustrations to document a picture album of class projects about the environment—a field trip, a visit by a resource person, a study of a topic related to ecology.

6. Communicate with the school principal, vice principal, or another teacher about an environmental concern or activity at school.

7. Contribute to a class dictionary or thesaurus about the environment.

8. Design a class or school bulletin board to recognize an author or artist who cares for living things and the environment.

9. Design a class or school bulletin board to show ways people care for the environment.

10. Design a classroom door cover with writing samples about the environment.

11. Design small ecological signs and posters to decorate your desk.

12. After going on a field trip, design a brochure for students in other classes who are preparing to take a similar trip. Include tips on planning the event, good manners as guests, being safe, responding to emergencies, staying close to a buddy, what to take, and the titles of interesting songs to sing and stories to tell on the bus, light rail, or train.

13. Discuss "Green Team" behavior on the schoolground (or school cafeteria or after school) and divide into "Green Team" groups to write a brief group handbook about what could be done by each child to maintain the environment.

14. Greet one another when arriving in the room and take time to give your friends the time of day with an ecology anecdote. As an example, write down a sentence with some information you've learned about caring for the environment that you want

to tell others to represent your "time of day" activity. As your name is called in roll call, give your written message to someone in the class.

15. Make individual and collaborative "ecological" books of different writing types—narrative, expository, poetry, and persuasive writing.
16. Make signs and posters about your environmental studies and display on classroom door or in school hall: what is being studied, what books are being read, and what was learned last week.
17. Plan for an upcoming field trip related to ecology, e.g., visiting a tree farm, and make lists of what needs to be done to prepare for the trip.
18. Publish an individual, class, or school newspaper about ecology.
19. Publish a class (or school) handbook about what helps the environment at school.
20. Publish an end-of-year class "ecological yearbook."
21. Publish programs and background notes for a class or school production about caring for living things and the environment.
22. Publish an ecological classroom magazine.
23. Record what signs are needed in the class or at school—perhaps more posters with captions are needed to advertise "Protect the Environment" or "Don't Dump" or other messages of environmental interest.
24. Write your ecological goals for the day/week—what you want to do and learn about environmental awareness.
25. Write in journals about what went on during the day that related to protecting the environment, and record some of the topics you may want to suggest for the next day's environmental news chart in the classroom.
26. Write about how far you got in reaching your goals related to caring for the environment for the day (or summarize what you learned about environmental awareness during the school day/week).

## 266 Language Arts and Environmental Awareness

27. Write a letter on behalf of the class to invite an environmental specialist to speak to the whole group.

28. Write down any questions you want to ask an environmental specialist during a class interview, using the questions to role-play some interview situations, and writing suggestions for improving your interviews to add to a collaborative class handbook about "How to Interview."

29. Write a letter to the editor of a local newspaper or to a government representative in the city, country, state, or nation to show concern/interest about something current related to an environmental news release.

30. Write suggestions for environmental improvements in the class and school to drop in a class or school suggestions box.

31. Write friendship cards with an ecology theme to say hello to a new student, good-bye to a child who is leaving, or get well to peers in the group.

32. Write brief autobiographical sketches to tell what you do to care for the environment. These can be included in the friendship cards as gifts for children who are newcomers; as lively, entertaining, cheery stories for friends who are ill; or as momentos for children who are leaving the area.

33. Write favorite poems related to living creatures on friendship cards or write down book titles of favorite endangered animal stories recommended for a recipient of a friendship card.

34. Write "Environmental News on a Chart" to review what was done/learned the day before in school about caring for the environment.

35. Others suggested by the children.

**Home Activity**

Invite your child to fill a small discarded clear container or box with some items from an earthworm's environment, and make layers of different colored earth. Your child can collect soil samples, grass, herbs, pebbles, cotton, stones, twigs, leaves, and so on. Have your child observe an earthworm in the container to see how long it takes the worm, a strong underground burrower, to stir the soil up into a well-mixed mixture. Have your child write his or her observations about the earthworm's contributions to the soil to display with the container or box.

- **Patent, Dorothy Hinshaw (1989).** *Children Save the Rain Forest.* Illustrated by Dan L. Perlman. New York: Cobblehill. Ages 9–11.

**Environmental context:** Importance of rain forest to global ecology

Patent's book gives a child information about the ecosystem of a tropical rain forest in Costa Rica and its living creatures, which include the strangler fig, white-faced monkey, and toucan. The differences among the various rain forests are mentioned along with their importance to our planet's ecology. The author discusses several factors that cause people to cut down the forests and points out that solutions to keep them from disappearing do not come easily. Full-color photographs.

**Activity: "Protecting a Disappearing Habitat"**

**Language arts focus:** To participate in a group discussion; to write a brief report; to use capitals and punctuation marks appropriately

Talk with the whole group about the history and the ongoing activities of people involved in establishing the International Children's Rain Forest organization. Discuss the economic and social factors that compel people to cut the trees in a rain forest. Ask the children to consider how they, too, can contribute to protecting this rapidly disappearing habitat. Have them put their thoughts in writing as a brief report. They may suggest not using aerosol cans, recycling, caring for the habitat of living creatures, and so on. Let them exchange papers and give feedback to one another about the use of capitals and punctuation marks.

**Home Activity**

Select a magazine illustration of a rain forest (or have your child draw a rain forest scene) and affix a small inexpensive mirror in the center of it so your child can see his or her reflection. Point out that your child can be a part of the worldwide community that cares for earth's rain

**268** Language Arts and Environmental Awareness

forests and can see him- or herself as part of this action by looking in the mirror. Invite your child to sketch or draw a scene to show what he or she can do to help care for the environment and display it beneath the mirror.

■ **Politzer, Annie (1972).** *My Journals and Sketchbooks by Robinson Crusoe.* Illustrated by the author. New York: Harcourt Brace Jovanovich. Ages 10 up.

**Environmental context:** Value of mapping the environment

Politzer's book includes a fictionalized account about a hero based on a real-life adventure, and in the text a reader "discovers" that Robinson Crusoe's "manuscript" has been found in a trunk in an old Scottish manor house. Brief journal entries date from October 3, 1659 to May 7, 1684, and the drawings show a map of the island on which Crusoe was stranded, sketches of the scenes in his unfamiliar environment, and a plan of his house with objects such as a "basket of turtle eggs" and "snares for rats" labeled for readers. The steps Crusoe followed to weave baskets and to make a ship in a bottle, indications of ways he interacted with his environment, are included. Black line drawings.

**Activity: "A Yard Map"**

**Language arts focus:** To draw a map and explain the map in writing; to read aloud written explanations; to rewrite sentences as needed

Mention to the children that some of the illustrator's drawings in the book show Crusoe's map of the island, and tell them they will have an activity to make a map of their own to depict an imaginary island they will create based on the environment in their backyard, front yard, or a nearby grassy area at school or in the neighborhood. Have them consider what living things will be in their island habitats. Discuss the question, "How many living things will be enough to create a viable food chain?" When the maps are drawn, have children explain their maps in writing and meet with a partner in the group to look at one another's maps and read aloud the explanations of their work. They should provide feedback about the food chains that were included or any unclear portions of the maps. If needed, encourage the original writers to rewrite sentences in their explanations. To provide feedback to one another, the children can participate in the following procedures:

1. Have one partner read his or her original explanation as the other partner writes down his/her observations and suggestions for revisions of the writing.

2. After the reading, let the listening partner tell his or her comments to the author, giving positive input and making suggestions for improvement. Mention to children that a listening partner can start feedback by beginning with compliments and positive comments about the writing. "Be fair" and "be honest" are suggested as additional guidelines. If needed, a "Partner Checklist for Writing Improvements" can be developed in a class meeting with suggestions by the children and used in the feedback partnerships.

3. The author partner can accept or reject the ideas with the goal of improving any weak spots to make the explanation stronger.

4. When an author partner gets suggestions for reorganizing the explanation, he or she may cut the written explanation apart in sentences or paragraphs. If desired, the author can move the pieces of paper into new arrangements until he/she determines the best order. The revised explanation can be taped to blank paper. If needed, the author can rewrite or copy the explanation until the writing flows smoothly on the page to the writer's satisfaction.

**Home Activity**

To help your child learn to proofread his or her writing with a tape recorder, show your child how the equipment is used and ask your child to dictate his/her writing into a tape recorder, pausing after each sentence. Then, have your child play back the tape and listen as he/she silently reads from the writing. The pause after each sentence on the tape gives your child the time to write further or to turn off the recorder while finishing the writing. As an option, you can read your child's writing aloud into a tape recorder, then play the tape and have your child follow along with the writing to proofread the words.

### 270 Language Arts and Environmental Awareness

■ **Pringle, Laurence (1975).** *Chains, Webs and Pyramids.* Illustrated by Jan Atkins. New York: T. Y. Crowell. Ages 9–11.

**Environmental context:** Food chains

Pringle's book describes the steps in nature in various food chains, food webs, and food pyramids and discusses their importance in the maintenance of life and the flow of energy in nature from one living thing to another. For example, a diagram of a food web shows all the energy pathways that are in it. A web that shows many energy paths is more congested than a simple food chain. Ecological pyramids beginning with food produced by plants are diagrammed with broad bases and narrow tops to show steps in a food pathway. An index is included. Black-and-white drawings for illustrations.

**Activity: "Food Pyramid"**

**Language arts focus:** To participate in a discussion; to diagram and write sentences related to topic

Discuss with the children the simple food chain of grass to cow to humans and tell children they will have the opportunity to transform this information into a diagram of an ecological pyramid. Point out that an ecological pyramid begins with food produced by plants diagrammed on a broad base, then shows steps going upward in a food pathway, and culminates in a narrow top. Diagram an example on the board similar to the following one:

**Food Pyramid**

Decomposers
Meat eaters
Plant eaters
Plants

Ask the children to transform the information in this food chain into a food pyramid diagram of their own.

As a follow-up activity, tell the children that sometimes they will see lists of items similar to the food pyramid in the printed material they read and that they can write sentences from this information. Tell them they will have an activity to use the list in the previous food pyramid to make it include more information so they can write food pyramid sentences. Copy the food pyramid on the board. Elicit the children's suggestions about examples to write on the right side of the pyramid list.

| Food Pyramid | Examples |
|---|---|
| Meat eaters | Cat |
| Plant eaters | Bird |
| Plants | Tree |

With the children's help, write some brief pyramid sentences on the board that include the information from the two lists. An example might be, "A cat is a type of meat eater." Have children dictate or write sentences for all of the pyramid items. Further, ask the children to look for lists related to environmental awareness in printed material and encourage them to show the lists to the whole group. Engage the children in writing several complete sentences from the examples in the lists they find.

### Home Activity

Present your child with the items in a particular food chain printed on index cards, and mix them up so they are not in the correct order. Read the food chain list together and have your child rearrange the food chain index cards in order. If appropriate, write a food pyramid with your child that leads up to your child's favorite foods.

■ **Pringle, Laurence (1995). *Vanishing Ozone: Protecting Earth from Ultraviolet Radiation.*** New York: Morrow. Ages 9–14.

**Environmental context:** Evidence of thinning ozone layer

Pringle's informative book involves a reader in learning about the hardworking scientists who collect evidence about Earth's crisis—its thinning ozone layer. The informative text explains the ozone molecule and goes on to describe the groups who affect the ozone situation, e.g., industrialists, environmentalists, and governments, who all have their points of view about what is happening to the ozone layer. Technical terms are included in the author's discussion about how the changing ozone can affect humans, animals, plants, and the supply of natural resources. Includes diagrams and maps. Black-and-white photographs.

**Activity: "Thinning Ozone"**

**Language arts focus:** To participate in buzz groups; to conduct research; to use appropriate capitalization and punctuation in writing letters

Have the children divide into buzz groups (small groups of three or four) and discuss ways they can take action on the thinning ozone layer, in preparation for writing on the topic. Let them research addresses of governmental agencies and environmental groups in local directories. Next, have the children write their letters of interest, making sure they use capitalization and punctuation where needed, and inquire about what is going on to attend to this issue. Have them include a self-addressed and stamped envelope for a return reply.

**Home Activity**

Invite your child to contact a local governmental or state authority to inquire about any ozone protection programs. Ask, "Are there any such programs in our area? If not, to whom could you inquire about the current state of the thinning ozone issue?"

- **Talbott, Hudson, and Mark Greenberg (1996).** *The Jungle Adventures of Alex Winters.* Illustrations by Hudson Talbott. New York: Putnam Group. Ages 9–11.

**Environmental context:** Rain forest habitat

In this story, Alex Winters, a sixth-grader, is on his way to visit his parents, both anthropologists, when his plane crashes in the Amazon jungle. Alex and the injured pilot are taken to the village of the Yanomamis, meaning "fierce people." He waits for the pilot to recover and writes daily diary entries to describe what happens and record how the Yanomamis exist day by day in their rain forest habitat. Full-color photographs.

**Activity: "Story Questions"**

**Language arts focus:** To use appropriate capitalization and punctuation in writing questions and answers about a story; to comment on use of capitals and punctuation marks

Ask the children to write their questions about the story on index cards and put them in a container. Encourage them to write ingenious and interesting ones: "What would it be like if Alex thought he was a pilot? What would it be like if Alex imagined he was larger than he was? If he were smaller? If he changed families and became the son of one of the "fierce" people? If in the middle of his adventure, Alex woke up and realized it was all a dream?"

Have the children each select a card and then write something about the question on it. Have the children trade cards and ask volunteers to read their questions and responses aloud to the whole group. Elicit comments from the readers about the use of capitals and punctuation marks.

**Home Activity**

Invite your child to make a paper jungle with construction paper, and green and purple lights, and then tape jungle sounds to play as part of the environment. Suggest that your child use tissue paper to make leaves and add dried flowers to the habitat. If desired, suggest that your child use gold glitter to sprinkle on the leaves to represent sunlight. Have your child write and describe what he or she did to make the jungle exhibit on an index card to place by the display. Encourage the use of capitals and punctuation marks where needed. Invite other family members to see the display.

■ **Thornhill, Jan (1992).** *A Tree in a Forest.* Illustrated by the author. New York: Simon & Schuster. Ages 9–11.

**Environmental context:** Importance of fallen log

Thornhill's book is a story about the life of a maple tree beginning as a sprout on a fallen log and growing into a shelter for animals. Over two hundred years later, the tree is weakened by storms and falls to the ground, where a new sprout grows from its decaying wood. The illustrations are suitable for a point-of-view discussion since they show the same location in different seasons in different years. Full-color illustrations.

**Activity: "A Point of View"**

**Language arts focus:** To summarize; to use appropriate capitalization and punctuation when writing from another point of view

Tell the children that they will have the opportunity to think of a possible role to take (other than their own) when writing a viewpoint about the value of fallen trees in the forests. Ask the children to think of ways to summarize what they have learned from one of several points of view and use capitals and punctuation marks where needed in the sentences. Talk about these points of view related to a study of a forest habitat and allow plenty of time for the children to consider different possibilities for selecting an audience and a form such as one of the following:

1. To select a point of view, could the children write from an animal's viewpoint? From the viewpoint of a fallen log or living tree in the rain forest? From the viewpoint of a scientist living today? From the viewpoint of a scientist who is concerned about cleaning up the environment?
2. To select an audience, who could the children write to? What aspect of the topic could be selected?
3. To select form, in which format do the children want their writing to take place—informal and casual letters, news articles, outlines, and reports? Have them also consider writing the letter in one of the following ways:
   - To someone other than the teacher;
   - As a conversation among two or more people;
   - As a newspaper article;
   - As a travel brochure;
   - As a telephone conversation;
   - As a script for a play.

After decisions are made, ask the children to develop their writing from a viewpoint other than their own. For example, to write from the log's point of view, the children can imagine that they are the log on the ground in daylight, at night, and in different types of weather. Some living plants and animals are nearby. They can write about what it feels like to fall to the ground and tell what this reminds them of—perhaps another tree that was destroyed by lightning or a forest fire. The log has its own private thoughts about what is happening. The log thinks about other situations that are like the one it sees happening around it. The log can tell what the other living things are doing.

To complete their writing activity, have the children write to someone other than the teacher and use a form different from the usual paragraph. Ask them to team up with a partner and read one another's writing and make suggestions for sentence revisions and additions, deletions, or changes related to the use of capitals and punctuation marks.

**Home Activity**

Invite your child to write from a viewpoint other than his or her own and prepare it for submission to one of the many children's magazines that publish a child's writing and art work. Have your child look at the list of periodicals in the appendix entitled "Periodicals That Publish Children's Work" and select one or two addresses to write for guidelines before submitting his or her writing for publication.

■ **Whitfield, Philip, Dr. (1989).** *Can the Whales Be Saved?* Illustrations from The Natural History Museum in Washington, DC. New York: Viking/Kestrel. Ages 9 up.

**Environmental context:** Ecological problems

Whitfield's book widely explores the social dimension of ecological problems such as toxic waste and acid rain and asks questions not only about the whales but also about the natural world and threats to its survival. The topics range from plants and animals that are successful in surviving to what an ordinary person can do to help save the planet's natural environment. The author suggests ways a reader can help: by putting earth first, taking part in conservation projects that help rain forest survival, conserving wildlife, using safe energy sources, and recycling scarce resources. An interested reader can begin in a simple way by not using aerosol cans, by recycling packaging, and by growing wild flowers for butterflies and insects. Glossary included. Black-and-white sketches and photographs for illustrations.

**Activity: "Questions and answers"**

**Language arts focus:** To use appropriate capitalization and punctuation in writing questions and answers; to conduct research

Have the children write their own questions about threats to living things or the natural environment and hand the paper to another child. You can emphasize the use of capitals at the beginning of questions and proper placement of the question mark at the end. The child who receives the paper writes the answers after researching the topic (you can emphasize the use of capitals at the beginning of answers and proper placement of the period or exclamation mark at the end). Have the questions and answers returned to the original question-writer and ask volunteers to write some of their questions on an overhead transparency to show the use of capitals and question marks and then read the answers aloud to the whole group.

**Home Activity**

Encourage your child to write his or her views about caring for the environment to people in the wider community—editors of newspapers, authors and illustrators of children's books, resource people, or representatives of government—and invite your child to write a letter of inquiry to one or more of these groups. Your child can inquire about the activities these organizations perform to promote environmental awareness and care for the environment and its inhabitants. Further, encourage your child to ask questions about the environment and what he or she can do to protect it. See Appendix I: Environmental Agencies and Organizations for addresses.

# Appendix I ▪ Environmental Agencies and Organizations

In the following list are addresses of some agencies interested in promoting ecological awareness and caring for and protecting creatures and the environment as valued living things and sensitive habitats.

American Forestry Association
    1516 P Street NW
    Washington, DC 20005

American Geological Institute
    422 King Street
    Alexandria, VA 22302

American Museum of Natural History
    Central Park West at 79th Street
    New York, NY 10024

Care for the Earth
    PO Box 289
    Sacramento, CA 94101

Center for Environmental Education
    881 Alma Real Drive, Suite 300
    Pacific Palisades, CA 90272

Center for Marine Observation
    1725 De Sales Street, NW
    Washington, DC 20036

The Children's Rainforest
    PO Box 936
    Lewiston, ME 04240

Coastal Conservation Association
    4801 Woodway Street
    Houston, TX 77036

The Cousteau Society, Inc.
    930 West 21st Street
    Newfolk, VA 23517

## 278  Language Arts and Environmental Awareness

Defenders of Wildlife
1244 19th Street, NW
Washington, DC 20036

Environmental Protection Agency
Environmental Education Division
Washington, DC 20460
c/o George Walker, Environmental Education Specialist
(for grants or projects that focus on improving teaching skills and educating the community about the environment)

Friends of the Earth
530 7th Street, SE
Washington, DC 20003

The Fund for Animals, Inc.
200 West 57th Street
New York, NY 10019

Greenpeace, Inc.
1436 U Street, NW
Washington, DC 20007

Hug the Earth
PO Box 621
Wayne, PA 19087

International Wildlife Coalition
70 East Falmouth Highway
Falmouth, MA 02531

National Arbor Day Foundation
100 Arbor Avenue
Nebraska City, NE 68410

National Audubon Society
950 Third Avenue
New York, NY 10022

National Geographic Society
17th and M Streets, NW
Washington, DC 20036

National Wildlife Federation
1400 16th Street, NW
Washington, DC 20036

The Nature Conservancy
1815 North Lynn Street
Arlington, VA 22209

New York Zoological Society
185th Street and Southern Boulevard
Bronx, NY 10460

Sierra Club
730 Polk Street
San Francisco, CA 94109

U.S. Environmental Protection Agency
Office of Communications and Public Affairs
401 M Street, SW. Pm-211B
Washington, DC 20460

The Wilderness Society
1400 I Street, NW
Washington, DC 20005

World Wildlife Fund, U.S.
1250 24th Street, NW
Washington, DC 20037

# Appendix II ▪ Periodicals That Publish Children's Work

*Boys Life.* Boy Scouts of America, 1325 Walnut Hill Lane, Irving, TX 75038. Interest in letters to the editor and jokes.

*Chart Your Course!* G/CT Publishing Co., Inc., Box 6448, Mobile, AL 3660-0448. Interest in different formats—poetry, plays, music, photography, artwork, activities.

*Chickadee.* 59 Front Street East, Toronto, Ontario M5E 1B3. Artwork, jokes, and riddles of Canadian children.

*Child Life.* Children's Better Health Institute, Benjamin Franklin Literary & Medical Society, Inc., PO Box 10681, Des Moines, IA 50336. Interest in health and reading.

*Children's Digest.* Children's Better Health Institute, Benjamin Franklin Literary & Medical Society, Inc., PO Box 10681, Des Moines, IA 50336. Interest in exercise, health, nutrition and sports, poetry, health questions, and expression of opinions.

*Cricket.* Open Court Publishing Co., 1058 Eighth St., LaSalle, IL 61301. Accepts letters to the editor and has poetry and art contests.

*Current Health I.* Curriculum Innovations, Inc., PO Box 310, Highwood, IL 60040. Accepts questions about health.

*Ebony Jr.* Johnson Publishing Co. Inc., 820 South Michigan Ave., Chicago, IL 60605. Sponsors annual writing contest, accepts poetry and artwork and letters to the editor. Intended for African American children.

*Faces: The Magazine about People.* Cobblestone Publishing Inc., 20 Grove St., Petersborough, NH 03458. Accepts letters and drawings related to geography, world culture, and society.

*Highlights for Children.* 803 Church St., Honesdale, PA 18431. Accepts letters to the editor, poems, pictures, jokes, stories, and craft ideas.

*Humpty Dumpty's Magazine.* Children's Better Health Institute, Benjamin Franklin Literary & Medical Society, Inc., PO Box 10681, Des Moines, IA 50336. Accepts artwork related to health and health habits.

*Jack and Jill.* Children's Better Health Institute, Benjamin Franklin Literary & Medical Society, Inc., PO Box 10681, Des Moines, IA 50336. Accepts jokes, riddles, poems and questions from readers about health, exercise, nutrition and safety.

*Muppet Magazine.* Telepictures Publishing Inc., 300 Madison Ave., New York, NY 10017. Accepts letters to editor and pictures, questions, and invention ideas.

*Odyssey.* Astro Media, Kalmbach Publishing Co., 625 E. St. Paul Ave., PO Box 92788, Milwaukee, WI 53202. Accepts questions, opinions, pictures, puzzles, and poems related to astronomy and space.

*Owl.* 50 Front St. East, Toronto, Ontario M5E 1B3. Accepts work of Canadian children related to Canada, environment, and nature.

*Pathways.* Inky Trails Publishing PO Box 345, Middleton, ID 83644. Accepts art, jokes, poetry, puzzles, and stories on wide range of topics.

*Penny Power.* Penny Power Magazine, Consumers Union, 256 Washington St., Mount Vernon, NY 10553. Accepts letters to the editor related to consumer information for children.

*Prism.* 1040 Bayview Drive, Suite 223, Fort Lauderdale, FL 33304. Accepts poetry, fiction, information, art and photographs.

*Ranger Rick.* National Wildlife Federation, 1412 Sixteenth St., NW, Washington, DC 20036. Sponsors annual contest about writing end-

## Appendix II 281

ing to a story and accepts questions related to nature, reading, and science.

*Shoe Tree*. PO Box 356, Belvedere, NJ 07823. Accepts children's work but be sure to write for current guidelines.

*Stone Stoup*. PO Box 83, Santa Cruz, CA 95060. Accepts artwork and writings related to ways children communicate.

*Story Friends*. 616 Walnut Ave., Scottsdale, PA 15683. Stories for children that reinforce Christian values.

*Turtle: Magazine for Preschool Kids*. Children's Better Health Institute, Benjamin Franklin Literary & Medical Society, Inc., PO Box 10681, Des Moines, IA 50336. Accepts artwork about health and health habits.

*Wee Wisdom*. Unity School of Christianity, Unity Village, MO 64065. Accepts letters to the editor, words and definitions, poems and stories.

# Index of Book Titles, Authors, and Illustrators

*Advice for a Frog* (Schertle & Green), 70
Aiello, Laurel, 177–78
Aldis, Rodney, 129
Alvin, Virginia, 204
*The Amazing Apple Book* (Bourgeois), 110
*Amazon Basin* (Reynolds), 132
Amon, Aline, 205
*And Then There Was One: The Mysteries of Extinction* (Facklam & Johnson), 66
Andreasen, Dan, 133
*Animation: How to Draw Your Own Flipbooks, and Other Fun Ways to Make Cartoons Move* (Jenkins), 128
Appelhof, Mary, 122
Archambault, John, 57
Armour, Richard, 3
Arnold, Tim, 227
Arnosky, Jim, 49, 137
*Around the Pond: Who's Been Here?* (George), 11
Aruego, Jose, 134
Atkins, Jan, 270
*The Atlantic Salmon* (Lavies), 32
Atwood, Ann, 36

Babbitt, Natalie, 41
Bailey, Linda, 138
Baker, Jennie, 187
Baldwin, Pamela, 68

*Balloons and Other Poems* (Chandra), 25
Bang, Molly, 140
Baron, Virginia Olsen, 45
Barron, T. A., 243
Bash, Barbara, 229
*A Basket Full of White Eggs: Riddle-Poems* (Swann & Goembel), 38
*Bats, Bugs and Biodiversity: Adventures in the Amazonian Rain Forest* (Goodman & Doolittle), 156
Bauer, Erwin, 257
Bauer, Peggy, 257
*Beastie* (McHargue), 260
Behn, Harry, 6, 35
Benet, Rosemary, 109
Benet, Stephen Vincent, 109
Benjamin, Lea, 128
Bierhorst, John, 104
*Birds in the Bushes: A Story about Margaret Morse Nice* (Dunlap & Ramstad), 65
"Birds in the Rain" (McCord), 22
*Black Sky River* (Seymour & Andreasen), 133
*Blow Away Soon* (James & Vojtech), 123
Bonnet, Bob, 144
*A Book of Americans* (Benet & Benet), 109
Bosse, Malcolm, 157
Bostock, Marian, 213
Bostock, Mike, 196

283

## Index of Book Titles, Authors, and Illustrators

Bouchard, Dave, 85
Bourgeois, Paulette, 110
Bowden, Joan Chase, 86, 92
Brady, Irene, 237
Bradshaw, Reagan, 258
Braren, Loretta Trezzo, 119, 175
Brickman, Robin, 220
Brinkloe, Julie, 230
Brown, Marc, 86
Brown, Mary Barrett, 143
Bruchac, Joseph, 89, 101
Brynjolson, Rhian, 222
Buchanan, Debby, 7
Buchanan, Ken, 7
*Buffalo Woman* (Goble), 107
Bunting, Eve, 8, 51
Burton, Virginia Lee, 231
Butterfield, Moira, 245

Caduto, Michael, 89, 101
Cameron, Elizabeth, 233
*Can I Help?* (Janovitz), 14
*Can the Whales Be Saved?* (Whitfield & Natural History Museum), 275
Carson, Rachel, 158, 247
*The Cartoon Guide to the Environment* (Gonick & Outwater), 254
*The Case of the Missing Cutthroats: An Ecological Mystery* (George), 148
Cassady, Sylvia, 26
Castaldo, Nancy Fusco, 119
Catrow, David, 197
*Chains, Webs and Pyramids* (Pringle & Atkins), 270
Chandra, Deborah, 25
*Chattanooga Sludge* (Bang), 140
Cherry, Lynne, 189
*Chessie: A Chesapeake Bay Story* (Wildlife Services), 193
*Chickens Aren't the Only Ones* (Heller), 13
*Chico Mendes: Fight for the Forest* (De Stefano), 212
*Children Save the Rain Forest* (Patent & Perlman), 267
Clement, Claude, 90

Cohlene, Terri, 105
*Come Back, Salmon* (Cone & Wheelwright), 190
*Compost! Growing Gardens from Your Garbage* (Glaser & Hariton), 121
Cone, Molly, 190, 196
Cooper, Ann, 201
*Creepy, Crawly Caterpillars* (Facklam & Facklam), 121
*Cricket Songs* (Behn), 35
*Crinkleroot's Guide to Knowing the Birds* (Arnosky), 137
*Crinkleroot's Guide to Knowing Butterflies and Moths* (Arnosky), 49
*Crocodile Smile: 10 Songs of the Earth as the Animals See It* (Weeks & Ehlert), 63
Crossland, Caroline, 10
Custer, Arthur, 19

Daly, Niki, 88
Davie, Helen K., 27
de Paola, Tomie, 91, 93
De Stefano, Susan, 212
*Deep Dream of the Rain Forest* (Bosse), 157
Dekker, Midas, 248
Demi, 36
*A Desert Scrapbook: Dawn to Dusk in the Sonoran Desert* (Wright-Frierson), 42
*A Desert Trip* (Steiner & Himler), 60
*Deserts* (Aldis), 129
Dewey, Ariane, 134
Di Fiori, Lawrence, 70
Dillon, Diane & Leo, 104
Donnelley, Effie, 195
Donnelley, Marlene Hill, 238
Doolittle, Michael J., 156
Downer, Ann, 144
*The Dragonfly's Tale* (Rodanas), 100
Dunlap, Julie, 65

*The Earth Book* (Jennings), 258
*The Earth Is Sore: Native Americans on Nature* (Amon), 205
*Earth Songs* (Livingston), 205
*Earth Verses and Water Rhymes* (Lewis), 17

## Index of Book Titles, Authors, and Illustrators  285

*Earthkeepers: Observers and Protectors of Nature* (Keene), 214
*Earthworms, Dirt and Rotten Leaves: An Exploration in Ecology* (McLaughlin & Shetterly), 262
*Echoes for the Eye: Poems to Celebrate Patterns in Nature* (Esbensen & Davie), 27
*Ecology* (Pollock), 167
Edwards, Hazel, 192
Edwards, Richard, 10
Ehlert, Lois, 63
*The Elders Are Watching* (Bouchard & Vickers), 85
Emerling, Dorothy, 201
Endicott, James, 57
Esbensen, Barbara Juster, 27
*Everglades* (George & Minor), 213
*Evergreen, Everblue* (Raffi), 78
Evyndson, Peter, 222

Faber, Doris, 206
Faber, Harold, 206
Facklam, Margery, 66, 146
Facklam, Paul, 146
Fielder, John, 243
*50 Simple Things Kids Can Do to Recycle* (Montez), 163
*Fireflies, Fireflies, Light My Way* (London & Messier), 18
Fisher, Aileen, 194
Fleming, Denise, 52
Florian, Douglas, 62
*Flower Moon Song* (Mizumura), 36
*The Flute Player: An Apache Folktale* (Lacapa), 97
*Fly with the Wind, Flow with the Water* (Atwood), 36
*Folks Call Me Appleseed John* (Glass), 95
Foreman, Michael, 122
*Forest Log* (Newton & Brady), 237
Franklin, Mark, 74
Fraser, Mary Ann, 250
*Freebies for Kids and Parents Too!*, 219
*Freebies: The Magazine with Something for Nothing*, 219

Fregosi, Claudia, 195
*Fresh Paint* (Merriam), 42
Friedman, Judi, 209
*The Friendly Wolf* (Goble), 108
Fritz, Jean, 210
Froman, Robert, 29
Frost, Robert, 31

Gal, Laszlo, 113
*Gaylord Nelson: A Day for the Earth* (Shulman & Rogers), 213
George, Jean Craighead, 148, 152, 154, 155, 213, 151
George, Lindsay Barrett, 11
Gershator, Phillis, 94
Gibbons, Gail, 252
*The Gift of the Tree* (Tressault), 61
"The Gift Outright" (Frost), 32
Gilmmerveen, Ulco, 120
Glass, Andrew, 95
Glaser, Linda, 121
Goble, Paul, 107–08
Goembel, Ponder, 38
*The Golden Hive* (Behn), 6
Gonick, Larry, 254
Goodman, Susan E., 156
Gordon, Bernard L., 68, 70
Gordon, Esther S., 68, 70
*Grandpa Art's Nature Songs for Children* (Custer), 19
*Grandpa's Mountain* (Reeder), 219
*The Great Ball Game: A Muskogee Story* (Bruchac), 89
*The Green Book* (Walsh), 179
Green, Mimi, 94
Green, Norman, 71
Greenberg, Mark, 272
*The Greenhouse Effect* (Hare & Khan), 71
Grindley, Sally, 122
Guiberson, Brenda, 54
*A Guide to Print and Nonprint Materials Available from Organizations, Industry, Governmental Agencies and Specialized Publishers*, 219

*Haiku: The Mood of the Earth* (Atwood), 36
*Haiku Vision* (Atwood), 36

## 286  Index of Book Titles, Authors, and Illustrators

*Hands-On Ecology* (Wong), 182
Hare, Tony, 71
Hariton, Anca, 121
Harlan, Judith, 158
Haseley, Dennis, 195
Heinrich, Berne, 255
Heller, Ruth, 13
Henricksson, John, 158
*Here Comes the Recycling Truck!* (Seltzer), 199
Heuer, Kenneth, 57
Hewitt, Kathryn, 8
*Hiawatha* (Longfellow & Jeffers), 16
*Hidden Pictures: Find a Feast of Camouflaged Creatures* (Woods & Palin), 135
Himler, Ronald, 55, 60
Hirschi, Ron, 257
Hodges, Margaret, 88
*Honi's Circle of Trees* (Gershator & Green), 94
*The House on Maple Street* (Pryor), 170
*How Come the Best Clues Are Always in the Garbage?* (Bailey), 138
*How to Make Pop-Ups* (Irvine), 129
*How to Raise Butterflies* (Norsgaard), 131

*I Never Told and Other Poems* (Livingston), 34
*If an Auk Could Talk* (Gordon, Gordon, & Baldwin), 68
*In a Spring Garden*, (Lewis), 36
*In the Eyes of the Cat: Japanese Poetry for All Seasons* (Demi), 36
*In the Forest* (Cooper & Emerling), 201
*In the Heart of the Village: The World of the Indian Bunyan Tree* (Bash), 229
*Insects Are My Life* (McDonald & Johnson), 236
*Into the Deep Forest with Henry David Thoreau* (Murphy & Keisler), 165
Irvine, Joan, 129
*It Rained on the Desert Today* (Buchanan, Buchanan, & Tracy), 7

*Jackrabbit* (London & Ray), 235
Jacques, Laura, 130
James, Betsy, 123
*Jan and the Great One* (Evyndson & Brynjolson), 222

*Janice Van Cleave's Earth Science for Every Kid: 101 Easy Experiments That Really Work* (Van Cleave & Aiello), 177
*Janice Van Cleave's Oceans for Every Kid: Easy Activites That Make Learning Science Fun* (Van Cleave & Aiello), 178
Janovitz, Marily, 14
Jaspersohn, William, 126
Jeffers, Susan, 16
Jenkins, Patrick, 128
Jennings, Gary, 258
"Johnny Appleseed" (Benet & Benet), 209
*Johnny Appleseed* (Lindbergh), 110
Johnson, Pamela, 66
Johnson, Paul Brett, 236
*The Jungle Adventures of Alex Winters* (Talbott & Greenberg), 272

*Ka-ha-si and the Loon: An Eskimo Legend* (Cohlene & Reasoner), 105
Kane, Henry B., 76
Kastner, Jill, 98
Keen, Dan, 144
Keene, Ann T., 214
*Keepers of the Animals: Native American Stories and Wildlife Activities for Children* (Caduto & Bruchac), 101
Keisler, Karen, 165
Khan, Aziz, 71
*The Kids' Nature Book* (Milord), 162
*The Kids' Wildlife Book: Exploring Animal Worlds through Indoor/Outdoor Experiences* (Shedd & Braren), 175
Knapp, Brian, 74
Koch, Michelle, 128
Kroll, Virginia, 130
Kudlinski, Kathleen V., 158

Lacapa, Michael, 97
Lasky, Kathryn, 196–97
Lathem, Edward Connery, 32
Lauber, Patricia, 216
Lavies, Barbara, 32
Lavies, Bianca, 159
Lawlor, Laurie, 108
Leaf, Munro, 78

# Index of Book Titles, Authors, and Illustrators 287

*The Legend of the Bluebonnet* (de Paola), 91
*The Legend of the Indian Paintbrush* (de Paola), 93
*Let's Reduce and Recycle*, 194
Lewis, J. Patrick, 17
Lewis, Richard, 36
*The Lincoln Writing Dictionary for Children*, 44
Lindbergh, Reeve, 110
*Listen to the Rain* (Martin, Archambault, & Endicott), 57
*The Little House.* (Burton), 231
*The Living Earth* (Schmid), 239
Livingston, Myra Cohn, 34, 205
*Loggerhead Turtle: Survivor from the Sea* (Scott & Sweet), 78
London, Jonathan, 18, 235
Longfellow, Henry Wadsworth, 16
*The Lorax* (Seuss), 22, 220
Luenn, Nancy, 55, 98

McCloskey, Robert, 20
McCord, David, 76
McDonald, Megan, 236
McHargue, Georgess, 260
McLaughlin, Molly, 262
*The Mammoth, the Owl, and the Crab* (Fregosi), 195
Martin, Jr., Bill, 57
Marzani, Carl, 160
Merriam, Eve, 42
Messier, Linda, 18
Miller, Moira, 36
Milord, Susan, 162
Minor, Wendell, 213
Mizumura, Kazue, 36
*Monarch Butterflies: Mysterious Travelers* (Lavies), 159
Montez, Michele, 163
Moore, Bobbie, 218
*More Cricket Songs: Japanese Haiku* (Behn), 35
*Mud* (Ray & Stringer), 22
Murphy, Jim, 165
*My Father Doesn't Know about the Woods and Me* (Haseley), 195

*My Journals and Sketchbooks by Robinson Crusoe* (Politzer), 268

*The Nature Book: Discovering, Exploring, Observing, Experimenting with Plants and Animals at Home and Outdoors* (Dekker), 248
*Nature's Green Umbrella: Tropical Rain Forests* (Gibbons), 252
*Natural History from A to Z: A Terrestrial Sampler* (Arnold), 227
*Nature and the Environment* (Faber & Faber), 206
*Nature in a Nutshell for Kids* (Potter & Croce), 168
*Nature Projects for Young Scientists* (Rainis), 172
*Nature Walk* (Florian), 62
Newton, James R., 237
*Night Tree* (Bunting & Rand), 51
*Night Visitors* (Young), 114
Norsgaard, E. Jaedicker, 131

*An Ocean World* (Sis), 5
Olive, Jim, 258
*Once There Was a Passenger Pigeon* (Gordon, Gordon & Di Fiori), 70
*Once We Went on a Picnic* (Fisher), 194
*One at a Time* (McCord & Kane), 76–7
*One Day in the Tropical Rain Forest* (George), 152
Orr, Richard, 245
Outwater, Alice, 254
*An Owl in the House: A Naturalist Diary* (Heinrich), 255
*A Package for Miss Marshwater* (Donnelly), 195
*The Painter and the Wild Swans* (Clement), 90
Palin, Nicki, 135
Parnall, Peter, 59
Patent, Dorothy Hinshaw, 102, 267
Peet, Bill, 77
*The People Who Hugged Trees* (Rose & Safflund), 110, 112
Perlman, Dan L., 267
*Persephone and the Springtime, A Greek Myth* (Hodges), 88

## 288    Index of Book Titles, Authors, and Illustrators

*Peter's Place* (Grindley & Foreman), 122
Pitman, Blair, 258
*The Poetry of Robert Frost* (Lathem), 32
Politzer, Annie, 268
Pollock, Steve, 167
*Pond Buddies* (Lasky & Bostock), 196
*Pond Year* (Lasky & Bostock), 214
Potter, Jean, 168
Pringle, Laurence, 218, 270, 271
*The Processing and Recovery of Jon Thomas— Cool Cat!*, 194
Pryor, Bonnie, 170

*Quiet* (Parnall), 59

*Rachel Carson: The Environmental Movement* (Hendricksson), 158
*Rachel Carson: Pioneer of Ecology* (Kudlinski), 158
Raffi, 78
*Rainforests* (Aldis), 129
Rainis, Kenneth G., 172
Ramstad, Ralph L., 65
Rand, Ted, 51
Ransom, Candice F., 213
Ray, Deborah Kogan, 235
Ray, Mary Lyn, 22
*The Real Johnny Appleseed* (Lawlor & Thompson), 108
Reasoner, Charles, 105
*Recycling: Meeting the Challenge of the Trash Crisis* (Alvin & Silverstein), 204
Reeder, Carolyn, 219
Reynolds, Jan, 132
*Richard Orr's Nature Cross-Sections* (Butterfield & Orr), 245
*The Ring in the Prairie: A Shawnee Legend* (Bierhorst, Dillon & Dillon), 104
*A River Ran Wild* (Cherry), 189
Rodanas, Kristina, 100
Rogers, Teresa, 213
Romanova, Natalia, 85
Rood, Ronald, 238
*Roomrimes* (Cassady), 26–27
Root, Kimberly Bulcken, 213
Rose, Deborah, 110, 112

Russell, Helen Ross, 129

Safflund, Birgitta, 110
*Sanctuary: The Story of Three Arch Rocks* (Fraser), 250
*Sand Castle* (Wegen), 241
*Save Our Oceans and Coasts* (Hirschi, Bauer, & Bauer), 257
Schmid, Eleonore, 239
*Science Fair Projects: The Environment* (Bonnet, Keen, & Zweifal), 144
Scott, Jack Denton, 78
*Sea Full of Whales* (Armour), 3
*The Search for Spring* (Miller), 36
*Seeing Things* (Froman), 29, 77
Seltzer, Meyer, 199
Seuss, Dr. *pseud.* (Theodore Seuss Geisel), 22, 220
Seymour, Tres, 133
Shaw-Mackinnon, Margaret, 113
Shedd, Warner, 175
*She's Wearing a Dead Bird on Her Head* (Lasky & Catrow), 197
Shertle, Alice, 70
Shetterly, Robert, 262
Shulman, Jeffrey, 213
*The Siberian Crane* (Friedman), 209
*The Silent Spring* (Carson), 158, 247
Silverstein, Robert, 204
Simon, Hilda, 223
Simont, Marc, 202
Sis, Peter, 5
*Small Poems* (Worth & Babbitt), 41
*Small Worlds: A Field Trip Guide* (Russell), 129
*Snails of Land and Sea* (Simon), 223
*Song of the Ancient Forest* (Luenn & Kastner), 98
*Sounding the Alarm: A Biography of Rachel Carson* (Harlan), 158
*The Spider Web* (Brinkloe), 230
*Spoonbill Swamp* (Gulberson), 54
*Spring Pool: A Guide to the Ecology of Temporary Ponds* (Downer), 144
*Squish: A Wetland Walk* (Luenn & Himler), 55

## Index of Book Titles, Authors, and Illustrators   289

*Squishy, Misty, Damp and Muddy: The In-between World of Wetlands* (Cone), 196
Steiner, Barbara, 60, 102
*Stickybeak* (Edwards), 192
Stone, Lynn M., 176
Strete, Craig Kee, 134
Stringer, Lauren, 22
*Sunflower House* (Bunting & Hewitt), 8
*Sunny Days & Starry Nights: A Little Hands Nature Book* (Castaldo & Braren), 119
*Sunset in a Spider Web* (Baron), 45
*Swallows in the Birdhouse* (Swinburne & Brickman), 200
Swann, Brian, 38
*Sweet Magnolia* (Kroll & Jacques), 130
Sweet, Ozzie, 78
Swinburne, Stephen R., 200

*Taking Care of the Earth* (Pringle & Moore), 218
Talbott, Hudson, 272
*A Tale of Antarctica* (Gilmmerveen), 120
*Ten Tall Oak Trees* (Edwards & Crossland), 10
*Theodore Roosevelt* (Fritz & Tomes), 210
*There Lived a Wicked Dragon: An Environmental Coloring Book for Children and Adults,* 194
*There's an Owl in the Shower* (George), 154
*They Thought They Saw Him* (Strete, Aruego, & Dewey), 134
Thompson, Mary, 108
Thornhill, Jan, 273
*Thunder, Singing Sounds, and Other Wonders: Sound in the Atmsophere* (Heuer), 57–58
*Tiktala* (Shaw-Mackinnon & Gal), 113
*Timber! From Trees to Wood Products* (Jaspersohn), 126
*Time of Wonder* (McCloskey), 20
*To Walk in Wilderness: A Rocky Mountain Journal* (Barron & Fielder), 243
Tomes, Margot, 210
Tracy, Libba, 7
*A Tree in a Forest* (Thornhill), 273
*A Tree Is Nice* (Udry & Simont), 202

"Trees" (Behn), 6
Tressault, Alvin, 61
*Tunafish Sandwiches* (Wolcott & Zander), 135

Udry, Janice May, 202

Van Cleave, Janice, 177–78
*Vanishing Ozone: Protecting Earth from Ultraviolet Radiation* (Pringle), 271
Vickers, Roy Henry, 85
*Volcano* (Lauber), 216
Vojtech, Anna, 123

Walsh, Jill Paton, 179
*Water Sky* (George), 155
Weeks, Sarah, 63
Wegen, Ronald, 241
*Wetlands* (Rood & Donnelley), 238
*Wetlands* (Stone), 176
*Whale Brother* (Steiner), 102
*Whales: Giants of the Deep* (Patent), 102
*What Do We Know about Rainforests?* (Knapp & Franklin), 74
Wheelwright, Sidnee, 190
*When the Whippoorwill Calls* (Ransom & Root), 213
*Where Once There Was a Wood* (Fleming), 52
Whitfield, Philip, Dr., 275
*Who Cares?* (Leaf), 78
*Who Really Killed Cock Robin: An Ecological Mystery* (George), 251
*Why the Sun & Moon Live in the Sky* (Daly), 88, 92
*Why the Tides Ebb and Flow* (Bowden & Brown), 86
"The Wind" (McCord), 76
*Window* (Baker), 187
*Wings Along the Waterway* (Brown), 143
Wolcott, Patty, 135
Wong, Ovid K., 182
Woods, Audrey, 135
*World Water Watch* (Koch), 128
*Worms Eat My Garbage* (Appelhof), 122
Worth, Valerie, 41

## Index of Book Titles, Authors, and Illustrators

*The Wounded Earth: An Environmental Survey* (Marzani), 160
Wright-Frierson, Virginia, 42
*Writing for Kids* (Benjamin), 128
*The Wump World* (Peet), 128

*You Come Too, Favorite Poems of Young Readers* (Frost), 31

Young, Ed, 114

Zander, Hans, 135
*Zen ABC* (Zerner & Zerner), 45
Zerner, Amy, 45
Zerner, Jessie Spicer, 45
Zweifel, Frances, 144

# Subject Index

Activist, wildlife, 5
Activities, class:
  language, 3, 6, 9, 10, 12, 13, 14, 16, 17, 19, 20, 22, 25, 27, 29, 31, 33, 34, 36, 39, 41, 42, 45
  listening, 49, 51, 53, 54, 55, 59, 61, 62, 63, 65, 67, 68, 70, 72, 74, 76, 77, 79
  folk literature, 85, 87, 89, 90, 92, 93, 94, 96, 97, 99, 100, 102, 105, 106, 107, 108, 111, 113, 114
  reading, 119, 120, 121, 122, 124, 126, 128, 130, 132, 133, 135, 136, 137, 139, 140, 143, 145, 146, 149, 153, 154, 155, 157, 158, 159, 160, 162, 163, 165, 167, 168, 170, 172, 175, 176, 177, 178, 180, 182
  speaking, 187, 190, 191, 192, 194, 196, 197, 199, 201, 202, 204, 205, 207, 209, 211, 214, 215, 216, 218, 219, 221, 223
  writing, 227, 229, 230, 232, 234, 236, 237, 238, 240, 241, 243, 245, 248, 249, 250, 251, 252, 254, 256, 257, 258, 260, 263, 267, 268, 270, 272, 273, 274, 276
Activities, home:
  language, 5, 7, 8, 9, 11, 12, 13, 15, 17, 18, 19, 22, 23, 26, 28, 31, 32, 33, 35, 37, 40, 42, 44, 46
  listening, 50, 52, 53, 54, 57, 59, 60, 61, 62, 63, 66, 67, 69, 71, 73, 75, 77, 78, 80
  folk literature, 86, 88, 90, 91, 92, 94, 95, 96, 98, 99, 101, 103, 105, 106, 108, 112, 114, 115
  reading, 120, 121, 122, 123, 125, 127, 129, 131, 132, 134, 135, 136, 138, 140, 142, 144, 145, 147, 152, 153, 155, 156, 157, 158, 160, 161, 163, 165, 166, 168, 169, 171, 173, 176, 177, 178, 179, 181, 183
  speaking, 189, 190, 191, 193, 195, 196, 198, 200, 201, 203, 205, 206, 208, 210, 212, 214, 215, 217, 218, 220, 222, 224
  writing, 228, 230, 231, 232, 235, 236, 238, 239, 240, 241, 244, 247, 248, 249, 250, 251, 253, 255, 256, 258, 259, 262, 266, 267, 269, 271, 272, 273, 275
Adjectives, use of, 154
Advertisement, use of, 25, 36
Air. *See* Pollution, air
Air Quality Clearinghouse (Wash., DC), 216
Alligators, 18, 54
Alphabet book, 233
Amazon Basin, 132
American Forestry Association (Wash., DC), 277
American Geological Institute (VA), 277
American Museum of Natural History (NY), 277
Animation in books, 128–29
Antarctica, 120
Ants, 115
Apples, 108–10
Attentive listening, 49, 50, 62, 63, 74, 76, 79

**291**

## Subject Index

Audio tape recorder, use of, 102, 112
Auk, 68

Balance scales, simulated, 133
Banner, ecological, 26, 46, 133
Bats, 156
Biodiversity, 156
Biodynamic Farming and Gardening Association (Wash., DC), 216
Biography, 158, 206, 207, 210, 212, 213, 247
Biologist, marine, 247
Bird(s): backyard, 65; decreasing numbers of, 89, 133; feeders, 17; habitat, 200; sanctuary, 16. *See also* Auk, Condors, crane, eagle
Bowerman Basin (WA), 257
Brainstorming, 100, 111
Bugs. *See* Insects
Butterfly: attracting garden, 53; habitat, 49, 53, 159; life cycle, 49; monarch, 49, 159; raising, 131; trail, 52

Camouflage, for protection, 134–35
Capitalization, use of, 227, 244, 254, 267, 274
Carson, Rachel, 158, 206, 247
Cartoons, 128, 254
Carver, George Washington, 212
Caterpillars, 146
Center for Environmental Education (CA), 277
Center for Marine Observation (Wash., DC), 277
Character dialogue, 90, 194
Chattanooga Creek (TN), 140
Chemicals and damage, 158, 206, 247
The Children's Rainforest Agency (ME), 277
Cities, growth of, 187, 231
Coastal Conservation Association (TX), 277
Compost, 94, 121, 122
Condors, California, 69
Conservation, 202; Hall of Fame, 215; laws, 71
Consumer products, 139

Contamination: human, 142; oil, 122. *See also* Pollution
Conversation, one to one, 93, 187, 197
Couplet. *See* Poetry
Cousteau Society, The (VA), 277
Crane: Siberian, 209; Whooping, 69
Creatures: caring for, 192; oviparous, 13; returned to wild, 130
Critical analysis, 221; listening, 54

DDT, danger of, 158, 206, 247
Data, gathering, 36, 51, 62, 158, 221
Decision-making, 198
Defenders of Wildlife (Wash., DC), 277
Desert: animals, 8; appreciation of, 42; ecosystem, 7, 60; habitat, 129; Sonoran, 42
Diary: entries, 255, 272; writing in, 250
Dictionary, use of, 44, 253
Discussion: panel, 114, 199; point of view, 122; round table, 201; small group, 99, 216, 271; whole group, 100, 102, 107, 122, 191, 214, 218, 241, 252, 254, 267
Douglas, Marjory Stoneman, 212
Dragonfly, 100
Drama, 8, 59, 196, 223
Drawing, 12, 95, 205, 235

Eagle, bald, 69
Earth: care of, 214, 258, 267; fate of, 271
Earthworms, 122, 262
Ecology: global, 160, 258; local, 259
Ecology quilt, 132, 256
Ecosystem: desert, 60; everglades, 213; forests, 9, 237; wetlands, 55
Endangered animals, 63; fauna, 209, 223; sea turtles, 78; shore birds, 120, 143; protection of, 78, 257
Energy alternatives, 74
Environment: futuristic, 180; humans' effect on, 8, 10, 219; long ago, 89
Environmental, changes, 170; hazards, 144; Search Paper I, 144; Search Paper II, 150; survey, 149–52
Environmental Education Specialists (Wash., DC), 278

## Subject Index 293

Environmental Protection Agency (Wash., DC), 194
Eskimo legend, 105
Essay writing, 106, 155, 252
Experimentation: with animals, 172, 248; with plants, 172, 248
Exploring, 248
Extinct animals. *See* Auk, Passenger pigeons
Extinction, 66

Field trip guide, 109, 129, 138
Fireflies, 18
Flag, ecological, 132–33
Flipbooks, 128
Food: chain, 135, 148; pyramid, 251, 270–71; web, 270
Forests, old growth, 98, 237, 273
Free material, 94, 194, 219
Free verse. *See* Poetry
Friends of the Earth (Wash., DC), 278
Frost, Robert, 32
Fund for Animals, The (NY), 278
Futuristic environment, 180

Garbage, 138
Garbage buster, 139
Gardening, 9, 14, 121; catalogs, 15
Goodall, Jane, 212
Goose, Hawaiian, 69
Greenpeace (Wash., DC), 216

Habitat: desert, 60; disappearing, 42; ocean, 4; pond, 11; rain forest, 156, 252; swamp, 18, 54; wetlands, 176, 196, 238; woods, 52, 61, 86
Haiku. *See* Poetry
Hands-on activity, 21, 182
Harmony of life forms, 18, 19, 110
Honeybees, behavior of, 6
How and why tales, and natural phenomenon, 97
Hug the Earth Organization (PA), 278
Human Ecology Action League (Wash., DC), 216

Humans: effect on environment, 8, 10, 182; relationships with animals, 230

Information: book, 140, 143, 145; listening for, 99; transforming, 140
Insects, 236
Interdependence (of humans and environment), 110, 111, 119, 132, 165, 220, 239
International Wildlife Coalition (MA), 239, 278
Interviewing, 162, 202
Inquiry, 170

Johnny Appleseed, 95
Journal writing, 232, 243, 253, 268

Leaf sculpture, 11
Legends: Eskimo, 105; Japanese, 90; Jewish/Middle Eastern, 90; Native American, 91, 93, 97, 100–01, 104, 107
Legendary character, 94–95
Letter writing: business, 120, 276; personal, 86, 123, 238, 248
Library, use of, 81, 174, 178, 218, 262
Life cycles, 33
Life forms, respect for, 41, 76, 110, 114
Listening: attentively, 49, 50, 62, 63, 74, 76, 79; critically, 54, 62; for directions, 77; for information, 55, 59, 68; to descriptions, 54; tto details, 65; to drama, 8, 59, 77; to points of view, 67; to procedures, 55
Littering, 250
Living creatures: appreciating, 76; caring for, 239
Loggerhead turtle, 78
Logging, 126, 173–74

Map: area, 190, 268; environmental, 131; noise pollution, 24
Mendes, Chico, 212
Metamorphosis, 159
Metaphors, use of, 25, 36
*Mitakuye oyasin*, 107
Mock trial, 68–69
Monarch butterfly, 159

## 294  Subject Index

Moth, Hawaiian, 146
Mural, use of, 3
Museum visit, 111
Mystery, ecological, 148, 251

Nashua River, 189
National Arbor Day Foundation (NE), 278
National Audubon Society (NY), 278
National Geographic Society (Wash., DC), 278
National Science Teachers Association (VA), 218
National Wildlife Federation (Wash., DC), 278
Native American: beliefs, 85, 102, 205; legend, 16, 91, 93, 97, 100, 101, 104
Natural phenomena, 90–92, 97, 104
Natural Resources, recycling,163–64
Nature: appreciation of, 32, 46, 87, 162; as motivation, 31; expressions, 32; observations, 12, 13, 36, 38, 45, 124; patterns, 27; rebuilding, 216; verse, 25, 26, 33, 34; walk, 60, 98, 175, 243
Nature Conservancy, The (VA), 278
Nelson, Gaylord, 213
New York Zoological Society (NY), 278
Newspaper: articles, 173, 215; headlines, 10; reading, 10, 173
Notebooks: environmental, 181, 249; naturalists', 202, 248
Nurse log, 86, 237, 273

Observations, use of, 12, 13, 36, 38, 45, 124, 248
Ocean: and coast, 237; pollution of, 122, 178
Oil spills, 178
Oral interpretation, 6
Overpackaging, 139
Owls, 154, 255
Ozone, vanishing, 271

Painting, 249
Panel discussion, 114, 199
Pantomime, 195, 211
Passenger pigeons, 70

Penguins, 120–21
Personal letter. *See* Letter writing
Pesticide Action Network (Wash., DC), 216
Plants, 93
Plastic, effect of, 138
Poetry: acrostic, 4; concrete, 29; couplet, 9; different-portrait poem, 5; ecological, 6; environmental polluter monster, 228; free verse, 22, 44; haiku, 34; honeycomb shape, 30; if/then, 5; nautilus shape, 30; one-word, 5; sijo, 45; sound, 50; surprise ending, 41; tower shape, 30
Pollution: air, effect of, 40; noise, 24; ocean, 122, 178; water, 190
Pond: creatures, 11; ecosystem, 196; life, 196
Population increase, 189
Posters: recycle, 200; thumbprint, 127; tree, 127
Prairie chickens, 69
Predictions, making, 62, 126, 165, 175
Profiles, children's, 212
Proverbs, 180
Punctuation, use of, 227, 244, 254, 267, 274

Questions and answers, 102, 273

Radiation, ultraviolet, 271
Rain: appreciation of, 58; value of, 146
Rain forests: Amazonian, 252; appreciation of, 74; ecology of, 156, 267; importance of, 24, 152; preserving, 252
Ranking, 172, 176
Reading: class newspaper, 204; critical, 121–22, 137, 143, 176; for descriptions, 154; for directions, 119, 149, 168, 177, 178; fact vs. opinion, 124; and guidelines, 145; to identify, 159; point of view, 106, 153, 187; to summarize, 119; to take notes, 157; and word webs, 140
"Recipe," environmental, 121
Recyclable items, 98, 163, 199
Recycling, importance of, 98, 163, 194, 199, 204
Report, writing a, 51, 114, 158

## Subject Index

Research, 16, 51, 63, 68, 94, 113–14, 121, 126, 167, 175, 182, 196, 199
Rhymes, 9, 13; "think clinks", 31; water, 17. *See also* Poetry
Riddles, 38–40
Rivers, wild, 189
Rocky Mountains, 243
Role-play, 180, 194, 195, 202, 232
Roosevelt, Franklin, 213
Roosevelt, Theodore, 207, 210, 250

Salmon: Atlantic, 32; coho, 190
Sanctuary, bird, 71
Sand castle, 241
Sand pictures, 241
Scale, use of, 133
Seasons, cycle of, 17, 22
Sierra Club (CA), 196, 278
Sierra Nevada (mountains), 173–74
Sijo. *See* Poetry
Similes, 25
Singing, 19, 63, 78
Sketchbooks, 154
Sketching, 154
Sludge, effect of, 140
Snails, 223
Soil, conservation, 240
Solar radiation, 260
Songs, 19, 63, 78, 89
Speaking, choral, 57
Spider, web, 230
Spoonbill, Roseate, 54
Story: how and why tales, 86, 88, 89, 92; round-the-group, 63, 241; telling, 87, 92; transformation, 97; writing, 28, 230
Swamp, 18, 54
Sunflowers, 8

Sustainable Cotton Project (Wash., DC), 216

Technology: effects of, 160; future, 167, 179, 216
Telephone conference, use of, 3, 8, 192
Thoreau, Henry David, 165
Tree: adopting a, 96; appreciation of, 6; as habitat, 61, 229; importance of, 6, 10, 75, 202; planting, 95, 96, 108, 126

Video, use of, 141–42
Vocabulary: about growing plants, 14; developing, 96, 108; expanding, 19–20, 90

Waste, toxic, 140
Water, pollution, 190; restorative power of, 20, 57; storm, 20; value of, 7, 57, 128
Water cycle activity, 141
Waterway, monitoring, 191
Wetlands, ecosystem, 55, 176, 196, 238
Whales, 3, 5, 102, 155, 155, 275
Wilderness Society, The (Wash., DC), 278
Wildflowers, protection of, 233
Wildlife: activist, 5; and fashions, 197; habitat, 235; protecting, 113; sanctuary, 257; understanding, 175
Wind: power, 21; value of, 123, 125
Woods. *See* Forests
Words: defining, 207; descriptive, 236; in web, 100, 238
World Wildlife Fund, (Wash., DC), 278
Writing: captions, 146; first-person report, 97; informative, 245; manuscript, 234; narrative, 260; news, 204; paragraph, 178, 229, 236; point of view, 237; procedural, 20; request, 218, 232

Yanomami people, 272